PRAISE FOR
NOT BY CHANCE ALONE

"An illuminating account of how a great thinker with insatiable curiosity overcame a difficult childhood through his love of social science."

—*KIRKUS REVIEWS*

"Elliot Aronson is our modern day Horatio Alger as revealed in this charmingly inviting memoir by one of psychology's premier contributors. This master storyteller weaves his personal narrative in and around the events and people that marked his life path that was destined for greatness, without help from the vicissitudes of chance."

—PHIL ZIMBARDO, PAST PRESIDENT OF THE AMERICAN
PSYCHOLOGICAL ASSOCIATION; AUTHOR OF *THE LUCIFER EFFECT*

"This is more than a delightfully written, warm, and wise autobiography by one of our greatest social scientists; it is also an unusually candid and thoughtful look at the way important new insights are born, mature, and come to be employed. Aronson's account of his life-long relationship with Leon Festinger, first as student and collaborator and then as life-long friend, is a must read for anyone who wants to get to the heart of social psychology."

—LEE ROSS, PROFESSOR OF PSYCHOLOGY, STANFORD
UNIVERSITY; AUTHOR OF *THE PERSON AND THE SITUATION*

"Absolutely wonderful. Elliot Aronson has long shown that he can write engagingly for a wide audience, and in *Not by Chance Alone* he has outdone himself. Not only was I captivated by Aronson's truly inspirational life story, but I also learned so much about the people, theories, and experiments that helped define the field of social psychology."

—ELIZABETH LOFTUS, DISTINGUISHED PROFESSOR, UNIVERSITY OF CALIFORNIA-IRVINE; PAST PRESIDENT OF THE ASSOCIATION FOR PSYCHOLOGICAL SCIENCE

"Arguably, Elliot Aronson is first and foremost a very gifted teacher. The clarity he brings to that enterprise is evident in his success as a distinguished researcher and as a writer (witness the enormous popularity of his engaging treatise on social psychology, *The Social Animal*). And it is well manifested in this fascinating life story of a professor's quest to improve the human condition by understanding the social forces that so powerfully influence our lives. For those interested in an inside look at the joys and frustrations of an intellectual life, this book is a wonderful read."

—LUDY T. BENJAMIN, JR., PRESIDENTIAL PROFESSOR OF TEACHING EXCELLENCE, PROFESSOR OF PSYCHOLOGY, TEXAS A&M UNIVERSITY

"Aronson's candid autobiography is an instructive and enjoyable read. In addition, the volume offers an informed perspective on the sweeping development of social psychology as a discipline over the past six decades."

—THOMAS F. PETTIGREW, RESEARCH PROFESSOR OF SOCIAL PSYCHOLOGY, UNIVERSITY OF CALIFORNIA-SANTA CRUZ

"Elliot Aronson's done it again—revealed deep human insights from a deeply human story."

—ROBERT B. CIALDINI, AUTHOR OF *INFLUENCE: SCIENCE AND PRACTICE*

NOT BY CHANCE ALONE

ALSO BY ELLIOT ARONSON

The Social Animal

Social Psychology (with Tim Wilson and Robin Akert)

Mistakes Were Made (But Not by Me) (with Carol Tavris)

Age of Propaganda (with Anthony Pratkanis)

Nobody Left to Hate

The Adventures of Ruthie and a Little Boy Named Grandpa
(with Ruth Aronson)

The Handbook of Social Psychology (with Gardner Lindzey)

The Jigsaw Classroom (with Shelley Patnoe)

Methods of Research in Social Psychology (with Phoebe C. Ellsworth,
J. Merrill Carlsmith, and Marti Hope Gonzales)

NOT BY CHANCE ALONE

My Life as a Social Psychologist

Elliot Aronson

BASIC BOOKS

A MEMBER OF THE PERSEUS BOOKS GROUP
New York

Published by Basic Books,
A Member of the Perseus Books Group

Books published by Basic Books are available at special discounts for bulk purchases in the United States by corporations, institutions, and other organizations. For more information, please contact the Special Markets Department at the Perseus Books Group, 2300 Chestnut Street, Suite 200, Philadelphia, PA 19103, or call (800) 810-4145, ext. 5000, or e-mail special.markets@perseusbooks.com.

Excerpt from the poem "My Daughter's Morning" is used with the permission of the author, David Swanger.

Library of Congress Cataloging-in-Publication Data
Aronson, Elliot.
  Not by chance alone : my life as a social psychologist / Elliot Aronson.
    p. cm.
  Includes bibliographical references and index.
  ISBN 978-0-465-01833-8 (alk. paper)
  1. Aronson, Elliot. 2. Social psychologists—United States—Biography.
3. Social psychology—United States. I. Title.
  HM1031.A76A3 2010
  302.092—dc22
  [B]
                                        2010011018
10 9 8 7 6 5 4 3 2 1

TO MY MOST
IMPORTANT
MENTORS:

Jason Aronson

Abraham Maslow

David McClelland

Leon Festinger

Vera Aronson

We work in the dark,
We do what we can,
We give what we have.
Our doubt is our passion,
And our passion is our task.
The rest is the madness of art.

—HENRY JAMES

CONTENTS

INTRODUCTION

Courtesy Ellen Suckiel

Elliot at ten and fifty-two.

In 1954, in my senior year at Brandeis University, I heard an invited lecture by the distinguished nuclear physicist Leo Szilard. Szilard reminisced about how in the 1930s, when he was teaching at the University of Berlin, he gradually realized that Hitler's Germany was no place for a Jew. One day he packed a small valise, hopped on a train, and fled the country. The train was practically empty. The next day the train was jam-packed, and it was stopped at the border and forced to turn back. Szilard's moral of the story was "You don't have to be much smarter than the average person— only a little bit smarter." In this instance, only one day smarter.

Well, maybe. My guess is that you also have to be incredibly lucky. As I reflect on my life, Szilard's story comes to mind because, as a psychologist, I am well aware that memory is an imperfect historian, and it tends to be imperfect in a self-serving direction. My aim is to be truthful, but what is the truth?

As I see it, there are essentially two ways to write an autobiography. One is to take credit for every good outcome: "I was smart enough to go to this prestigious university and choose to marry that wonderful woman and study with this professor and go to that leading graduate school so that I could apprentice myself to that prominent scholar, and then I wisely accepted that perfect job." The other way is to attribute everything to the vicissitudes of chance: "My God, I have been incredibly lucky. At every step of the way I simply happened to be in the right place at the right time." But both accounts are true. In my own case, most of the good things that happened to me were the result of being in the right place at the right time—in my career, in my choice of a life partner, and in the friendships and professional relationships I formed—and I also was adept at making pretty good use of the opportunities that presented themselves to me.

In my life the professional and the personal have been inextricably intertwined. The Great Depression, World War II, the McCarthy witch hunts, the civil rights movement, the years of sexual liberation and the clarion call to "make love, not war," women's liberation, the extremes of political correctness on the Right and the Left—all of these events left a deep impression on me, though sometimes I found myself out of step with the times. I loved the human potential movement and its efforts to "break down barriers" between people in the 1960s and 1970s, but that philosophy crashed and burned during the "respect my boundaries" 1980s. My active, highly visible commitment to civil rights and freedom of speech got me death threats and charges of being a "nigger lover" in Austin, Texas, where I was instrumental in bringing about a fair-housing ordinance. That same commitment also brought me protests and charges of being a "racist" in Santa Cruz, California, where I protected the right of Arthur Jensen to present his justifiably unpopular argument that racial differences in IQs are innate.

Social psychology, a field that examines how circumstances, generations, cultures, ideas, and guiding principles get inside individuals and shape their actions, has infused my life. It has provided me with a powerful lens through which I have been able to view the events around me and understand myself, my family, and my times. How, I wondered, does any man become a good father if his own father was absent, physically or psychologically? Traditionally, psychology has emphasized the power of genetics or of early childhood experiences—you will become your father whether you want to or not. In contrast, social psychology attempts to understand the power of your generation's influence, your own experiences, and how you interpret them. When I was fourteen, I was a pretty good baseball player and a member of a championship team. Yet although we played some of our games on weekends close to home, my father never came to see me play. He loved baseball, but not enough to come to one of our games. It didn't bother me at the time, because, in those days, hardly *anybody's* father came to see his kid play. When I became a father, however, I had a strong desire to see my kids play, and that evoked a longing in me; I realized, for the first time, how much I wished my dad had come to one or two of my games. It would have made me so happy, and, I thought, it would have made *him* happy as well. I felt the loss, but only in retrospect. Being immersed in social psychology gives me a perspective that mitigates the common impulse to confuse how we feel now with how we felt then. It defuses any impulse I might have had to feel angry at my father for not showing up, and blaming him retrospectively.

So, how much of our lives is determined by luck, a random opportunity, chance? How much comes from the genetic hand we are dealt at birth? How much from what we make of the chances we get?

I was thirteen years old when World War II ended, when I first heard about the Holocaust and saw newsreels of the horrifying, gaunt figures liberated from concentration camps. And I remember thinking that if it had not been for my grandparents' desperation and courage that brought them to America at the end of the nineteenth century, I would have been among those victims. I, too, could have died in a concentration camp. My stomach churned at the realization that *it could have been me*. I was flooded with gratitude toward my grandparents for having had the guts to get out when they did.

So my very survival as a Jew was a matter of luck, but, of course, luck was not the whole story. Insight is also important, as is the ability to take advantage of luck. For example, my mother, like most Jewish mothers of her day, wanted me to become a doctor, but, figuring that I lacked the brains and drive to become one, she kept pressing her second choice on me: If I couldn't become rich on my own, I could marry rich. In particular, I could marry Barbara, my first college sweetheart, whose father owned not one but *two* five-and-dime stores. My mother was so delighted with the prospect that *she* fell in love with Barbara—or, rather, with Barbara's father's stores. "He'll give one of those stores to you!" she kept reminding me. I had no conscious idea at the time how stupid it would have been for me to marry Barbara (for the sole purpose of having my own five-and-dime store), but my intuition got me out of there. Where does that come from, that intuition, that hunch, that sets a person on one course and not another?

Consider this: As a student, I had three mentors. As an undergraduate at Brandeis, my mentor was Abraham Maslow. As an M.A. candidate at Wesleyan, it was David McClelland. As a Ph.D. candidate at Stanford, I worked with Leon Festinger. In a study rank-ordering the one hundred most eminent psychologists of the twentieth century, those three men were among the top fifteen. The probability of a student working with such distinguished mentors, solely by chance, is extremely remote. Yet I didn't go to Brandeis to work with Maslow; I went to Brandeis because it was the only university that gave me a scholarship. I met Maslow because I wandered into his class quite by accident. Then I went to Wesleyan at the eleventh hour, as a last resort, because I had no other prospects. I had never even heard of McClelland. Finally, I did not go to Stanford because of Festinger; indeed, I spent most of my first year at Stanford trying to keep out of his way. So what is the role of chance? And how does one take advantage of lucky breaks?

Luck was certainly on my side, but it was more than chance that got me to fall in love with both scientific social psychology and the human potential movement. I was attracted by the notion that human personalities and abilities are not carved in stone. Granted, our genetic propensities impose limitations (I will never be as smart as Albert Einstein or as athletically gifted as Michael Jordan). But social psychology rests on the assumption that people are not locked in by their genetics or by their early childhood deprivations. Clinical psychology is about repair. It says, "You were damaged in childhood, but we can fix it—a little." Social psychology is about change. It says, "Okay, you had a bad childhood, but let's change your environment, change your motivation, and give you new opportunities, and you can transcend your origins, your self-defeating attitudes, your prejudices." I was excited by the idea that people can grow and improve—that a shy, relatively untalented eighteen year old like me, who grew up in a financially and intellectually impoverished household, could pull himself up by his own bootstraps, get educated, find mentors, catch fire.

My mother was wrong when she tried to guide me into a marriage that would have led me to the ownership of a five-and-dime store. But she was merely being prudent, operating from her own experience in the Great Depression and the facts at hand. When I was entering college I was not a promising student, and my chances of achieving success seemed slim. Yet if I had gone on to marry a woman I didn't love and to own a small business I had no interest in managing, I would have failed both as a husband and as a merchant. But how was my mother to know that I was soon to discover a field of interest that not only would excite me but I would, in turn, excite? How was she to know that after Barbara, I would meet a remarkable young woman and that we would live in magnificent harmony for fifty-five years (and counting)?

It is not accidental that the kinds of psychology that attracted me—"hard-nosed" experimental social psychology and "soft-headed" encounter groups—were both American inventions. In 1835 Alexis de Tocqueville, the brilliant French historian and observer of the American scene, wrote in his masterpiece *Democracy in America*: "[Americans] have all a lively faith in the perfectibility of man; they judge the diffusion of knowledge must necessarily be advantageous, the consequences of ignorance fatal; they all consider society as a body in a state of improvement, humanity as a changing scene, in which nothing is, or ought to be, permanent; they admit that what appears to them today to be good, may be superseded by something better tomorrow." This quintessential American belief in the power of change and self-improvement—

that a factory worker's son can become a professor, that people who hold deep-seated prejudices can in fact transcend them, and that the way things are is not the way they have to be—has been the dominant theme of my work and of my life.

For the past fifty years as a teacher, I have tried to impart this way of looking at things to my students. Early in my career I came to understand that this was the single most precious gift I could ever give them. Students are continually asking themselves, "Who am I?" My goal was to get them to reframe the question into "Who do I want to become?" Once they arrive at their own answer, they must also learn that getting there won't come by chance alone.

CHAPTER ONE

Growing Up in Revere

Elliot and Jason, 1940.

P arents love to tell stories about their children. What they don't realize is that their children are listening. One of the earliest stories I remember my mother telling about me—a story she often repeated to her friends—was of taking me to the park in the baby buggy in cold weather, when I was about a year old. "Other babies' cheeks would turn a healthy, rosy color," she would say, "but Elliot's would become ashen, and his lips would turn blue. He was such a sickly child." As a preschooler, every time I heard her tell this story, I could feel her embarrassment that I wasn't the beautiful baby that other mothers had. It made me want to apologize.

I was born in 1932 in Chelsea, Massachusetts, a slum city just across the Mystic River from Boston. Chelsea was brimful of junkyards, rag shops, and oil storage tanks. When I was three years old, my family moved to the adjacent equally slum city of Revere. Nestled between the Suffolk Downs horse track and Wonderland, a greyhound racing track, Revere was teeming with small-time gamblers, bookies, and assorted Runyonesque characters. Its major industry was gambling. But the saving grace of Revere was that it was on the ocean and had a good swimming beach and a boardwalk, with a real, honest-to-goodness wooden roller coaster. My advice to young people is, if you have to live in a slum, make sure it's on the ocean.

While reminiscing about his boyhood in Brooklyn, comedian Sam Levenson once told Ed Sullivan, "We were poor, but we didn't know we were poor." That's touching, but it was not my experience. We were poor, and we knew it. I have vivid memories of going to bed early and hungry so that we could ward off the cold in our unheated home by covering ourselves with blankets and overcoats, of stuffing my shoes with cardboard to cover the holes in the soles because we couldn't afford to have them repaired, of never having new clothes but always wearing whatever my older brother had outgrown. I remember our family moving in the middle of the night because we were in arrears in our rent. I remember my parents' bitter quarrels about money and my father's failure as a provider.

My father, Harry Aronson, had emigrated from Russia in 1909, when he was eight years old. He quit school at the age of thirteen and began peddling socks and underwear from a pushcart in Boston. Eventually, he earned enough money to open a small dry-goods store, where he still peddled socks and underwear, but from behind a counter. My mother, Dorothy, was the eldest of ten children, all of whom were born in this country. Her parents had also come from Russia. Her father, Ben Feingold, a tailor, gradually moved up to the middle class by opening a tuxedo-rental store ("Feingold's—The Best One!" was the store's logo). Her brothers worked hard to put poverty behind them; they became doctors, dentists, chiropodists, and small-business owners.

My parents married in 1927. My mother felt she was marrying beneath her on two counts: My father never got past the fifth grade, whereas she prided herself on having graduated from high school, and he was a greenhorn, whereas *she* had been born in America. But she was already twenty-seven—in those days almost too old to find a husband—and at least Harry was the well-to-do owner of a dry-goods store. He even drove a late-model car. Shortly after they married, he acquired a second store, and so for a while they lived comfortably. My father was proud of having worked his way up from selling goods in a pushcart to owning his own stores. Their first child, Jason, was born in 1929, shortly after the stock market crashed; I, in 1932; and our sister, Paula, six years later.

In 1935, at the height of the Depression, my father lost his stores, and the bank foreclosed on our home. We became destitute, living in poverty until well after America entered the war. Our house was intellectually impoverished as well. Neither of my parents was interested in ideas; they never discussed politics, music, art, history, or current events. In spite of my mother's pride in having finished high school, I never saw her reading a book. The only books in our house were the Old Testament and some Hebrew prayers. My mother's major form of entertainment was the daytime soap opera, especially *Helen Trent*; *Our Gal Sunday*; and *Just Plain Bill, Barber of Hartville*. My father's major form of entertainment was gambling. Unfortunately, he was a compulsive gambler who would bet on anything from horses to dogs to baseball to how many cars would pass by the corner of Shirley Avenue and North Shore Road within a three-minute window.

My mother never forgave my father for our descent into poverty. She blamed it on his gambling and on his being a poor businessman, because he refused to fire his employees when the store was losing money and habitually extended credit to deadbeats. "As soon as they made any money, they shopped at other stores so they wouldn't have to face you!" she would accuse my father. "Besides, how could you have paid an employee when your family was going hungry?"

My father attributed our poverty to the Depression—to the fact that his blue-collar customers had lost their jobs and needed help. Once, when I was about ten, he tried to explain his point of view to me. "What else could I have done? They were my only customers. They didn't have money! If I didn't give them credit, I'd have had no customers at all. And how could I fire anyone who worked for me and depended on me?" That was why, he said, he eventually couldn't pay his rent and lost the stores. I was not sure whether my father was a victim of the worldwide Depression or whether he would have survived financially if he had been a better businessman—one who didn't gamble.

My parents' descent into poverty caused my mother enormous shame and embarrassment. Her husband's older brother, Aaron, managed to keep *his* store; her father, Ben, managed to keep *his* store; why couldn't her husband? I can barely imagine how difficult it was for her to accept charity, but it was the only way we could survive. And I can understand why she was always so worried and angry: It's Massachusetts, it's bitterly cold in winter, you can't heat the house, you have three small kids, and everyone is hungry all the time. Once in a while a relative would drop in with a bag of apples or oranges, which was a real treat. But I mostly remember my mother putting aside her pride and standing in line for the weekly handouts of bread and cereal at the welfare station across town. We went there together; I, age three, would ride in the stroller on the way there, and walk alongside her on the way back with the stroller filled with supplies. I don't know if I remember those walks or if she created my memories with her stories.

My mother used to tell one story that epitomized the humiliation she felt during those years. My father's oldest brother, Uncle Aaron, and his wife, Goldie, both worked in Aaron's store. It was 1937, the year I started school, and my mother took the trolley car to their store in East Boston to buy school clothes for Jason and me. At the counter Goldie wrapped the clothes in a bundle. Taking them, my mother said, "Goldie, we can't pay now, but I promise we will in a few months." Goldie grabbed the bundle out of her hands and said, "You can have these clothes when you pay for the last bundle you bought from us." My mother was dumbfounded. She told and retold this story a lot, acting it out—how Goldie snatched the bundle back from her, put it under the counter, and stood there resolutely with her arms folded across her ample chest. My Uncle Aaron, a meek little man, would witness the scene silently, not daring to overrule his wife, avoiding my mother's gaze. My mother would always end the story by saying, "You know, there was nothing in that bundle for me, and nothing of great value—just a few things for the children—a shirt, pants, some socks." She would make a meal out of that story, which underscored the fact that my uncle was still in business when my father wasn't, how she had to take that long trip on the trolley for nothing, the humiliation she suffered at my father's hands. She apparently didn't notice that she was faulting my father for the same generosity she expected Goldie to extend to her.

My father was often unemployed for months at a time; when he was able to find a job, it was temporary and often involved manual labor such as highway construction for the Works Progress Administration. Late one night I woke up to go to the bathroom. Still groggy, I passed the kitchen and saw my father in tears, sitting alone at the table, his head in his hands. I can only guess how defeated he must have felt at having been reduced to doing manual labor after years of owning his own stores. But that was nothing compared to the misery of not having a job at all, and so he did whatever he could. For a while he worked as an insurance agent, going door to door selling nickel-and-dime life-insurance policies to poor people, but after Prudential caught him having embezzled two hundred dollars, which he promptly gambled away at the racetrack, he was fired. (My father saw this as borrowing the money, which he thought he would quickly repay after the next race, when his horse would surely win.) His father-in-law, Ben

Feingold, paid Prudential the money so my father wouldn't go to jail. To pay off that debt, my father worked at Feingold's, delivering tuxedos. He hated the job, mostly because he hated working for Ben, who would constantly remind him of how he had saved him from prison. But jobs were hard to come by, especially for unskilled former merchants who had narrowly avoided prison on charges of embezzlement.

My father's money problems were only half of his troubles; the other half was my mother's nagging him incessantly about their money problems. She never let him forget that by losing his stores and our home, he had deprived her of her feeling of security and, along with it, her pride. She often reminded him that she could have married Max Pincus, who, as the sole owner of a successful hardware store, was "sitting pretty." The dinner table was their battleground. My parents had monumental fights, and night after night they followed the same pattern as if it were choreographed. She would badger him; he would erupt in anger, slam his knife and fork onto his plate, and storm out of the house, trudging off to hang out with his friends in the card room at the Elk's Club or Mike the Barber's—not that Mike actually gave many haircuts; the three barber chairs he had in the shop were primarily a front for the gambling in the back room. (Much later it occurred to me that my father might have been using the fights as a vehicle to get to Mike's.) He would not return home until long after we kids went to bed. When he was employed as a day laborer, he needed to leave for work long before Jason and I woke up to get ready for school. Thus, we would usually not see him again until the next dinnertime, when the nagging and anger would often pick up where it had left off. As soon as my mother's nagging would begin, Jason would give me a bleak "here we go again" look, and we would hunker down until the knife and fork would clatter and the door would slam. We would then continue with dinner, but with a lump in our throats.

How often did these incidents replay themselves? Three times a week? Three times a month? I do not trust my memory. The scenes were so dramatic, and traumatic, that they are emblazoned on my mind with a vividness that makes them seem as if they were a daily occurrence, though I am reasonably certain that's an exaggeration. What I do know, with hindsight, is that once the cycle got started, it was hard for them to break out of it. If my mother felt an overpowering need to vent her pain and frustration at my father, I'm sure she figured that the best opportunity was dinnertime while he was seated at the table, temporarily immobile, with his napkin tucked into the top of his shirt and his fork raised toward his mouth. From my father's perspective, I'm sure he felt anguish at his own failure and at having fallen out of the middle class. He almost certainly didn't need to be reminded of it, much less of Max Pincus, let alone at dinnertime, when—as he frequently said at the top of his lungs—he expected to have "a fuckin' moment of peace and quiet at the end of a hard fuckin' day."

"*You* think *you* had a hard day?" she would shout back. "How do think it was for me, having to walk three miles to the welfare station with all the neighbors watching?" At that he would launch himself out of the house in anger, staying away until after my mother was asleep, leaving her no opportunity to get to him until the next dinnertime. And then the cycle would repeat.

Naturally, as a child, I didn't understand their dynamics. Looking back, I am convinced that whatever love my parents may have felt for each other in the early years of their marriage had been bleached out of their relationship by the time these battles began. Yet I suspect that, deep down, they had some empathy for each other but lacked the ability to communicate in ways that might have been supportive rather than overflowing with blame, self-pity, and vexation.

When the war began my father finally got a job as a semiskilled factory worker. The pay wasn't great, but the work was steady. On the side he worked as a small-time agent for a big-time bookie in the numbers racket, taking bets from fellow factory workers. His money woes diminished, but not his quarrels with my mother.

I was a painfully shy child and adolescent. In school I never volunteered to speak up, and when called upon I stammered and blushed and was barely able to respond to the question being asked. One afternoon, when I was in third grade, the teacher became angry at the class and ordered each of us to write "I will not make noise in class" fifty times before she would allow us to go home. I wrote about thirty of them when my pencil broke. I was too scared to ask the teacher if I could sharpen the pencil, so I sat there quietly as other children handed in their papers and left. I dreaded that I would be stuck there forever and imagined my mother, frantically wringing her hands and pacing around in our kitchen, wondering where on earth I could be. In desperation I tried to gnaw a point on the pencil with my teeth. It wasn't working. Finally, I summoned all my courage, walked up to the teacher's desk, held up my pencil, and murmured, "May I please use the pencil sharpener?" She snatched the pencil out of my hand, scrutinized it, and snapped, "Just as I suspected. You bit off the point just so you could have an excuse to disturb me." I stood there, mute, too mortified even to defend myself. That was decades ago, and it still makes me cringe to remember it.

In contrast, Jason was a star. In the Feingold family there were a lot of uncles and aunts, and all of them awaited his arrival, their first-born nephew, with great anticipation. They were young adults, not quite ready to begin families of their own, so Jason immediately became their special toy. What a great little kid he was: bright as a penny, strong, vigorous, joyful, and a natural entertainer. And the more attention he got, the happier and more self-assured he became. I remember their happy kvelling over him: "Sing, Jason! Dance, Jason! Show Uncle Leo the picture you drew, Jason! Knock on wood, he's a regular Norman Rockwell!" They fawned all over the little bastard.

Did I resent my big brother? You bet I did. At family gatherings, on the playground, everywhere we were together, his charisma ignited the atmosphere and highlighted my own inadequacies. In the summer of '39, when I was seven years old, the Feingold family organized a Sunday picnic by a lake in eastern Massachusetts. All my uncles and aunts were there. Jason and I were having fun throwing a baseball around, feeding each other pop flies and ground balls, when a few of our uncles came over, announced that they were going to rent a rowboat to go fishing, and invited Jason to come along. Not only were they not inviting me, but they were depriving me of my one playmate. Desolate, I meekly asked if I could come along. Uncle Mike said that he was sorry, but there wasn't enough room in the boat and, besides, I was too young to enjoy fishing anyway. My eyes filled with tears; I tried hard to hold them back, but to no avail. Uncle Nat said, "Aw, let's let him come; we'll make room." And so I went.

We were on the boat for about two and a half hours. It was pretty boring, but at least I got to be with my brother. When we arrived back at the shore, Uncle Herbie asked, "Well, Elliot, did you have a good time?"

"Yeah," I said.

"I guess it paid to cry," Uncle Eddie remarked.

"*Sha!* Let him alone," said Uncle Leo. His perfunctory kindness came too late. I was heartsick and wished I hadn't gone.

I hated the image my family had of me, largely because it was accurate. One Saturday afternoon I went to the movies. The serial they were showing that month was based on the comic-book character Captain Marvel, who in everyday life was Billy Batson, a meek, nerdy teenager. When danger arose Billy would shout the magic word "SHAZAM," and in a puff of smoke he would be transformed into a big, strong, tough superhero. Unlike Clark Kent, a.k.a. Superman, Billy Batson wasn't born super. He couldn't leap tall buildings in a single bound, he was not more powerful than a locomotive, and, if you shot him, the bullets would not bounce off—they would kill him. That's what made the character so interesting to me: Billy had to transform himself, and his transformation was always temporary. I arrived home from the matinee, infused with Billy Batson and Captain Marvel. I tied an old bath towel around my neck as a cape, got up on the third step of the porch of our apartment house, stretched my right arm out in front of me and my left arm behind me, shouted "SHAZAM"—and leaped bravely off the porch. I landed awkwardly and sprained my ankle. I limped into the house, and my mother said, "What did you do this time?"

A few days later we went to a family gathering, and as I limped in one of my aunts asked, "What happened to Elliot?" An uncle answered, "He thought he was Superman and tried to fly by jumping off the porch." "Elliot . . . *Superman?*" said another. The whole group burst into laughter. I tried to explain that I wasn't trying to be Superman, only Captain Marvel, but they weren't listening.

Jason would have been a tough act to follow for any younger sibling, let alone a klutz like me. At school, where I was forever three years behind him, the teachers knew me as Jason's little brother and assumed that I was like him. I was a pretty good student in elementary school and junior high school, but I lacked the star quality that the teachers seemed to expect. I could read the disappointment on the face of my first-grade teacher as she discovered that I wasn't as quick, wasn't as charming, wasn't as bright, and wasn't as assertive as Jason, and, in the jargon of the schools, didn't have the "leadership skills" that he did. None of this, of course, was Jason's fault. I never consciously held it against him, but at times I envied his charisma and wished I didn't have an older brother. But, even as a child, I was all too aware that my inadequacies were my own and would have been there even if my brother had never existed. Although I was overshadowed by Jason, I knew that if that shadow were magically removed, I would have been revealed as a shy, uninteresting kid with mediocre talents.

But regardless of my flashes of envy and jealousy, I loved and admired him. He loved me too, and showered a lot of attention on me. It was Jason who showed me how to dribble a basketball and how to throw a football with a perfect spiral. It was Jason who informed me that excessive masturbation would not cause blindness or hair to grow on the palms of our hands (common fears among novice masturbators at the time). It was Jason who taught me how to appreciate the subtleties of a ride on the roller coaster. And it was Jason who taught me how to throw, catch, and hit a baseball. When I was very young we played on a diamond that was strewn with lumpy soil, pebbles, and weedy grass—a far cry from the manicured lawn and smooth surfaces of Fenway Park. A sharply hit ground ball on our diamond would often take unpredictable bounces. My natural tendency was to try to field a grounder by positioning my body to the left or right of the ball, so that if it took a strange hop it would not hit me in the face.

Jason would have none of it. Hour after hour, he would hit me ground balls until I learned to overcome my fear and put myself in the direct path of the ball. This skill that I learned as a boy paid great dividends in adolescence, when my ability as a ballplayer became a major source of gratification and, in those awkward teenage years, just about my only source of self-esteem.

Most of all, though, I loved having Jason there to lead the way, offer advice, and fight off bullies. "Just wait 'til my big brother gets ahold of you—he'll kick the shit out of you, you big ox!" I'd yell to some older kid who was tormenting me. And kick the shit out of them he did. We were the only Jewish family in our tough neighborhood, which was made up mostly of working-class Irish Catholics who were virulently anti-Semitic. Indeed, most of the neighborhood kids behaved as if Jason and I were personally responsible for the Crucifixion. Jason was a big, strong guy, so they gave him plenty of room. But I, being skinny and rather frail, bore the brunt of their hatred of Jews. I was frequently faced with the choice between fighting and running—between feeling brave but getting beaten up, and feeling cowardly but remaining unbloodied. Jason was around to protect me enough of the time to earn my gratitude and resentment. It was nice to have a bodyguard. It was degrading to need one.

And I sure needed one when walking home from Hebrew school, which was located in a small Jewish enclave on the other side of town. Jason graduated from Hebrew school when he was thirteen; after that, I was on my own. In fall and winter it was dark when I walked home, and so I was forever trying to find creative routes, zigzaggy paths that would take me away from the greatest areas of danger. But in spite of my best efforts, I was frequently waylaid, pushed around, and occasionally roughed up by gangs of teenagers shouting anti-Semitic slogans at me. I remember sitting on a curb after one of those incidents, nursing a bloody nose and a split lip, feeling very sorry for myself—and wondering how it was that these kids could hate me so much when they didn't even know me. I wondered whether they had been born hating Jews or had learned it from their parents and priests. I wondered whether, if these kids would get to know me better (and discover what a sweet and harmless little boy I was), they would like me more. And if they liked me more, would they then hate other Jews less? I wish I could say that being the target of bullying made me a more empathic kid. I wish I could say that my experience goaded me to spring to the defense of smaller kids when they were being pushed around. Spring to their defense? Hell, no. So eager was I to distance myself from other targets that I actually joined the bullies, determined to convince the bigger, tougher, more aggressive kids that I was closer to them than to their victims. I took no joy in taunting weaker boys. It was my feeble attempt to buy an insurance policy against being taunted myself.

When I completed Hebrew school at last, my mother suggested I go out and earn some money to help the family. I could begin, she said, by doing what Jason had done at my age: going around to various drugstores and asking if they needed a soda jerk. Jason had worked in a drugstore for three years. (I followed in his footsteps literally—same schools, same teachers, same attempted jobs.) "But none of the stores have 'Help wanted' signs in the window," I protested.

"There's always room for a good worker," she replied, instructing me to go inside and inquire about work anyway. For me, this was an excruciating assignment. I did it, though, and was promptly rejected by four different stores. When I came home and told my mother that there were no job openings, she said, in a derisive tone, "Yeah, and I know how you asked. You probably said,

'You don't need any soda jerks or anything, do you?'" It was a cruel thing to say, but she wasn't far off.

Finally, I did manage to land a job in the produce department at the Elm Farm Supermarket. My job was to keep the shelves stocked, spray the vegetables to make them look good, and sort potatoes and onions into five-pound sacks. I thought I was doing my job pretty well, but I was fired after a few months because I didn't know how to look busy when I had nothing to do and all of the five-pound sacks that I filled were about a quarter pound over. "That costs the corporation money," the manager fumed. And so, at fourteen, I already felt like an abject failure. So young, and yet so untalented!

My father and I did not have a lot to say to each other. We did a few father-son things: He took me to Fenway Park in 1946, where, for fifty-five cents, we could sit in the center-field bleachers and watch the Red Sox play ball, in the era of Ted Williams, Bobby Doerr, and Dom DiMaggio. He taught me how to drive a car, and did it with a degree of patience that astonished me. We lived in the same house for almost seventeen years, and I can recall only one serious conversation between us, the one in which he told me his version of how he lost the stores. He never told me about his childhood, his education, his relationship with his brothers and sisters, or his hopes and aspirations for himself or for his children. All through my adolescence I used to have recurring fantasies about taking long walks with him, during which we would talk deeply, earnestly, and lovingly about important things. The setting was almost always bucolic: a meadow, the woods—places we never visited in reality. When I was in my fifties these fantasies became nightmares. I would awake in a cold sweat, unable to forgive myself for having asked my father so little, for knowing so little about him. Why didn't I ever ask him about his life? The simple truth is that I believed I was of little interest to him, and I sensed his constant disappointment in me. "Why can't you be more like so-and-so?" he would say, always of some kid who had three jobs and a newspaper route, and never missed a violin lesson. "Why are you always wasting your energy playing baseball and basketball?" In those days Jewish parents believed that any activity that was unproductive intellectually or financially was a total waste of time. Children should be working to earn money, studying to get ahead, or practicing the violin to become Jascha Heifetz.

But on a deeper level, I didn't ask my father questions because I was afraid of him, of his brooding, punitive presence that could easily erupt into wrath. Whenever he was angry he seethed more ferociously than anyone I had ever seen. Years later, watching the actor Lee J. Cobb fuming, clenching his fists, and losing his temper in the film *Twelve Angry Men*, I exclaimed, "Oh, my God—that's my father." Although my father never actually punched me, he often shook his fist at me in a way to make me fear he would, and his anger was almost always disproportionate to the crime. *"Ikh vel dir bald geybn a flyask in punim s'zol shoklen dayne tseyn,"* he would say in Yiddish ("I will give you such a smack in the face that it will loosen your teeth"). He was the designated family punisher. One beautiful spring afternoon I got caught up in a baseball game, and the next thing I knew I was already a half hour late for Hebrew school. So I decided to keep playing and then hung out with the guys so that I could get home at exactly the time I would have normally. Unfortunately for me, the school called to find out where I'd been. Busted. My father put the phone down and erupted, pounding his fist on the table.

"What the hell is the matter with you? We don't have enough troubles without your adding to them?"

"But Dad! All the other kids were . . . "

"I don't give a shit about the other kids. You are not like the other kids, and besides they are none of my business. If you ever do anything like this again, there will be hell to pay!"

Between his disappointment and his anger, I knew he didn't think highly of me. If he loved me, I was never sure of it.

But then there was the night of the concussion, when I was about fifteen. While going for a rebound in a basketball game, I was hit on the top of my head by an opposing player who had a cast on his arm—which he was effectively using as a weapon. I was knocked out for thirty seconds. When I came to, I sat on the bench for about five minutes, felt better, and played the rest of the game. Hours later, in the middle of the night, I was awakened by the sound of my own groaning. I had an excruciating headache. My brother, who slept in the same room, went to wake up our parents. But when I tried to explain to them what had happened, I could produce only gibberish. My thoughts seemed clear enough, but they came out as meaningless sounds. I felt I was speaking through somebody else's mouth. It felt eerie. But I wasn't scared; I knew I could *think* clearly. But the look of anguish and horror on my parents' faces frightened me.

My father turned to my mother and in an agonized voice said, "We've lost our son."

I wanted desperately to calm their fears. I mustered all the concentration I could and, with what felt like superhuman effort, I exclaimed, "Aahhhmmmawwwrrrlllwrrride!" It was my sorry attempt at "I'm all right." It could not have been less reassuring. Fortunately, after a few hours, the aphasia subsided, and I could explain to them what had happened, whereupon they immediately started blaming me: "How could you have been so stupid to keep playing after you were knocked out?" Yet for years thereafter, whenever I thought back on my childhood and wondered (as I often did) about whether my father loved me, the memory of his voice saying "We've lost our son" never failed to reassure me. A touching story . . . yet it also shows that if I have to reach that far into the bag to come up with evidence of my father's love or concern for me, I had good reason to feel insecure about my place in our family.

In 1949, when I was a junior in high school, my father was diagnosed with an aggressive form of leukemia. One day he mentioned that he was worried about losing weight and might see a doctor; three months later he was dead. He was only forty-seven. In the weeks leading up to his death, more than ever I yearned to talk to him, to learn from him. There were all kinds of things I needed to understand. Mostly, what I wanted to know was my father's own story—his history. Yet even though I knew he was dying, I could not speak to him. I didn't know how to ask. I feared his impatience and anger. My father had always been worried and preoccupied with earning a living; now he was worried and preoccupied with dying. He didn't seem to have any time for what I feared he would have regarded as idle chatter with me, but I never bothered to find out. I sat by passively and made all kinds of excuses for not asking him what I so desperately wanted to know. I didn't feel important enough, entitled enough, to ask him questions when he was well; how could I possibly intrude into his thoughts and wishes now that he was sick?

I drove my mother to the hospital every evening to see him during visiting hours. I would come up to the room with her and say hello, but then, unable to think of what else to say to him, feeling awkward, and wanting to give them privacy, I would drift over to the window and remain there, looking out, for the duration of her visit. One evening, shortly before his death, when he realized that he was not going to recover from his illness, he began to talk openly to my mother. Oblivious to my presence, my father expressed his regret to her that he was dying so young, leaving the family without any money in the bank or any source of income. He particularly regretted leaving his children financially vulnerable. He wasn't terribly worried, he said, about "the baby," his eleven-year-old daughter, Paula, because he felt she would eventually find a husband who would take care of her. And he certainly wasn't worried about "the big guy" (Jason, already in college, whom he described as "a real go-getter"). But, he told my mother, he was deeply concerned about "the little guy" (me) because he felt that without his support and constant prodding I wouldn't amount to much. His remarks stung, but I pretty much agreed with his deathbed assessment of my future.

Ten years later I was at a going-away party that my friends were throwing for me. I was happily married, I had just received my Ph.D. in psychology at Stanford, and I was about to head east to take a position as an assistant professor at Harvard. I got drunk and walked outside. It was a particularly beautiful night; all the stars were out. I remember crying as I looked up at the stars and told my father that he could now rest easy; I had already achieved so much more than he could ever have imagined. This was an odd thing for me to do. I must have been *very* drunk, because I don't believe in an afterlife, much less in the possibility of communicating with dead people. But I longed for him to know that "the little guy" was on a path where he might eventually amount to something, after all.

The philosopher Jean-Paul Sartre once said that from the moment we spring out of the womb, we are "doomed" to freedom.

What did he mean by "doomed" if not that freedom is heavy, that we pay a price for it in suffering and loss? We do not become free at the moment we are born. For some people it doesn't happen until they are well into middle age, because a man is not totally free until his father dies. For me, that freedom came at age seventeen, and I still remember, along with the grief and despair I felt at losing him, a surge of liberation from his disapproval, disappointment, and anger. At the time the relief I felt blindsided me and evoked intense guilt and confusion—you are not supposed to feel relieved when your father dies. Years later I came to understand those feelings. A dark presence had been lifted from my world.

Yet, all my adult life, I have wished I had been able to know more about my father. I have wondered whether, if he had lived to a ripe old age and seen the success his goofy boy made of his life, he would have been proud of me at last, talked about his own feelings at last, told me the story of his life at last. But perhaps his death freed me to become the man he feared I never would be.

CHAPTER TWO

Boardwalk Morality

Courtesy RevereBeach.com

Roller coaster and amusement stands, Revere Beach Boardwalk, 1947.

"Do you really think that they'll think I'm old enough?"

"Yeah, fourteen is a little young for this work, but don't worry about it, kid. As soon as old Abe Shaw sees you, he'll give you a job. I guarantee it."

It was 1946. I was surprised by Jason's confidence in me, yet it made me feel a bit less scared. But only a bit; my palms were still sweating, and my voice was still up somewhere in my throat as I walked toward Revere Beach. I arrived at the boardwalk early, but already there was a long line of kids waiting outside the back room at the penny arcade. They were there to be interviewed by Abe Shaw, the guy who managed most of the rides and arcades in the amusement park. Abe had been there forever and had earned a reputation for being a shrewd manager and a tough boss who took no shit from anyone, not even his Mafia bosses.

I was dismayed to see that there were about three times as many kids waiting in line as there were summer jobs. Besides, most of them looked to be at least sixteen years old, the legal age for working at the amusement park. My palms began to sweat even more as some of the older guys in line looked at me contemptuously. "So why had that fucking Jason been so confident that old Abe would give me a job right away?" I thought to myself. I considered walking out and heading back home. But I couldn't bear to imagine the look of disappointment on my mother's face when I told her that I had left without even trying.

Boy, was I dumb. It slowly dawned on me that Jason had been teasing, using the oldest boardwalk joke in existence—"As soon as old Abe Shaw sees you, he'll give you a job." Of course he would.

If he *saw* you, he'd give you just about anything you asked for—because, as everybody knew, old Abe was blind as a bat and hadn't seen anything in forty-five years. He was a legendary figure, rumored to be able to size you up without even being able to see you. His office was in the rear of the arcade building, and his door was always open—not out of friendliness, but so he could hear the sound of the pennies and nickels clinking into the arcade machines. It was said that if Abe listened closely for about fifteen minutes at the peak of the evening, any evening, he could guess the night's receipts with uncanny accuracy.

"*Next!*"

My turn finally came. I walked into the dingy office and stood in front of the desk while Abe pretended to be looking out the window. I stood quietly for three or four minutes and then cleared my throat. Abe spun around, looked straight at me, and said, "You don't have to make noise, sonny. I know you're there." I gasped. Abe picked up a pencil from the desk, moved a pad of paper in front of him, and said, "What's your name, sonny?" By this time, I was completely undone; how could a blind guy so easily find a pencil and paper on his desk? And what use could he have for them anyway?

"El . . . El . . . Elliot Aronson."

"Well, Aronson, don't you think you're a little young for this kind of work? You don't look more than fourteen, maybe fifteen, years old, tops."

"Uh . . . I th . . . th . . . th . . . th . . . think I can do it, sir."

"Oh, you th-th-th-think so? Well, we'll see. We'll try you on the milk-bottle game. The pay's sixty cents an hour. Report to Louie tomorrow night, six o'clock sharp.

"*Next!*"

"So, Jason, if he's blind, how the hell could he see that I am only fourteen years old?"

"Blind bastard was just showing off. I bet he asked you for your name right off, right?"

"Yeah. But he doesn't know me from Adam, and he didn't ask for my age. I swear to God! How could he know my age? That's what I want to know!"

"Keep your shirt on. A couple of nights ago when I was leaving work, I told him my kid brother would be coming in applying for a job. I said you were a good little kid and a hard worker. So he was lying in wait for you and was probably set to hire you. And he knows that I'm seventeen, so he probably guessed that you were two or three years younger than me. He knew if you were twelve, you wouldn't be applying for a job, right? So he figured fourteen or fifteen would be a good guess. End of mystery."

"But why would he want to go through all that, just to confuse a little kid?"

"Like I said, just showing off. Look, Abe is blind, right? And he's got some weird talents that only blind guys have, like he can hear better than most people. So he knows somebody's in the room—right? 'Cause he heard you walk in. And he knows where you're standing because he can hear you breathing. So, because he can do some things that are only slightly out of the ordinary, he's become famous for having a sixth sense. He likes that, right? So he tries to add to that legend by faking more dramatic stuff—stuff that he really can't do. But he pretends that he can by taking a calculated guess based on information he has, but that you don't know he has. And he says it as if he's sure as hell. And the next thing you know, the kid in front of him—*you*, simple bastard that you are—is dazzled by his magic."

"But what if he's wrong?"

"Nothing! If he's wrong about your age, you correct him, and you don't think much about it one way or the other. After all, who expects a blind guy to be able to guess a person's age? But if he's right, you get all impressed, and you go around telling everybody who'll listen what a supertalented hotshot old Abe is. And the next thing you know, we have a living legend on our hands. Don't you see? He can't lose."

Jason was right on this one, but blind Abe had other foibles too, some of which weren't quite so harmless. Like the way he used to grab little kids by the balls when they came into his office. He pretended that he was just horsing around, but none of us ever believed that. We all knew he was serious, but we kept quiet about it. All for sixty cents an hour, a penny a minute. Quite a bargain, for him.

Abe and his cronies stiffed us boardwalk workers to boot. They would stop counting our time the minute we closed the doors, but there was always another forty-five minutes of cleanup to do that we never got paid for. And if we ever checked in a nickel short, they docked us the nickel. Nobody ever complained, though. Not just because we needed the money, but because we knew there were fifty kids in line waiting for our jobs. Besides, we figured the bosses had the power and therefore the right to jerk us around.

But we got even, thanks to what Jason called "boardwalk morality." For example, everybody I knew who worked on the boardwalk used to clip—a euphemism for stealing. But boardwalk workers never thought of it as stealing. Stealing was wrong; that's when you shortchanged a customer. It was wrong for two reasons: First, most customers were poor slobs like us and couldn't afford to be cheated. Second, if you thought about shortchanging anyone, you would never try it on the untrusting customers who counted every cent in change as if their lives depended on it. No, the only customers you could get away with cheating were those who trusted you. And what kind of a guy would cheat someone who trusted you? That's why any kid who was known to cheat customers was held in contempt by the other boardwalk workers.

But clipping wasn't stealing; it was getting even—getting even with a bunch of rich, dishonest bastards who underpaid you and who watched you like a hawk. Clipping therefore had to be subtle and skillfully done. Anyone who was caught was fired immediately, as happened to Noman Pasternak. Noman's real name, of course, was Norman, but one day, when penciling his name on the starched lapel of his working jacket, something we all did, he unwittingly left out the "r." From then on, we all called him "Noman."

Noman worked on a penny-pitch game in the arcade, where the customers tossed pennies, trying to get them to lodge in a shallow bowl floating in a tub of water. If they succeeded, they won a chintzy little prize—such as a balloon shaped like Mickey Mouse that could stand up on cardboard feet. Nine times out of ten, the tossed penny would skip out of the bowl and land in the water. One night after work several of us dropped into a boardwalk deli run by Abe and his associates. Noman ordered a corned-beef sandwich and promptly paid for it with thirty-five wet pennies. The next day, when he reported for work, he was sacked on the spot.

––––––––––––

The boardwalk was a two-mile microcosm of a complex city, crowded with colorful characters, all kinds of games and rides, nightly shows, and food stands galore, their pungent smells inter-mingling in the air—including frozen custard, pizza, hamburgers, cotton candy, fried clams, and Joe & Nemo's hot dogs. And the sounds! The roar of the roller coaster, the screams of its riders, filled the air. At first I worked the milk-bottle stand, where the customer got three baseballs to throw at five hollow aluminum bottles stacked on a small table. (They weren't real baseballs, of course; they were cheap sawdust-packed nickel bricks that we had to wrap in tape so that the covering wouldn't fall off after a day.) If you knocked the five bottles off the table with three balls, you'd win a cockamamie plastic Hawaiian lei; with two balls, a cheap wooden cane. But if you succeeded in knocking them all off with one ball, you would get the best prize on the boardwalk—a teddy bear. But not just any teddy bear. "No sirree," I'd say, "but a big, fat, cuddly Mumbo Jumbo teddy bear. That's right, ladies and gen-tlemen, we're playing for the big one, the Mumbo Jumbo teddy bear. Come on over! Three balls for a quarter. How about you, sir? Don't you want to win a Mumbo Jumbo teddy bear for the little lady?"

Almost anyone could win himself a lei. And quite a number of people could win a cane. But the probability of knocking all those bottles off the table with one ball was almost zero. "I'm sorry, sir," I'd have to tell customers time and again, "you can't just knock them down; they have to be all the way off the table." It would have been extremely difficult to throw a single ball hard enough and true enough to knock all the bottles off with one pitch, even if the game had been honest. But Abe Shaw didn't take any chances. The thing was rigged. The two end bottles on the bottom row had about an inch of lead poured into them, so that when the ball hit one of them it sort of keeled over in a dead faint and laid there on the table without budging.

The bottles flopped down in such an unnatural manner that it's a wonder everybody didn't get suspicious right away. A few people did, but Abe had worked out a contingency plan. He had instructed me and the other workers how to handle that situation: A guy might say, "Hey, the bottom bottles are made out of lead!" At which point I would assume a long-suffering look of resignation, walk over to a newly stacked set of bottles, grab the middle bottle from the bottom row, and present it to the complainer for his inspection. This gesture was designed to be so winningly forthright that no one thought to quibble about whether the other bottles might be leaded. It worked every time.

My biggest problem, though, was not with suspicious customers but with frustrated ones. There were four tables of milk-bottle games, each in its own alley. After spending several dollars vainly trying to win his girl a Mumbo Jumbo teddy bear, players were likely to feel exasperated, embarrassed, and angry. And, since they didn't care much about the second and third prizes anyway, after missing with the first ball, they had two spare balls that they had no real use for. So they found a use for them: hurling them at me while I was busily setting up the bottles in the next alley. The first time it happened, I didn't know what hit me. I felt a searing pain in the small of my back, and spun around in shock and fury only to see the smiling face of my tormentor, claiming, in mock apology, that the ball got away from him.

Of course, I didn't believe a word of it. But my options were limited; these guys invariably had ten years and eighty pounds on me. Besides, deep down, I believed they had a right to be angry because they were being gypped. I struggled with that one, trying to protect myself and also trying to figure out where I fit into this world.

"They're right to be mad, goddammit," I'd complain to Jason.

"So what the hell are you complaining about?"

"Why me? I didn't do anything wrong. I don't deserve to get hit with a fucking baseball. I get sixty cents an hour here. I'm not the one that's cheating them."

"Of course you are."

"No, I'm not. Well . . . okay, I am, but I'm not getting rich off them."

"Justice, he wants. On the boardwalk, no less."

"Damn right! What's wrong with that?"

"Look, El. Don't get all self-righteous all over me, willya? Part of what you're getting paid for is to be insulation, and you know it. When's the last time Abe Shaw got hit with a fucking baseball?"

"That prick!"

"He's not such a prick. He's just playing the system. And that's the way the system works. When a person gets some dough together, he can walk around in his house in his shirtsleeves in the middle of winter without being cold because he can afford insulation. In our house everybody is wearing eleven sweaters, and we're still shivering and freezing our asses off. Abe Shaw can pay for insulation. On the boardwalk his insulation is you and me, and everybody else that works for him. We stand between him and the big guy throwing baseballs. It's a shitty job, and I hate it and I can see that you hate it too, and I'm glad you hate it. Some of these guys don't seem to mind it, and I feel really sorry for them," he continued. "But look, don't pretend that you don't know what's happening. If you start pretending, you're really lost. Abe is a crook, but he's pretty honest with us. He tells us what he's going to pay us, and he tells us what he wants us to do. And we can take it or leave it. Just don't whine about it."

During Jason's talk I was staring down at my feet, nodding occasionally, and letting the words flow over and around me. It reminded me of the delicious sensation of climbing into a nice warm bath after a day out in the cold. (In our house nothing nice was ever simply called by its name. There was never anything as simple as a warm bath. It was always a *nice* warm bath. Conversely, nothing was ever simply unpleasant, such as a draft of cold air coming through cracks in the window frame; it was always a *terrible* draft.) I loved listening to Jason. The world was a confusing place. Nothing was as clear as I wanted it to be and as it was in the movies, where the good guys wore white and always behaved politely and the bad guys always needed a shave and could never look you in the eye. In the real world I tried to identify the villains, spot the phonies, and, by the way, cast myself in the role of the hero. But I suspected that I was kidding myself, that the world was more complex than I wanted it to be, though I wasn't entirely certain what I was leaving out of the picture.

Every once in a while Jason turned on a spotlight for me. He illuminated the unspoken rules of the boardwalk, where you shouldn't believe your eyes, where what you saw was not the truth, where the games were rigged, where you always needed to look behind the curtain if you wanted to know what was really going on. I was grateful to him, so how did I express my gratitude? I punched him as hard as I could on the arm. "How did you get to know so much?"

"Don't be a smart-ass, El. Nobody likes a smart-ass."

I was anything but a smart-ass. I was timid, often confused, but I kept trying to understand. I did appreciate Jason's insights, but they were usually delivered as lectures, with an attitude of know-it-all pomposity that made it difficult for me to swallow the lesson whole. I always wished that the message would come in a beautifully wrapped package, so that I could embrace the whole thing without all those feelings of ambivalence.

Nonetheless, during the first eighteen years of my life, Jason was just about the only person in my family to see me as a bright and talented youngster with a lot of potential; he was undeterred by all the evidence to the contrary. He taught me that hard work could be fun, and that having fun was important. He taught me to take myself seriously, but not too seriously. By example, he showed me the joy of poking fun at my own foibles and blunders and that humor could be found in anything. For years after the aphasia brought on by my concussion, he would mimic the way I tried to say "I'm all right"—a flawless imitation of Charles Laughton's Quasimodo, the Hunchback of Notre Dame. Also by example, he taught me how to play the hand I was dealt, in poker as in life, like a mensch—that is, with a minimum of whining or complaining.

The boardwalk was full of other lessons besides the cynical ones, if you were ready to observe them. One lesson came from the brilliant divers at the aquatic show, who could do triple somersaults in the air before gracefully entering the water, making barely a ripple. After their act a clown would appear on the high dive, wearing a baggy swimsuit that hung down to his knees. He would peer over the edge tentatively and then back away. He would try again, look down in feigned fright, step backward toward the edge, go too far, and fall, arms and legs flailing. The audience would be helpless with laughter. "What an idiot!" my buddy exclaimed.

It took me many nights of observation before I realized that far from being a clumsy buffoon, he was the most talented diver in the show. I came to appreciate how much hard work he put into appearing so clumsy, while entering the water safely at the last second. Years later, when I became a college professor, laboring for hours to prepare lectures that seemed casual and spontaneous, I would think fondly of that clown diver and the lesson his performance taught me: If it looks easy, it probably isn't.

My milk-bottle game was on the boardwalk just down from the biggest arcade, where Abe Shaw's office was. You would enter the arcade to find, on your right, pinball games, a fortune-telling machine, and the penny-pitching game where Noman worked. On your left was Pokerino, thirty individual tables that ran in a long row from the front of the arcade all the way to the back. In Pokerino you didn't compete with other players. You sat at your own table and rolled a ball into one of its pockets, labeled with card names—jack of spades, king of hearts. As the board lit up, you'd try to roll the ball into the pocket that would give you the best poker hand. It took some skill to win this game, but mostly luck; that ball took some strange bounces.

The only grown men on the boardwalk who made more than $3 an hour were the mike men on the major games, such as Pokerino and Fascination. A good mike man was worth his weight in gold (or, more accurately, in nickels), because a lot of money was riding on how quickly he could break the ice—that is, on how quickly he could get those first few people off the street and into the arcade. These guys were charming, witty schmoozers, and we all admired the hell out of them. The least-experienced kids worked the simplest games, so I was thrilled when, at age sixteen, I was offered a promotion, to make change at the Pokerino tables.

One cold and rainy night, with hardly any patrons on the boardwalk, the mike man at the Pokerino tables stepped down from his perch and asked me if I wanted to take over until closing time. This was a fantasy come true. I had been observing him, listening to his spiel over and over until I had it memorized. I even found ways to improve upon it, while rehearsing for hours in front of a mirror. So when he gave me a chance, I was ready. This is what I came up with my first night behind the mike:

Walk right in, sit in, get a seat, get a ball. Play poker for a nickel. Five cents. There are no bells to start you or stop you. You play your own individual game. You win your own individual prizes! And we're playing for the biggest, the best, the grandest prizes on the boardwalk. It's so easy to play and win a game. You put a nickel in the slot, and you get five rubber balls. You roll them nice and easy, under the glass, over the incline, and into the various marked pockets. Any three of a kind or better poker hand, and you are a winner. So walk in, sit in, play poker for a nickel. Five cents. Hey! There's three jacks on table number 27. Pay off that lucky winner! And a full house on table number 16!

That was me! There I was, smooth as silk. Actually, there was nobody in the arcade. There wasn't anyone sitting at table number 27 or table number 16. I had somehow figured out that the only way to attract people was to make it sound as if others had already been pulled in by the game. And sure enough, a few people wandered in and began to play. Within a half hour it seemed like half of the sparse crowd wandering the boardwalk was playing Pokerino. Abe Shaw came out of his office and asked his assistant what was causing the commotion. "It seems to be Elliot doing his spiel," the assistant reported. "Make that kid a mike man," said Abe, and my career as a barker began. I got a raise to $1.50 an hour.

Even while I was doing it, though, I questioned how I could have made it as a mike man. I was convinced that my shyness was a permanent social handicap: I always had been shy, and I always would be shy. Yet on the boardwalk I was able to assert myself and behave with grace and even boldness. My success behind the microphone delighted me, but also confused me. Who was I, really? Being able to ask that question raised the possibility that, one day, I could become more like my big brother than I had previously dared to dream.

CHAPTER THREE

Learning to Learn

Elliot at Brandeis, 1950.

My uncle Fred knew exactly what I should do when I faced the two most momentous decisions of my life, and his advice was wrong both times.

When my father died I was about to enter my senior year of high school. His death precipitated a family conference—not from the Aronson side but from the tight-knit Feingold side. The Aronsons would never dream of calling a family conference or of trying to dictate a course of action for one of their kin, but the Feingolds did it all the time. Accordingly, it was natural for my aunts and uncles to gather in our living room to consider the question: What is to become of Dorothy and the children? Almost all of them attended, as well as my mother, Jason, and Paula, who was then about twelve. Uncle Fred, the dentist, who was the oldest and wealthiest of my mother's brothers, presided. And, as the self-appointed head of the family, he dominated the meeting. He proposed that Jason, who was entering his second year at Brandeis University, stay in college. I should finish high school and then get a job, so that I could support my mother and sister and help finance the rest of Jason's education.

It seemed like a reasonable plan to me, but Jason immediately saw through the facade of familial concern to the real issue—money, and how not to spend it on us. The Feingolds might be willing to augment whatever savings my mother had for one year, until I was able to work full-time, but then they would be free of us. Jason said, "Screw that! Elliot is going to go to college, and it's not going to cost any of you a red cent. He and I can both work our way through school."

"What about your mother and sister?" Uncle Fred asked.

"Ma knows how to work," Jason replied. She had in fact worked as a stenographer before she married, although of course she had not had a job in more than twenty years.

My mother took all of this in, but said nothing. I think she did not want to cross either her brother or her oldest son; she may have been a little afraid of both of them. Uncle Fred was skeptical of Jason's plan and annoyed with his insubordination; he was accustomed to getting his way in family discussions. Noisy argument ensued, but Jason was resolute. His year at college had opened a world of possibilities for him, and he wanted me to enter that world, too. He feared, reasonably, that once I went from high school into the workforce, I would not turn back. The meeting broke up unhappily. When the uncles and aunts left, Jason turned to my mother and said, "Ma, you can do it." And she could. Within a few months she had a job selling dresses in Chandler's, a fine department store on Tremont Street in Boston, and was enjoying it.

Jason not only had to convince Uncle Fred but also had to convince me. I hated high school, because, with few exceptions, the teachers were burned out and boring (my history teacher often came to class drunk). They didn't think I was worth much, and I can't blame them: I got mostly Bs and Cs, without working very hard. Jason gave me a pep talk about exerting more effort in my senior year so that I would stand a chance of being admitted to a good university. In my heart of hearts, I thought the effort would be useless. I didn't think I was smart enough, and even if I got admitted, I couldn't afford to go; I was not about to ask Uncle Fred for a loan. Jason tried to convince me that I could earn a scholarship as he had done. "But I'm not as smart as you are!" I protested.

He grabbed me by the shoulders and said, "Look, schmuck, do you want to spend your life pushing a baby buggy down Shirley Avenue?"

That was a chilling image. For years, with a mixture of sadness and fear, he and I had observed guys in their early twenties who had married their high school sweethearts, were soon saddled with children, had taken miserable dead-end jobs, and were pushing that baby buggy down one of the main streets of our town. The mere thought of that fate scared me into trying harder. By the middle of my senior year I had pulled my grades up a little, but the big surprise came when I took the SAT exams. I astonished my teachers, and myself, by getting an astronomical score. And so I applied to a few colleges, all in the Boston area. I was accepted at Boston University, Northeastern, and Brandeis, which had been founded just two years earlier but was achieving national recognition as a first-rate college. The fact that Jason was already at Brandeis gave me a moment's pause—once again, being judged as his little brother, arriving in the wake of his stellar achievements. He was on the Dean's List, he was elected as the very first president of the student union, he would go on to be the editor of the first yearbook, and he was founding director of the campus satirical revue, *Hi Charlie*. But Brandeis made the decision easy by offering me a one-year full-tuition scholarship and a part-time job that allowed me to pay most of my room and board. I would be working five nights a week at the campus snack bar, making milkshakes and grilling hamburgers.

The summer after high school graduation, I did not go back to the Pokerino tables. I found a way to make more money, working on highway construction for the Commonwealth of Massachusetts. During that summer I did a lot of thinking about the transition I was about to make. From my experience as a mike man on the boardwalk, I had learned that, somehow, entering a new situation would give me an opportunity to try to re-create myself. In high school I never went to a prom; I had never even dated, being too shy to ask a girl out. Because my fellow students saw me as shy, they contributed to my self-concept, and my self-concept in turn constrained my behavior. (Later I learned there is a name for this phenomenon—the self-fulfilling prophecy.) But going to college would wipe the slate clean. In a new environment I could try to become the person I wanted to be. I figured that if I behaved as if I were not shy, the new people I met would see me as an outgoing guy.

And so, arriving at Brandeis in the fall of 1950, I hit the ground running—socially, anyway. I made some close friends. Most of the guys I was hanging out with were tough, smart, and verbally aggressive, skilled in sarcasm and the witty put-down, and I saw from the start that to keep up with them I would have to become a good counterpuncher. At home I used to cry easily. Here, to protect myself, I started building a shell. I also began dating, and within a few months, I discovered that I was attractive to women. I started going steady with Barbara, who was pretty and popular, and my view of myself as an awkward, inept teenager slowly faded. Barbara told me that her friends were calling us the cutest couple on campus.

I worked every evening from seven to ten at the snack bar. Curfew at the girls' dormitory was eleven. Barbara would come into the snack bar shortly before it closed, so that we could be together for that hour. In those days there was no place to go for making out, let alone for making love. We couldn't go to a dorm room, as men were not allowed in the women's dorms. We couldn't go to a hotel or motel, even if we could have afforded it, because you had to be married, and desk clerks were suspicious of nervous teenagers who weren't wearing wedding rings. So most of our sexual activity, such as it was, took place in the back seat of cars or in a small coin-operated laundry room that was frequently empty (and dimly lit). For the first months of our relationship we necked and petted, often to orgasm, but we didn't go "all the way" until one evening when we were in the back seat of a friend's car. Usually, Barbara would press her thighs together and whisper "no no no" at the ultimate moment, but this time she didn't. She opened her legs, and I slid in. It was my first time. I felt an exhilaration that filled my whole body. I also felt enormous gratitude that she had allowed me to enter her. At the crucial moment I withdrew and ejaculated into my hand.

Moments later she turned to me and said, "Did you put it inside?"

"Couldn't you tell?" I asked.

"No! Of course not! You actually put it inside me? That's awful!"

"But I thought it's what you wanted."

"It's *not* what I wanted. I'm a virgin—or I was." And she began to cry.

"My God, Barbara, I'm really sorry."

My exhilaration and gratitude deflated rapidly and were replaced by guilt, contrition, and confusion. How could she not know? I drove her to her dormitory, kissed her good night, and thought about what had happened. I was naive, but not that naive. Of course she knew; she had to know. It dawned on me that we were caught up in a sexual drama and we would each have to play our parts: She would pretend to have been unaware of the penetration, and I would pretend that I didn't know that she was pretending. For the next few months, from time to time we made love "accidentally." Then, without discussing it, we dropped the pretense.

One night, when I left Barbara and arrived back at my room after eleven, I found Jason waiting for me.

"With Barbara *again*?" he asked. "You know, you don't have much time to study as is. You have to make use of whatever time you have free, instead of fucking around with Barbara every night. You could flunk out of this place."

"What is this?" I said. "Am I living in the same dorm with my father? Lay off."

"I'm not your father, I'm your brother, and I want you to get the most that you can out of being here."

"I *am* getting a lot out of being here."

"Okay, have it your way," Jason said, going out the door, "but at least be careful." And with that, he tossed me a package of Trojans.

Jason's concern about my study habits was justified, but not because of Barbara. Soon after I got to Brandeis I discovered that I had never learned how to be a student. I didn't even know the first thing about taking notes. I would sit in class, listening to the lecture, scribbling furiously. By the time midsemester exams came around, I pulled out my lecture notes and found they were virtually unintelligible. I did poorly on those tests, but I learned something from the experience. From then on, at the end of every class, I would find a little nook—sometimes even the nearest stairwell—read over my scribbled notes, and neatly summarize them in a page or two. At the end of the semester, when it was time to prepare for the final, my notes described the heart of the course. More than that: They revealed the scope and pattern of the professor's thinking and the way his lectures dovetailed with the readings. I had taken the first step toward mastering the art of getting to the essence of a topic. When I was boiling down my lecture notes, I could see the professor's thought process and where he was heading. I found I was also learning to love to learn, and, perhaps most important, I was learning to think critically and challenge unsubstantiated assertions. For the first time in my life I understood what it was to be a student. In the second semester of my freshman year, I was earning straight As.

My political awakening at Brandeis was just as intense—in fact, it had begun before classes even started. One night during freshmen orientation week, I was having a discussion in the dorm lounge with Steve, one of the older students who were advising us. The topic was Senator Joseph McCarthy, and our discussion quickly grew heated. Like just about everyone I knew back home in Revere, including all of my teachers and fellow students, I thought McCarthy was a hero. In my final year of high school he had been giving speeches, to everyone from Republican women's groups to the U.S. Senate, claiming that the State Department was infested with Communists in high positions. McCarthy would dramatically hold up a sheet of paper, declaring, "I have in my hand a list of their names!" and expressing outrage that the State Department would allow such dangerous people to be making foreign policy decisions.

When I was in high school our teachers had told us that Communists had infiltrated the State Department, so I was filled with anxiety and gratitude for Joe McCarthy. Moreover, because I believed that the Soviet Union was evil and sinister, it followed that any American Communist was a potential spy who should be exposed and punished, and McCarthy seemed to be doing just that. No one I knew would have disagreed with that position. My history teacher (who happened to be sober that day) had quoted former ambassador Joseph Kennedy's claim that McCarthy was both a war hero and a peace hero. The only newspaper my parents, friends, and I read was the *Boston Daily Record*, a Hearst tabloid, which intensified the fear of the Communist threat and hailed McCarthy as the savior of democracy. The whole issue seemed like a no-brainer; all we needed to do to protect ourselves was root out the Commies. And McCarthy had their names. Case closed.

At Brandeis, I discovered that I had been living in a hall of mirrors. To my astonishment Steve and most of the freshmen in my dorm not only considered the issue debatable but were convinced that McCarthy's claims were wild and irresponsible, and that the senator himself was more of a menace to our democracy than anyone in the State Department. They pointed out that the numbers on his list kept shifting. He told one group that the State Department had 205 "card-carrying members" of the Party, to another group it was 87 or 79, to the U.S. Senate it was 57.

"And notice," Steve shouted at me, "that he never actually *named* anyone on his list!" I fought back, lamely, arguing that even if there were only one, it would be one too many. Steve retorted that the Tydings Committee had determined that McCarthy's so-called list was a hoax, and there were no spies in the State Department.

I was dumbfounded. This may have been the first time that a belief that I thought was absolutely right had been challenged, and not just challenged but treated with derision. What was this Tydings Committee anyway? How could anyone consider Senator McCarthy to be a menace? Wasn't he a patriot? Maybe, I remember thinking, Steve and some of the other guys were Communists themselves. But soon I realized that this debate was not simply a matter of opinion or taste, like whether you liked a particular movie, or you believed Joe DiMaggio or Ted Williams was the better all-around ballplayer. This was a matter of cold facts, on a crucial question at that. Either McCarthy had a list of documented Communist spies or he did not. It dawned on me that I might need to find a way to dig into the evidence for myself. I should no longer rely on what other people thought, whether they be my peers and teachers at Revere High School or my liberal classmates at Brandeis University.

During our argument, Steve suggested, at the top of his lungs, "Why don't you read the *New York Times* instead of the *Daily* fucking *Record*?" That idea alone was astonishing, a reflection of my naïveté. My initial thought was, "Why should I read the *New York Times*? I'm from Boston; I'm not from New York." But privately I made the decision to take his advice. The next day I went to the college library and began following McCarthy's exploits in the *Times*, where I learned that Steve had been right about how much the *Boston Record* had distorted and omitted.

Over the next few months I learned that the Tydings Committee, a Senate subcommittee that had investigated McCarthy's allegations, had concluded that there were no Communists in the State Department, which in any event had adequate screening devices in place. And then I read something that shocked my innocent freshman mind even more: When the Tydings Committee's report was brought before the entire Senate, the vote as to whether to accept its conclusions split precisely along party lines. So perhaps it *was* a matter of opinion after all! Just as Red Sox fans favored Ted Williams and Yankee fans favored Joe DiMaggio, Republican senators unanimously had accepted McCarthy's charges against the State Department while Democratic senators had unanimously repudiated them.

Wow, I thought, so this is college. I guess not all learning takes place in the classroom. It was a revelation to me that facts can be distorted by ideology and that knee-jerk patriotism, the kind I had brought with me from Revere, can blind us to immoral behavior in our leaders. I vowed to try to keep an open mind and, wherever possible, do my own digging. Although I considered the Soviet Union to be a serious threat to democracy, I also learned, for the first time, that many thousands of Americans had become members of the Communist Party in the 1920s, '30s, and '40s for humane, idealistic reasons and how incredibly simpleminded I had been to think that all of them were traitors or spies. During the first months of my freshman year, I felt intensely ambivalent. On the one hand, I wanted my country to be safe, and in the 1950s the threat of a nuclear holocaust was palpable. On the other hand, I was beginning to understand the monumental importance of civil liberties. All the things I learned in high school history and civics classes, about what a great country this is, were of little consequence if this great country was depriving law-abiding citizens of their freedom of speech, their right to have their own political opinions, and their right to work without harassment. I realize how obvious that lesson sounds to anyone who came of age after 1965, but in 1950, a scant five years past the end of what we called The War, there were no nuances about the word "patriotic." The more I studied McCarthy's tactics, however, the more I saw what a ruthless, erratic school-yard bully he was, willing to drag people and their reputations through the mud in a manner that was both careless and uncaring. His investigations were fishing expeditions designed to intimidate and humiliate his victims.

The summer of 1951, back in Revere, I spent some of my free time hanging out at Bob's Variety Store with some of my old pals from our neighborhood baseball team. Mostly, we talked about sports and sex. But when the topic of Communism came up, I blurted out my reservations about Joe McCarthy and his tactics. Out of the corner of my eye, I saw Billy MacDonald wink at Al Ross. "What?" I asked.

Billy laughed and said, "Do they teach you that stuff up there at the college?" I got defensive and started to explain that anyone who followed the issue closely in the newspapers would know . . . and then I stopped short and said, "Yeah, I guess so." And I realized that Billy was half right. They didn't actually teach me that stuff "up there at the college," but I sure learned it there. If I had stayed in Revere, my attitudes would undoubtedly have remained stagnant.

That summer, while Billy and I were once again swinging a pick and wielding a shovel on a highway construction crew, I received two letters from the dean of students. The first came in late June and congratulated me on my sterling grades during my freshman year. The second arrived a week later, informing me that, due to a shortage of funds, the university could no longer offer me financial aid. I was crushed. I surmised, with some bitterness, that the dean was reserving their meager scholarship money for incoming freshmen; he probably figured that I was already hooked. If so, he was right. I was so much in love with learning that nothing could have kept me from going back to Brandeis.

I earned enough money over that summer to pay for tuition, but I could not afford to pay for a dorm, and the university was too far away from Revere for me to commute. I tried sleeping on the floor of Jason's room, until my presence was detected and reported by the cleaning crew. I was summoned to the dean's office and informed that the rules of dormitory use were strict and inflexible. If I were caught again, I would be expelled.

So I spent that first semester of my sophomore year sleeping wherever I could. When the weather was fine, I slept in the woods surrounding the campus; when it rained, I slept on the back seat of any unlocked parked car I could find. One night I awoke from a sound sleep because the car I was in had started moving. The driver, a guy named Harvey, and his girlfriend were driving to a popular necking spot called the Duck Feeding and Parking Area. (The students referred to it as the Duck Peeding and Farking Area.) Needless to say, they were unaware of my presence in the back seat. What to do? I decided it was prudent to keep quiet. But twenty minutes later, when I heard the sound of zippers being unzipped, I decided I had better make my presence known. I gently cleared my throat. They leaped up, startled, as if a police siren had sounded. Harvey turned, saw me, and said to his girlfriend, "It's okay, honey. It's only Elliot." Apparently, my unorthodox sleeping arrangements were well known to my fellow students. They generously drove me back to campus, so I could find another car for the night.

I felt like I was hanging on to my education by my fingernails. During the day the only place serving food was the campus cafeteria, but you had to have a meal contract to eat there. If I wanted lunch, I had to scrounge food from one of my friends, under the watchful eye of the cafeteria manager, Mr. Grim (I swear, that was his real name), who, like the cleaning crew in the dorms, was ever alert for interlopers. When he turned away, my friend would surreptitiously shove his plate in my direction, and I would eat whatever I could as fast as I could. It was hardly gracious dining, but it kept me nourished. In the evenings I might get lucky and devour an illicit hamburger from the snack bar where I worked.

This history is beginning to sound like something out of Dickens or, closer to home, like the romantically embroidered stories my grandfather used to tell me about his walking to school barefoot through blizzards in czarist Russia. In my case, there was nothing romantic about it, but I was willing to endure these minor hardships. I almost never cut class, even when the professor was boring. That would have been akin to working hard to earn the money to buy a ticket to the theater and then not showing up. During that fall semester I managed to save enough money from my job to rent a room off campus. I was able to come in from the cold during the most brutal part of the Massachusetts winter.

During the winter semester I had to declare a major. I thought seriously of literature or philosophy, both of which were exciting the hell out of me. But, remembering my father's despair during the Depression, and having no idea whether another one was around the corner, I thought it might be smart to study something more practical, something that might help me land a job after college. So, with reluctance, I declared economics as my major.

My relationship with Barbara, which had lasted a year and a half, had run its course. In those days most students didn't have casual relationships that lasted more than a few months: You broke up, or you became engaged to be married. We both realized that although we liked each other enormously, we did not want to spend our lives together. And so we parted.

One afternoon I was having a cup of coffee with an attractive young woman I was hoping to get to know better. Suddenly, she looked at her watch and realized that she was late for class. I decided to walk along with her, hoping that she and I might sit in the back of the lecture hall and hold hands. It turned out that the class was Introductory Psychology, being taught by some guy named Abraham Maslow, a new professor who had just arrived at Brandeis. As it happened, Maslow was discussing the psychological aspects of racial and ethnic prejudice. Much to my astonishment, he was raising questions like the ones that had puzzled me ten years earlier, while I was sitting on that curb in Revere, nursing my bloody nose, wondering why all those Irish Catholics hated Jews so much. Where does prejudice come from? Is it inborn or is it learned? Can it be changed through good experiences with a member of the disliked group, or will the prejudiced person just dismiss it as the exception that proves the rule? Until that moment, I had no idea that there was a field of study that addressed such questions. I was enthralled. So I let go of the young woman's hand and started taking notes. I lost the girl but found my bliss. The next day I switched from economics to psychology.

Brandeis in those years was a small, informal college on a bucolic campus. It had first opened its doors in 1948, and when I got there two years later, there were only five hundred students—none of whom were even seniors yet. The four full-time faculty members in the Psychology Department had their offices not in an ordinary academic building but in a cozy, charming cottage on Ridgewood Terrace at the edge of campus. The faculty would hold seminars in the living room, and students would hang out there, reading and talking with our professors, getting to know them quite well. Once I started majoring in psychology, I spent a lot of time in that cottage. I studied primarily with Maslow, who was both an inspirational teacher and a visionary thinker. He was charismatic, but his charisma was not the flamboyant kind that people often associate with the word, but gentle and compelling. He spoke softly and thoughtfully, frequently pausing for several seconds in the middle of a sentence—he'd look up at the ceiling, making a little tuneless and almost soundless whistle, while he sought precisely the right word—but his listeners hung on every one of them. I got a great deal out of his lectures, but I most enjoyed our conversations.

At the time, psychology was dominated by two great forces: behaviorism and psychoanalysis. Maslow's revolutionary view was that neither approach truly captured the essence of humanity or the possibility of what human beings could become. He was particularly contemptuous of behaviorists, believing that the study of rats and pigeons in what he regarded as the restricted, artificial conditions of the laboratory could never ask, let alone answer, important questions. And he objected to what he considered the unduly gloomy portrayal of humanity through the eyes of psychoanalysis, with its emphasis on neuroses, defenses, existential anxiety, and unconscious conflicts.

As an alternative to these two dominant perspectives, Maslow proposed that it was time for psychology to develop a third force, one based on a humanistic, philosophical approach to human nature and motivation. He believed that psychologists needed to observe and interview healthy, mature people to find out what they were feeling, what they were thinking, and how they dealt with life's challenges. How did they survive, indeed transcend, adversity and deprivation? Maslow arrayed human needs along a hierarchy, from the lowest, basic needs for food, water, and safety, to a single glowing, transcendent motive at the top, which he called self-actualization. Maslow considered self-actualization to be the ultimate goal of all human beings, and he wanted psychologists to understand how best we can achieve it.

I immediately resonated to the concept of self-actualization because it addressed the notion of transcendence, which I linked to my hopes for my own life and to understanding my own history. Even then, however, I knew the concept was slippery; Maslow kept shifting the definition in his writings and conversations with us. I guess I was already an incipient scientist, because I kept trying to pin him down. Once I confronted him and asked whether by "ultimate goal" he meant that people had a conscious desire for self-actualization. He hemmed and hawed, whistled (tunelessly!) and looked at the ceiling, and then said, "I think 'desire' is too strong a term because self-actualization is nothing a person strives for; he sort of slips into it after satisfying the other needs in the hierarchy. The journey toward self-actualization is a never-ending process and is never fully achieved except, perhaps, by saints."

"I guess that leaves *me* out!" I said. Maslow laughed and said, "Me, too!"

Well, maybe. At one seminar, Maslow listed some of the major characteristics of individuals whom he regarded as being at the top of the hierarchy, people in the process of self-actualizing. These qualities included spontaneity, the ability to face unpleasant facts and difficult challenges with a minimum of stress, an interest in solving problems, openness to experience, a lack of prejudice, the ability to laugh at themselves, the ability to love without possessiveness, and a strong sense of autonomy—the ability to go their own way in spite of opposition. Maslow's description of the self-actualizing person sounded suspiciously close to how Maslow might have described himself, and a few of us teased him about it. He insisted that this list was derived from empirical research, though his notion of *empirical* was, shall I say, somewhat casual. His research, he said, consisted of observing and interviewing hundreds of people and examining the lives of exemplary individuals like Albert Einstein, Eleanor Roosevelt, Frederick Douglass, and Jane Addams. I agreed with his candidates for self-actualization, but it was only years later that I understood the fatal flaw in his reasoning: It was circular. How do we know whether Einstein et al. are self-actualized? Because they have the qualities of a self-actualized person. And what are the qualities of a self-actualized person? Those that Einstein et al. display.

By today's standards Maslow would not be considered a scientist. Science requires that you state your theory in a way that it can be tested and shown to be wrong. Maslow's theories were not even specific enough to allow others to test them. When I pressed him about the questions that he (and the nine-year-old Elliot Aronson) had raised about prejudice, his only answer was that he was certain that it was not innate, that it was learned, and that it could be modified; that empathy and altruism could be fostered if the environmental conditions were right. But he had no specific answers as to how we might bring this about.

Although I found Maslow's answer disappointing, I learned something even from my disappointment. I wanted him to have all the answers, to be the perfect father I never had, and he didn't quite fit the bill. "Get over it," I'd admonish myself. "He gives you plenty." Maslow was my first mentor, the first older man I was close to, the first to show concern for my personal as well as academic progress. Once, after taking me aside to compliment me on a presentation, he cautioned me about the sharp-tongued, sarcastic qualities that I was developing as part of my masculine survival strategy. "Your sharp edge is not venomous," he observed, "but it keeps people at arm's length." I was flattered by his interest in me, but I wasn't ready to give up that edge just yet. It disguised the shyness I still felt most of the time. .

What Maslow also gave me was a vibrant and powerful humanism, which he lived as well as preached, and which made him exciting to be with. Many of his lessons stayed with me for the rest of my life, and of these the most important was his optimistic orientation toward human beings and their potential to grow, learn, improve. Society too, he taught us, could become healthier. That optimism got into the very marrow of my bones. From Maslow, I acquired the determination to apply psychological wisdom and knowledge toward the betterment of the human condition. I only dimly realized it at the time, but that was a tremendous gift.

But Maslow's greatest gift to me was yet to come. In my senior year he hired me and another student to serve as his assistants and errand runners. The other student was a remarkable young woman named Vera Rabinek. She was Maslow's absolute favorite, for he saw her as someone who was already far along the path to self-actualization. Besides, he was playing matchmaker. At that time Vera was being ardently courted by two first-year graduate students in psychology. Maslow didn't think either of those guys were right for her and probably thought I might be able to dislodge them.

Vera had grown up in Hungary, survived the Holocaust, and emigrated at the age of seventeen. She was brilliant, gorgeous, and fairly glowed with a quality that I would call serenity. During my first three years at Brandeis I had admired her from afar but had not gotten to know her. She was far more sophisticated than I. She and her friends were the campus literati, and she seemed way out of my league. But after Maslow had thrown us together as his assistants, we gradually got to know each other; within a few months we had become close friends.

The two of us could not have taken more different routes to get to Brandeis, but it was several months before Vera told me her story. She was born in 1930 and had an idyllic childhood, living in the center of Budapest, a stone's throw from the opera house, which she frequently attended. But in the 1940s Hungary's home-grown Nazi affiliate, the Arrow Cross, with the complicity of the country's totalitarian government, began murdering some Jews and deporting others. Vera's older brother, George, was seized and sent to Buchenwald. Vera barely managed to avoid capture and deportation herself, although she had some harrowing close calls, until the Soviet army finally broke through and drove the Germans out of Hungary. In 1947 she arrived in the United States, where she was taken in by a foster family in Baltimore. Her understanding of English was poor, and she spent the first several weeks of high school in tears because she had no idea what anyone was saying. But she was a quick study. In 1950 she graduated fifth in her class and won a four-year scholarship to Brandeis.

I would later observe that many Holocaust survivors struggled for years with the cynicism, rage, and bitterness their experiences engendered—toward Nazis, toward Germans in general, toward all humanity. But some, like Vera, went another route, deciding to seize the beauties of all that life had to offer. We would be taking a walk and she would pause to watch a group of children at play. To me, it was just a bunch of kids, but Vera helped me focus on the beauty and wonder of the scene. To Vera, nothing was ordinary; every sunset was a gift. She also sharpened my appreciation of extraordinary works of art, such as a Schubert trio, a Mozart opera, or a Van Gogh painting. These were illuminating lessons for a young man like me, who had not grown up with art and music and lacked much of an aesthetic sense. Before long, the same intuition that cautioned me against Barbara now drew me to Vera: how wonderful it would be, that little voice said, to spend your life with someone who, having seen the worst that the world has to offer, finds joy and beauty in everything around her.

Vera had a directness that was irresistible. Unlike Barbara, and the few other women I had seriously dated after her, Vera did not play the gender game by the conventional rules of the time. She put her cards face up on the table. When she said no, she didn't mean "maybe in an hour or in a week or in a month, as long as I can pretend I don't know what is happening." And eventually, when she said yes, she was clear about why and what it meant for her, and for us. I fell in love with her, and, miraculously, she with me.

Decades later I learned that it was not only Maslow who had been pulling for me in the "who will win Vera's hand?" sweepstakes; the rest of the psychology faculty was also. Ricardo Morant, who had been a new assistant professor when Vera and I were first dating, told me that every Psychology Department faculty meeting would include an analysis of who they thought might be ahead in the quest for Vera Rabinek. Morant was also happy to remind me that Vera got an A in his course in experimental psychology—and I got a B+.

Vera and I decided to marry, but there was a roadblock. I had resolved not to get married until I had a clear idea of what I was going to do with my life, and as graduation approached, I was more confused than ever. Because Maslow had been pointing me toward a career in clinical psychology, I dutifully applied to a few graduate programs and was accepted. To gain experience as a clinician, as well as earn my keep, I had been working summers and weekends as an orderly in the neuropsychiatric ward of St. Elizabeth's Hospital in Brighton. One of my duties was to assist with electroshock therapy (ECT). I had to brace the patient's shoulders and hips so they wouldn't get dislocated during the convulsions that accompanied the treatment. I came to care about several of the patients, was happy for them when they were released from the hospital as cured, and dismayed to see them return a few months later. I saw that the treatments available at the time— psychoanalysis, ECT, or heavy-duty tranquilizing drugs—were temporary at best and did not do much for people with severe mental illnesses, such as major depression or schizophrenia. The hospital was a revolving door. Patients were admitted, got buzzed, felt better, went home, relapsed, and then came back. This observation shook my idealistic hopes about what I could accomplish as a clinical psychologist. Not seeing an alternative, I rejected the offers to go to graduate school.

Even then, I held the belief that every person needs to know two things—one, where am I going? and two, who's going with me?—in that order. There I was, in the spring of my senior year, about to graduate in a month, with no plans for the future. I knew who I wanted going with me, but I had no idea where I was going.

And then I caught a lucky break. Three weeks before graduation Maslow received a letter from David McClelland, the chairman of the Psychology Department at Wesleyan University. McClelland ran a small master's program in order to have teaching assistants for the undergraduate courses, but that year no one had applied. McClelland was desperate and wrote to Maslow, asking if he knew of any bright psychology majors who had no postgrad plans. Maslow simply tacked McClelland's letter to the bulletin board outside his office, where Vera was quick to spot it. Uncharacteristically, she ripped it off the board. She ran to find me and handed it to me, saying, "Abe must have meant to give this to you! It has your name all over it." I thought, "Perhaps it does. I won't become a psychotherapist, but maybe at Wesleyan I could pick up the skills to become a good college teacher." I phoned McClelland immediately. A few days later we borrowed a car, drove to Wesleyan, and spent the afternoon with him. We hit it off. Not only did he offer me a half-time teaching assistantship on the spot, but he also offered Vera a full-time position doing research in his lab. Suddenly, we were financially secure, and I knew where I was going. There were no further impediments to our getting married—except Uncle Fred.

My mother liked Vera, but because of her obsession with long-term financial security, she had misgivings about my marrying someone who lacked the family resources that Barbara had. My mother confided her worries to her sisters, and it was agreed to convene another meeting of the Feingold family, at which Uncle Fred once again presided. He summarized the family's concerns. "I think you're making a big mistake," he told me. "Marriage is

hard enough when it's between two people from the same back-
ground. But Vera is foreign born—*Hungarian!*—and who knows
anything about her parents? They don't even live in America. She
has no money, no hope of any inheritance. And neither do you."

My aunts and uncles had not seen much of me since I went
away to college and began to flourish. What Uncle Fred didn't say
out loud was that in their eyes, I was still the ineffectual little boy
they had always known, the one who would never become Captain
Marvel.

Once again, Uncle Fred's advice was wrong. Marrying Vera was
the best decision I ever made. But if it had not been for the timing
of McClelland's letter, my guess is that I would have enlisted in
the army to mark time and think about my future. Without a clear
career path, I would not have married Vera, at least not at that
time, and I might have drifted into a far different line of work. To
borrow from Leo Szilard's story, I would have missed the train.

That summer after our graduation Vera and I pooled our meager savings to buy our first car. One of my former baseball teammates from Revere, who had become an auto mechanic, found us
an old, beat-up Nash for $140 that he said was in great shape
under the hood, except that the transmission was shot. He generously volunteered to scour all the automobile graveyards in the
area until he could find a junk transmission in good shape. After
several days he came over, held up a greasy-looking thing, yelled
"Eureka! Thirty-five dollars!" and installed it. From that day on
Vera referred to that transmission as her engagement ring.

Our wedding was joyous but not in the usual way. By Feingold
family standards, it was a terrible affair. They favored lavish wed-
dings—complete with tuxedos (of course!), evening gowns, brides-
maids galore, a six-course banquet, and a five-piece band—whether
or not the bride's parents had the means to pay the piper and the

caterer. To be fair, the Feingolds were hardly alone in their notions of what a proper wedding should be, but Vera and I opted for simplicity. It was not our intention to disappoint the family or swim against the tide, but we firmly believed in living within our means, and we were turned off by the whole idea of conspicuous consumption. We just wanted to be married; the ceremony itself and the party that followed were unimportant. The compromise was a stand-up reception, held in my mother's living room where my aunts and uncles mingled with our friends, sipping off-brand liquor and chomping on lox, bagels, and the ubiquitous sponge cake. My relatives left early; our friends stayed late.

But first came the ceremony. As it happened, there was an unintentional note of hilarity in the otherwise formal proceedings. My grandfather Ben Feingold had insisted that the ceremony be conducted by an Orthodox rabbi. Although that would not have been our first choice, in the interest of maintaining some semblance of family harmony, we acquiesced—rather graciously, as I recall. For his part, as a thoughtful nod in the direction of our "modern ways," Ben found a young rabbi. "I didn't think you would want one of those ancient, stooped Old Country schnorrers with a white beard down to his knees," he said. The rabbi he chose was young, all right. Ours was his first wedding. He trembled noticeably, stammered, and kept pausing while he frantically dug into his pocket to fish out his notes. I sneaked a peek at Jason, our best man, who was biting his lower lip and turning crimson as he gamely tried to suppress laughter. The sight of Jason trying not to laugh made me chuckle, and that started a chain reaction: Vera burst into laughter and was joined by my friends who were holding the poles of the bridal canopy, causing the canopy to shake violently. Uncle Fred was not amused.

With no time for a honeymoon, Vera and I were off to Wesleyan two days later, as the fall semester was about to begin. We drove from Revere to Middletown in our beat-up Nash. The car wasn't much to look at, but it got us there, and, as my baseball buddy had promised, it served us well during our entire stay.

CHAPTER FOUR

A Wesleyan Honeymoon

Newlyweds.

D id I say Vera and I didn't have a honeymoon? Wrong. Our stay at Wesleyan was a two-year honeymoon. We set up housekeeping in Veterans Village, a cluster of converted army barracks owned by the university, located in a rural area but only a mile or two from campus. Each apartment consisted of a bedroom, a living room, a kitchen, and a bathroom. The university provided us with a bed, a table, and four chairs, and all for thirty-eight dollars per month, utilities included. We added the brick-and-board bookcase that was de rigueur for graduate students at that time. The inexpensiveness of that apartment, combined with the fact that Vera and I were both employed, meant that, for the first time in either of our lives, we could open a savings account.

The barracks were not well built. The buildings were poorly insulated, the floors creaked, the doors were not plumb, and the walls were thin and didn't quite reach the ceiling. When we got to know Rich and Arlene, neighbors in the adjacent apartment, they asked us the name of the novel that Vera and I were reading to each other in bed at night. It was Thomas Mann's *Magic Mountain*.

"Oh," said Rich. "From what I can gather, it's a fascinating story. Arlene and I often stand in our bathroom for a half hour at a time, listening to you read. By the way, I missed a part. Did Settembrini really kill Naphta in that duel?"

"No," I replied. "As often happened in these tests of honor, Settembrini purposely fired his shot into the air. But then Naphta trumped Settembrini by putting a bullet in his own head, thus ending their duel." After dutifully filling Rich in, I began to blush

as the realization struck me that if they could listen to us reading
in our bed, what else could they overhear? Vera and I realized that,
honeymoon or not, we would need to try to cavort more quietly
in the future.

But lack of privacy was a small price to pay in exchange for the
feeling of community in Veterans Village. Our fellow tenants were
all young married couples; most were graduate students, and some
were young faculty members. There were frequent potlucks, vol-
leyball games, and general all-around schmoozing. It was a lot like
dormitory life at Brandeis except that everyone was older, more
serious, and more married. Some of our neighbors had babies,
some had toddlers, which made us think seriously about having a
child. I was only twenty-two years old, and there I was, already
considering becoming a father. Why not? If many of our neighbors
could start raising a family, why couldn't we?

As I look back, I am amused at how ready I was to become a
husband and father. Just two years earlier, when I was a junior at
Brandeis, I had decided never to marry. It was not a quiet decision,
either. I frequently proclaimed my aversion to marriage out loud,
to my friends, acquaintances, and anyone else who would listen.
Vera recalls that I announced my no-marriage decision to her
when we were just beginning our friendship, almost as a warning
to her. I had almost never seen a happy marriage up close. My own
parents were hardly a loving couple, and, apart from Uncle Leo
and Aunt Lillian, I never saw a sign of romance or even mutual
affection among my many aunts and uncles. Because divorce was
rare among middle-class Jews at that time, the older couples I
knew seemed to be plodding unhappily through life hooked together, like a pair of oxen pulling a heavy wagon. Moreover, my
first college romance, with Barbara, was uninspiring. Being married to her would have meant joining that wagon train.

Then I met Vera, and my resolution to remain a bachelor for life dissolved in her sunlight. And now here we were at Veterans Village, surrounded by happily married young people who were going to school and raising families. So much change in such a short time, and I had a lot to learn. When it came to marital disagreements, for example, I was something of a wild animal, not unlike my father. Growing up, I had learned only one way to deal with the frustrations of a domestic dispute: raising my voice and pounding the table for emphasis. Vera, though, had grown up in a family where disagreements were discussed calmly and thoughtfully; her father was a gentle, timid man who would never dream of raising his voice. Indeed, he would much prefer to lose the argument than raise his voice in anger. Our two incompatible notions of how to argue crashed into each other, and it didn't take me long to discover that my behavior frightened Vera.

One night, during a disagreement about an inconsequential matter, I got so frustrated that I stormed out of the house, slamming the door behind me. Halfway down the stairs I stopped and said to myself, "What the hell are you doing—and where the hell do you think you are going? Damn it, schmuck, you are not your father!" I walked back up the stairs and into our living room. "I'm sorry," I said, and I was. Seeing the effect of my anger on Vera had startled me into self-reflection. I was confused; isn't anger what men do? Wasn't the only alternative to become meek and obsequious, to back down as Vera's father had done? Yet my explosive fury hurt Vera and made it hard for her to listen to the substance behind my shouting, preventing us from dealing with the causes of our disagreements. I realized I would have to find a way to express my feelings honestly. It took time.

My primary male role model for domesticity was Mike Wertheimer. Mike was a young assistant professor in the Psychology

Department, living with his wife, Nan, who was also an experimental psychologist, and their two toddlers. He was not only a first-rate teacher and researcher but also an excellent father, way ahead of his time in taking a great deal of responsibility for child care. He would frequently wander over to our apartment with his two-year-old daughter, Karen, perched on his shoulders, while pushing Duffy, his nine-month-old son, in a stroller, and invite me to join him for a cup of coffee or a walk around the neighborhood. Vera and I spent a lot of time with Mike, Nan, and their kids, hiking in the mountains, picnicking, and just hanging out. They made parenthood look very inviting. The Wertheimers were our first dinner guests. Vera was teaching herself to cook, primarily through trial and error, trying to remember how her mother had prepared meals in prewar Budapest. Before long she developed a great chicken paprikash, and was delighted when Mike ate everything on his plate and then used his bread to mop up any remaining trace of gravy. Vera considered him the perfect guest.

The atmosphere of the Veterans Village community shaped our direction as a young married couple. But it was the Wesleyan campus, and especially the Psychology Department, that gave us our first taste of what it might be like to live the life of a college teacher. For both of my years at Wesleyan, I was the only student in the graduate program. In many respects, this was a disadvantage. I had no peers to interact with, share ideas and anxieties with, and complain to about the faculty, the workload, and the weather. I also had no comparison group. How could I assess how well (or poorly) I was doing if I had no one with whom I could compare myself? Moreover, there were no graduate seminars, as there had been for master's degree candidates in previous years. Thus, my graduate training consisted entirely of doing supervised research.

But the advantages of my situation far outweighed the disadvantages. Because I was more advanced than the undergraduates, and because I had no fellow graduate students to hang out with, the faculty treated me like a colleague—a very junior colleague, to be sure, but a colleague nonetheless. I had easy access to every member of the psychology faculty for casual conversations. We frequently ate lunch together, and in midafternoon, when some of the members of the Psychology Department wanted a break, we'd stroll over to Downy House, a charming, wood-paneled coffeehouse, where we were frequently joined by faculty from other departments. One frequent visitor to the unofficial psychology table was David McCallister, a distinguished anthropologist, and another was the inimitable Norman O. "Nobby" Brown, who had just completed his masterly analysis of Freud, *Life Against Death*. They followed the lead of my psychology "colleagues" in discussing things with me as if I were a fellow faculty member.

The tone of this egalitarian treatment was set by David McClelland, the department chairman, who treated both Vera and me with warmth and kindness from the very outset of our stay at Wesleyan. A few days after our arrival at Veterans Village, knowing how sparsely the apartments were furnished, he invited me to borrow desks, chairs, and lamps from the Psychology Department. And then, when he saw that I had no way to transport the bulkier furniture, he helped me load a heavy desk into the back of his station wagon, drove me to the barracks, and, huffing and puffing, helped me carry it up two flights of stairs. I will never forget his generosity.

Dave had an easygoing, casual demeanor. As my mentor and Vera's boss, he was extraordinarily easy to work for. He was clear about what he expected us to do, but he left the details of how and when to do it entirely up to us. Indeed, he always seemed pleasantly surprised whenever we entered his office with a completed task in hand. He was the first Quaker I'd ever met, and a serious one—"thee-ing" and "thou-ing" with his wife and children in a sweet and affectionate way. Yet this good-natured guy was not only the departmental chairman but also its most distinguished member. At thirty-seven he had already written a successful textbook in personality, as well as a little book that had a big impact, *The Achievement Motive*. Dave, the quiet Quaker, spent his life studying achievement motivation and exemplifying it.

Dave had developed a reliable technique for measuring the degree of a person's achievement motivation (which became abbreviated as "nAch"). He would show test subjects an image of people in everyday life, like a middle-aged man and a young man in a rural setting, leaning against a fence and chatting, and ask them to write a structured story about who the people are, what is happening, and what the outcome will be. Dave and his assistants would then score the essays for achievement imagery: Were the men talking about repairing the roof, planting flowers, or going to the movies? Was the older man trying to convince the young man to go to college as a way of opening up opportunities for himself or to focus on raising a prizewinning cow at the next county fair? If you consistently wrote about self-improvement, inventing something, getting a promotion, scoring the winning touchdown, and so on, you would be deemed to have higher achievement motivation than if your stories were about people talking about the movies or sharing a sunset. The strength of the achievement motive, McClelland argued, is captured in the fantasies the test taker reveals. "In fantasy anything is at least symbolically possible," he wrote. "A person may rise to great heights, sink to great depths, kill his grandmother, or take off for the South Sea Islands on a pogo stick." Needless to say, people who are high in achievement motivation don't write about sinking to great depths or retiring to the South Seas.

At the time I met McClelland, the research on achievement motivation was already producing some fascinating results. Dave and his associates had found that achievement motivation was a better predictor of college success than IQ. And, in a deceptively simple study in which children played a ring-toss game, they showed why that might be. Imagine you're a child and you get to stand wherever you want to pitch a ring onto a peg. Will you stand up close and be guaranteed success, even if that success won't be very gratifying? Will you stand way back so that you are sure to fail, since after all you aren't particularly good at this skill? Children who scored low in achievement motivation did one or the other, standing either directly on top of the peg or clear across the room. But the kids with high nAch consistently chose to stand at a moderate distance from the peg. At that distance, with practice, they could sharpen their skills and eventually become adept at the task. According to McClelland, they were like successful entrepreneurs; they took a moderate risk for reasonably high reward. In this instance, the reward is the gratification of improvement and eventual high scores.

Vera was McClelland's full-time research assistant. She immediately mastered the coding system for scoring achievement motivation in people's stories and became the standard by which Dave judged the efficacy of other scorers. Dave was constantly expanding the kind of evidence that might reveal signs of achievement motivation. Why, he wondered, were some countries full of high achievers and others low achievers? This question led him to Max Weber's classic essay linking the rise of capitalism to the Protestant ethic, the belief that God looked favorably on those who work hard and are able to delay immediate gratification for greater gain in the future. McClelland reasoned that if Weber were right, then Protestant countries should be trying to infuse their youngsters with achievement motivation to a greater extent than Catholic countries. To test this hypothesis, he asked Vera to gather a random sample of elementary school readers that were currently popular in several countries. She found several bilingual foreign students and oversaw them as they translated these books into English. Vera then scored these stories for achievement imagery in much the same way she had previously scored adults' spontaneous stories in response to pictures. The data confirmed Weber's speculation: Children's readers in Protestant countries were loaded with achievement imagery, while such imagery was scarce in Catholic countries.

For my own research with Dave, I took up his challenge of helping him find a nonverbal measure of achievement motivation. This would allow him to test children who were too young to be able to read and write, to determine how early in a child's life the motive appears. An interesting challenge, but where to start? You can't start with children, because you need to correlate your nonverbal measure with the standardized verbal test of achievement. Some psychologists had suggested that personality traits reveal themselves nonverbally in the way people walk, the way they draw pictures, in the slant of their handwriting, and so on. I was skeptical, but I dutifully scoured the stacks at the college library in search of books or articles that might enlighten me. Most of what I found was not terribly convincing, but then, while rummaging around, I discovered a little gem in the *Psychological Review* for 1896. It was the report of an experiment, titled "Cultivated Motor Automatism: A Study of Character in Its Relation to Attention," by Gertrude Stein. Yes, *that* Gertrude Stein. She conducted the experiment while she was a student of the great American psychologist William James. Stein's experiment was the first serious attempt to investigate the phenomenon of automatic writing. She rigged a sling from a rope attached to the ceiling and placed her subject's arm in the sling. It was fitted with a stylus so that when the subject moved his arm, the movement was recorded on the paper below. She instructed her subjects to relax completely. She predicted that the markings on the paper would reflect the person's unconscious thinking. Her results were inconclusive, but the experiment was her first step in applying James's notion of "the stream of consciousness" into her own subsequent creative writing.

I also dug up a little book that, among other things, contained photographs of a page from original musical scores by two famous composers. I don't remember the name of the author or the book, but the two scores were memorable. One was written in a very neat, tidy, and orderly manner, while the other was scrawled tempestuously across the page. The author informed us that one had been composed and transcribed by Beethoven and the other by Mozart and then (rather smugly, I thought) invited the reader to guess which was which. The difference was striking, and the identification was obvious, confirming, the book's author said, his theory that personality is revealed in handwriting (in this case, score writing). When I showed the book to one of my neighbors, a graduate student in music, he found it fascinating. So did I. But I realized that, from a scientific perspective, the author's demonstration was meaningless. If we are allowed to cherry-pick examples that confirm our theory, there is no way that we can be wrong. I wondered how many tempestuous composers there were who wrote in a neat manner. One pair of composers, carefully preselected by the theorist, does not a confirmation make.

Although I found no single piece of research on so-called graphic expression to be convincing, the overall thrust of the research was just barely provocative enough to motivate me to take a closer look on my own. I began to think about what form of graphic expression I could investigate. Well, how about doodling? Everybody doodles. I found it at least conceivable that the way people doodle might reflect something important about their personality. But what would I do, lurk around telephone booths and grab the callers' notepads? I needed to find a way to get people to doodle under standardized conditions and then try to see if people with high nAch produce doodles that are reliably different from those produced by people with low nAch.

Here is how I decided to do it: I drew a complex doodle consisting of straight lines, circles, S-shaped lines, multiwaved lines, fuzzy lines, and ellipses. I then projected it on a screen for two seconds and asked a group of college students to copy it as best they could. Because two seconds was not nearly enough time for the students to get a clear idea of the doodles on the screen, what they drew was less a copy of what they saw than an expression of how they usually doodled.

We had already given these students the standardized nAch test. I now selected the doodles of those students on the high end of the nAch continuum and spread them out in a single row across our living room floor. Next I took the doodles of those on the low end of the nAch continuum and spread them out in a row parallel to the first. Vera and I then crawled around on our hands and knees looking for anything that distinguished the two rows. It was Vera who spotted the first major difference: The lines and geometric figures of the high nAch students were mostly discrete, made with a single bold stroke of the pen, while those of the low nAch students were fuzzy, overlaid, and repetitive. For example,

where high nAch students would draw a circle, the low nAch students would draw the same circle going around and around five
or six times. I discovered some other differences: Where students
with high nAch would draw an S-shaped line, those with low nAch
would draw it as multiwaved; high nAch students tended to fill
up the page with doodles, while low nAch students left a lot of
blank space, especially at the bottom of the page. The doodles of
people high in nAch, I concluded, were more efficient. They expressed as much as possible with the least effort. Why make a
multiwaved line when the same statement can be made with one
S-shaped line? Why overdraw a circle when the same circle can
be made with one round stroke? Why waste space, when one can
fill it?

Of course, that was a post hoc interpretation. I didn't predict
any of the doodle differences, so they easily could have been caused
by chance alone. What I needed to do next was cross-validate, testing my hypotheses on an entirely new group of subjects. I did the
research. And got the same results. There was a significant corre-
lation between achievement motivation and the way people doodled, in exactly the way that Vera and I had found while crawling
around on the living room floor. I developed a precise technique
for scoring doodles and was able to train my undergraduate research assistants to use it with great reliability. The relationship
between doodling and nAch continued to hold.

In his own research McClelland found that for people high in
nAch, the feeling that comes from a job well done is far more important than financial rewards, praise, or recognition. They are
forever seeking to improve their performance and to take on
greater responsibility at work, not for the status but for the challenge. As he and I chatted over coffee at Downy House, he often
expressed his belief that people with high nAch are the ones who

make things happen. Six years later, in his masterwork, *The Achieving Society*, McClelland argued that the major difference between successful and unsuccessful nations lies in the achievement motivation of its citizens. In it, he cited and extended Vera's research on children's readers in underdeveloped countries, and he expanded my research on graphic expression in a highly creative (some might say "far out") way: He applied my coding system to the decorative paintings on ancient Greek vases, as photographed and collected in the *Corpus Vasorum Antiquorum*. Sure enough, he found that vases that were produced and painted just prior to historical surges in Greek achievement were characterized by a greater use of efficient forms of graphic expression—such as S-shaped lines and filling more space—than those painted during more quiescent epochs. Greek vase painters were showing signs of high nAch in much the same way that twentieth-century college students were.

Actually, while I was at Wesleyan I devoted most of my energy not to research but to teaching. I can best describe what I was doing as teaching myself how to teach. Because I was employed as a TA, for the first time in my life I started to look at the process of teaching in an entirely different way, not from a student's perspective ("Hey, am I going to understand this stuff and get a good grade here?") but from the teacher's perspective ("How can I help these students comprehend this complex material?"). I was fortunate in having three excellent role models: Dave McClelland, Joe Greenbaum, and Mike Wertheimer. Stylistically, they could not have been more different from one another, but each was a first-rate instructor. Mike was extremely well prepared; he would come in with a sheaf of notes from which he would deliver a clear, formal lecture that was thorough and precise, but he left little room for spontaneity. Joe was an entertainer; he was funny and erudite, and referred often to movies and literature, but he always managed to bring his examples back to the essence of the course. McClelland was casual; he would walk in without notes and chat informally but with obvious expertise. I was impressed by all three of them, and, over the years, my own teaching style became a blend of their methods. I learned to be so well prepared that I could afford to be casual and responsive to the momentary mood of my audience; I learned how to hold my students' attention by keeping them entertained, not with jokes but with stories—some funny, some touching—that I would weave into the lesson in such a way that they illuminated and expanded on it. I learned to draw on material from life, literature, philosophy, films, and the day's news.

Halfway through the spring semester of my first year, Mike Wertheimer invited me to give a guest lecture in his Introductory Psychology course. I had a whole week to get ready, and I used all of it. I was so well prepared that I felt confident enough to walk in without notes. I printed a brief outline on the blackboard, which was more for my own benefit than for the students. As I faced the class and waited for them to settle down, I could feel my heart pounding. But as soon as I started to talk, my shyness and my nervousness vanished—just as they did when I sat behind the microphone at the Pokerino tables at the Revere Beach Boardwalk.

Vera had asked me if I would mind if she sat in. We both saw this as an important event, and I very much wanted her to be present. But in those days Wesleyan was an all-male school; it would have been impossible for Vera to slip into the classroom and sit, unnoticed, at the back of the room, and frankly I was embarrassed at the prospect of the students grinning when they noticed that Elliot's wife had come to hear him lecture. It was stupid of me, and I now regret that decision, but, with reluctance, I asked Vera not to come. Vera understood my discomfort completely, but she couldn't stand the idea of missing the first lecture of my life. So as soon as the class started, she sat on the floor just outside the classroom, opened the door a crack, and eavesdropped. The students seemed to enjoy my talk; they laughed at all my attempts at humor and were solemn at all the serious and touching things I described. As soon as the lecture ended, and before the applause died down, Vera ran back to her office before any of the students could spot her. Mike Wertheimer, always thoughtful and considerate (and not knowing that Vera had been eavesdropping), made a beeline to her office and said, "Your husband was superb!" A few minutes later I came into Vera's office, hugged her, and said, "This is what I want to do for the rest of my life."

Learning about the classroom from the perspective of the teacher also illuminated an experience that had deeply touched me when I was at Brandeis. In my senior year I had enrolled in a small seminar called Logic and the Scientific Method, taught by the distinguished philosopher Aron Gurwitsch. Gurwitsch, an austere man in his midfifties, smoked incessantly during class, inhaling through a long, black cigarette holder, and spoke with a heavy accent that was a blend of Russian and German. He was stern and impatient, always on the verge of losing his temper with any of us if we failed to immediately grasp some of the complex material he was presenting. Yet I found him to be an excellent teacher. From Professor Gurwitsch's rather harsh Socratic prodding, I learned the art of critical thinking and the importance of challenging entrenched ideas with logic and evidence.

One afternoon, as I was leaving Gurwitsch's class, the professor spotted me with a thin little book under my arm and asked me what I was reading. I handed it to him. It was the English translation of *L'homme machine*, written in 1748 by the French physician and philosopher Julien Offray de La Mettrie. I had been assigned this book and was supposed to give a report on it for a seminar in the history of psychology. I had accepted the assignment with reluctance, because I had never heard of La Mettrie and I was hostile to his general notion that humans are programmed like machines in their thinking and behavior. But once I got into it I found the book enthralling. La Mettrie wrote with passion and precision, and his ideas about human nature were revolutionary for his era. Moreover, because he was a materialist writing in Catholic France, I realized that writing that book must have been an act of great intellectual courage. Gurwitsch glanced at the first few pages and grunted.

"Do you like this book?" he asked.

"I *love* it," I replied enthusiastically.

"Oh," the professor said. "Et croyez-vous que l'homme est une machine?"

"Absolutely not! I disagree with all of his conclusions, but I am impressed by the sheer brilliance of his reasoning," I said.

Then a remarkable thing happened. Gurwitsch's entire face softened, his eyes glistened, and he leaned forward. He put his hand on top of my head and gently squeezed it, with obvious affection. "Good boy," he said softly.

It was the first time a professor had ever physically touched me and with such warmth. But, more important, Gurwitsch had shown me, almost wordlessly, that it was a good thing—perhaps even a noble thing—to be able to love a book, an idea, with which you disagreed. At Wesleyan, taking the first steps on the road to becoming a professor myself, I gained an even greater understanding of what his gesture, face, and tears were conveying. It was nothing less than the profound satisfaction a teacher feels when a student really gets it.

During the summer after our first year at Wesleyan, three important things happened. The first was that Vera and I decided to have a baby. Vera had always wanted to have children, many children, and the fact that so many of our friends at Veterans Village were happily raising young kids made it look easy. Moreover, I was now sure what I wanted to do professionally: teach psychology at the college level. I would get a Ph.D. and become a professor at a small college. I would not have to do much research and could do for my students what Abe Maslow and Aron Gurwitsch had done for me. Being launched on a clear career path, I could see no reason Vera and I shouldn't start raising a family.

The second thing that happened was that Dick Alpert and Ralph Haber, two Ph.D. candidates at Stanford who were McClelland's former graduate students, came back to Wesleyan, joining Vera and me to work on one of McClelland's research projects. During that summer the four of us became close friends, and we have remained close ever since. Ralph was to become a distinguished cognitive and forensic psychologist, contributing research on perception and memory as well as serving as an expert witness on the unreliability of eyewitness testimony. Dick went to Harvard as a developmental psychologist but was to leave academia and become the influential spiritual leader Baba Ram Dass. (I respect his transformation, but I have never stopped calling him Dick, and whenever we meet I eventually get around to telling him, much to his delight, that he hasn't changed all that much since 1955.)

The third thing that happened that summer was that Dave McClelland told me, in confidence, that although it wasn't official yet, he was expecting an offer from Harvard to become professor and director of the psychological clinic in a year. He wanted to know if I would be willing to join him at Harvard as a graduate student and his primary research assistant. I said that I was honored by his offer and would certainly consider it. But I told him that I was also intending to apply to Stanford, which looked good to me because Dick and Ralph were so happy there. Dave said that Stanford was a terrific university—"I think they call it the Harvard of the West," he joked—and that I couldn't go wrong no matter which place I chose.

When Stanford accepted me and offered me a teaching assistantship for the first year, Vera and I spent a long time making the decision. We agreed that it would be easier and safer to go to Harvard because Dave and I were fond of each other and because he was so easy to work for. Cambridge was also familiar territory; it was only a few miles from my mother and sister, a few miles from Brandeis and Maslow. Being on the East Coast would also mean that I could see more of Jason, who was a graduate student in political science at the University of Chicago. Stanford, in contrast, seemed remote. I had never been west of the Mississippi. Hell, I had never been west of Philadelphia.

But the one thing that made Harvard most attractive also was my greatest concern: Dave McClelland. As much as I liked and admired Dave, I felt that I had already learned most of what I could from him, and I wasn't excited about doing still more research on achievement motivation. If he brought me to Harvard, he would have had every right to expect me to work with him; once there, it would be difficult and perhaps even disloyal to switch mentors. Stanford, though, was virgin, unknown territory. Aside from Dick and Ralph, I knew no one there and would be obligated to no one. To Dave's great credit, he never applied any pressure, nor did he try to influence my decision in any way. When I told him my choice was Stanford, he said that he was disappointed but that he completely understood my decision and wished me well.

It didn't take long for Vera to become pregnant, and the baby was due in early March 1956. Our old Nash was becoming unreliable, and I began to have nightmares about the damn thing breaking down on the way to the hospital. Besides, if we were going to drive to California in the summer, we knew the old Nash would not be up to the challenge. So, in February, we decided that it would be prudent to buy a new car. A year earlier one of our neighbors in Veterans Village had bought a brand-new Volkswagen, and none of us could get him to stop talking about its virtues. It is hard to believe, but, at that time, 99 percent of all cars on our nation's roads were American. The VW burst on the scene with a reputation for reliability and fuel efficiency. What's more, we might even be able to afford the $1,560 for a new one. Well, not quite. We were about $300 short. Then it dawned on me: my bar mitzvah money! I was bar mitzvahed in 1945, with the war still raging. In those days war bonds were a tidy bar mitzvah present because they cost only $18.75; ten years later they would be redeemable for $25. So my aunts and uncles could give me a $25 present for only $18.75. I cashed in the bonds, got $175 for the old Nash—exactly what I had paid for it eighteen months earlier—and bought the new car.

And just in time. On leap-year night of February 29, Vera went into labor. It had started snowing that afternoon and was still snowing as we, shivering with excitement, climbed into our spanking-new VW and drove to the hospital. In 1956 husbands were considered to be a nuisance in maternity wards. As soon as Vera checked in, they hustled me out of the way and put me into a tiny, windowless waiting room that had all the charm of a prison cell. When I arrived, another expectant father was already there, smoking and pacing the floor. We exchanged pleasantries:

"Your first one?"

"Yeah."

"My third. Nuttin' to it," he said nervously.

He then offered me a cigarette, and we both smoked and paced like expectant fathers in Hollywood films of that era. About five hours later a student nurse stuck her head in the room and asked me if I wanted to see my son. They didn't allow me to hold him, but I could view him through a window. I then went in to see Vera, who was groggy and still reeking with the smell of ether, the anesthetic favored by most hospitals at that time. But she was deliriously happy. We looked at each other and cried. We could hardly believe it. We had brought a new being into the world. We were parents.

We decided to name our son Hal, after my father. In the naming of a child, the Jewish tradition is to choose the name of a beloved person who is no longer alive as a way of preserving the memory of that person. Typically, the child gets the identical Hebrew name as the deceased and an English name that begins with the same letter of the alphabet as the deceased's English name. We wanted an *H* name for my father, Harry, but why not Henry, Harold, Howard, Horace, Hubert, or Hyman? We chose the name Hal because we hoped our son would be as wild and adventurous in his youth, and as judicious and wise in adulthood, as was Shakespeare's memorable Prince Hal.

In naming my son after my father, I thought that I was merely making my mother and my grandfather happy by observing what had been, to me, a meaningless ritual. But the name had a surprising impact on me. When I picked up my new baby, fed him, burped him, changed his diaper, held him close, and said his name, I often thought about my father and the difficult roller coaster of a life he had led. How he started with nothing, worked hard, pulled himself out of poverty, opened a successful business, and moved into the middle class; how he lost it all, slid back into poverty, and felt the humiliation of being rescued from prison by the father-in-law he disliked. And how, just as he was beginning to get himself together, he died feeling like a failure, a man who had let down his wife and kids. The birth and naming of my infant son opened my heart to my father and his plight. For the first time since my father's death, he became a frequent visitor in my thoughts and dreams.

I loved watching Vera with Hal. Everything she did with the baby flowed effortlessly. She took about a month off from work, and then, in early April, we brought Hal into the psychology building, and each of us took turns caring for him while the other worked. At coffee time we brought him to Downy House and put him in the center of the table in his basket. As we sat around the table talking psychology, each member of the group would occasionally tune out of the conversation to do a little cooing, baby talking, and chin chucking.

In early June, after the Wesleyan commencement, Vera and I packed up and left Veterans Village. Our plan was to drive cross-country to Stanford, but first we spent six weeks as the guests of Dave and Mary McClelland at Yelping Hill, a fifty-acre compound in the Berkshires. The compound consisted of several small cabins, which the McClellands owned with several of their friends. Vera and I did a little work for Dave, but mostly we played with Hal and chatted with the residents and their constant stream of interesting guests. Our favorite was a young artist, a few years older than us, who stayed in a cabin near ours. Dave and Mary had introduced him as Maurice, but he asked us to call him Mark. We had already seen Mark's droll and charming illustrations in one of our favorite children's books, Ruth Krauss's *A Hole Is to Dig*. Vera and I spent a lot of time with him hiking, swimming, picking wild blueberries, discussing psychology, and lying on our backs at night, in a meadow, watching star showers. He confided to us that he was taking a leap from illustrating other people's books to writing and illustrating his own, and that he had already finished one; sure enough, the following spring he sent us a signed copy of *Kenny's Window*. A few years later we were delighted to learn that our summer friend had won the Caldecott Medal for a book that turned out rather well. It was called *Where the Wild Things Are*.

At last we were ready for our journey west. We bought a big map demarking almost every national and state park. We bought sleeping bags, air mattresses, and a Coleman stove, so that we could occasionally eat something hot and sterilize Hal's baby bottles. Our plan was to sleep under the stars every night unless it was raining, a plan that lasted until another of the McClellands' friends took pity on us in our hopeless naïveté. "You will wake up every morning soaking wet from the dew," he said. "Look, I just bought some new camping gear so, here, take my old pup tent."

The pup tent duly packed, we rigged the back seat of the VW with Hal's crib mattress. (I figured that he might as well get used to sleeping in cars. Someday, he might be a penniless student at Brandeis.) And off we went.

CHAPTER FIVE

Becoming a Social Psychologist

Leon Festinger in action (top).

Jason, Vera, and Hal at Indiana Dunes, 1956: "You guys did it; you really did it."

Vera and I had decided to camp our way across the country for reasons of beauty and economy. When we needed to sleep, if the nearest campground was uninteresting (as most were), we would spend only one night, get an early start the next morning, and continue westward. But whenever we were near a scenic place to camp, like a national park, a lakeside state park, or a charming village, we might spend three or four nights. We had decided that our first stop would be not for beauty but for family. We headed for Chicago, where we could visit with Jason and spend a few nights in his bachelor's apartment on South Harper Street.

While driving through Pennsylvania, we heard a news bulletin on the car radio, announcing a polio epidemic in Chicago. At that time no word struck as much fear into the hearts of parents as "polio." Vera and I knew that it was a highly infectious viral disease that frequently caused paralysis, especially in children, and that it spread rapidly in large urban centers. Jonas Salk had recently developed an effective vaccine against the disease, but it was not yet in wide use. Of course, we realized that the chances of Hal's contracting polio were remote. Nevertheless, as new parents, we decided to err on the side of caution and steer clear of Chicago.

Instead, we invited Jason to join us, camping out at Indiana Dunes State Park, about fifty miles from Chicago. For Jason, who was a creature of comfort, the idea of sleeping on the ground filled him with dread, so he agreed to come but only for the day. He enjoyed his visit and playing with his nephew so much that, to his credit, he decided to spend the night. At first he tried to sleep outside the tent in my sleeping bag and air mattress while Vera and I shared her sleeping bag in the tent. But soon Jason was complaining that he heard a rustling sound and, in spite of our assurances to the contrary, insisted, only half in jest, that there were grizzly bears nearby waiting to attack him. He pleaded with us, also only half in jest, to let him sleep in our tent. I will not attempt to explain how three full-sized people managed to squeeze into a two-person pup tent. I would not recommend it.

We crawled out of the tent at five o'clock in the morning, groggy and giddy, to attend to Hal sleeping a few feet away on his comfortable mattress in the back seat of the car. (Our putting him to sleep in the car while we were in the tent nearby may seem strange and even neglectful by today's standards, when many parents would handcuff their infants to their wrists as a defense against would-be kidnappers. But in those days everyone tended to trust strangers rather than fear them.) As the sun was rising, Jason, with tears in his eyes, kept looking from Vera to me to Hal, and said, "You guys did it; you really did it." Jason, who was destined never to have a child of his own, seemed overwhelmed by the mere fact of Hal's existence. He kept reaching out and stroking Hal's head with infinite tenderness and affection.

In the evening Jason decided to drive home so that we could all get a little sleep. As we were embracing, saying good-bye, he said, "Just think. Only ten years ago, you and I were slaving away for Abe Shaw, and, chances are, ten years from now, with a little luck, you and I will both be professors somewhere—maybe even at the same college—wearing tweed jackets with suede elbow patches, smoking pipes, and having students hanging on our every word. It's a miracle!" I agreed with him, but for me the bigger miracle had already occurred during those two days: Jason no longer saw any need to act as my father, as he had done at Brandeis, making sure that I kept my eye on the ball and my nose to the grindstone. And he was no longer playing the role of big brother, as he had been while we were growing up in Revere, leading the way, showing me how to do things, defending me from bullies. Now, for the first time, he was treating me as his equal. Indeed, if anything, he was looking up to me, as someone who was not only a promising graduate student but a husband and father as well.

Although Jason hated sleeping on the ground, Vera and I grew to like it more and more as our trip progressed. Our favorite layover was Rocky Mountain National Park, where we stayed for an entire week. Hal was the hit of the campground. Each morning as we crawled out of our tent, we found a cluster of campers with their noses pressed against the VW's windows, waving and cutting up and eventually succeeding in getting Hal to smile at them. Their antics were a great benefit because they usually kept Hal entertained and happy, allowing us an additional twenty minutes or so in the sack. By the time we reached Nevada, however, we were yearning for a soft bed and a hot shower. We stopped at a small motel in the gold-mining town of Battle Mountain, and it was there that our second son, Neal, was conceived.

When we arrived in Palo Alto, we phoned Dick Alpert, who had volunteered to find us an apartment near the Stanford campus. But try as he might, he couldn't find a place he thought we would like, so he decided to move out of the small cottage he had been renting and, with his landlord's permission, ceded it to us. When we objected he laughed and said that he was living below his means anyway. Stanford had just made him an acting instructor for one year (while he was finishing his dissertation), and our coming had provided him with an excuse for upgrading his living arrangements.

The cottage was a delight. It was located on Homer Lane, a dirt road on the edge of the Stanford golf course in an area that was evolving into an artists' colony. Although it was too small for the three of us, it had enormous charm, and we worked hard to use the available space efficiently. There was one bedroom at the far end, which we assigned to Hal so that, with the door closed, he could sleep without being disturbed. A large floor-to-ceiling bookcase divided the living room at the front of the cottage from the kitchen and dining area. To keep the living room free for guests, we placed our bed in the dining area, just two steps from the dining table. The running joke among my pals was, "Elliot arranged the furniture so that he wouldn't need to walk very far to go from eating to sleeping."

That winter, early 1957, we were joined by Vera's older sister, Lili. Lili had remained in Hungary after the Holocaust because, like many Jewish survivors at the time, she was optimistic about the egalitarian promise of Communism; more important, she was a serious music student, and wanted to continue her studies with Zoltán Kodály at the Liszt Academy of Music in Budapest. By the time she became disillusioned with the totalitarianism of the Soviet regime, however, the Iron Curtain had closed and emigration was impossible. She remained trapped until the Hungarian revolution of 1956; during that turmoil she managed to escape, making her way to America and eventually to us. She slept in the living room on the couch, and when Neal was born in May, she was a great help. However, the cottage, which had been too small for the three of us, now contained five. One day the landlord dropped in, took one look around, and gave us thirty days to get out. We ended up spending the rest of our time in Palo Alto at another army-barracks arrangement on the grounds of the Stanford Research Institute. We considered it luxurious—it had two bedrooms. Eventually, Lili began giving piano lessons and was earning enough to move to her own apartment.

In December 1958 our daughter, Julie, was born. That's right, three kids in three years! Vera had always wanted to raise a family while we were still young, and she convinced me that, although it would be hard work, it would also be fun. As usual, she was right on both counts. My favorite chore was feeding the infants in the wee hours of the morning. Vera was breast-feeding, but, because she needed her sleep, it was my job to wake up for the four o'clock feeding, prepare the supplementary bottle, and feed the infant. Although I did this for all of the newborns, I particularly remember how great it felt with Julie, holding her close to me, cuddling, and administering the bottle as if the milk were flowing from my own woefully inadequate breast. Early on, after a change of diaper and a half-hour feeding, Julie would go back to sleep, and so would I. But by the time she was three or four months old, she refused to go back to sleep, and there she would be, wide awake, playful and eager to start the day. When I tried to pull away to catch another hour or two of sleep, she would hold tight. Although I was dead tired and longed to crawl back into bed, she gradually charmed me into wakefulness—and I would put the coffee on.

Many years later my good friend, poet David Swanger, beautifully captured my feelings about the early ritual with Julie in these lines from his poem "My Daughter's Morning":

> *For her, I bring the day:*
> *warm milk, new diaper, escapades;*
> *She lowers all bridges and*
> *sings to me most beautifully*
> *in her own language, while*
> *I fumble with safety pins.*

During the first week of classes Robert Sears, the Psychology Department chairman, called an orientation meeting of all first-year graduate students. After greeting us warmly and providing the usual information about required courses, he changed expression. He looked grim, cleared his throat ominously, and asked us to take a good look at our fellow students. "At this time next year, about half of the people you are looking at will be gone," he said. "Because we aren't good at predicting graduate student success, our policy is to admit twice as many students as we intend to retain." There was absolute silence in the room. Acute anxiety makes no noise.

That afternoon I asked Ralph Haber, who was beginning his third year in the program, whether Sears had been serious. "Oh, yes," said Ralph. "In my first year almost two-thirds of my classmates were told not to return. Some of them were quite bright and did well in their course work. But surely *you* have nothing to worry about." I nodded, but inside I was petrified, thinking, "Ralph has no idea how much I don't know about psychology." I was stunned by the contrast between this welcome and the one I had received at Wesleyan. "So this is what it's like in the big leagues," I thought.

During that first year I did pretty well in the required courses, but my performance, especially in the two mandatory statistics courses, could hardly be called dazzling. I worked hard in those statistics courses, but, unlike many of my peers, I never quite got a feel for it, and earned low Bs in both of them. And the mere fact that there were *two* required statistics courses, I assumed, meant that the Stanford faculty considered the subject to be of paramount importance. I felt I was in real danger of being among the 50 percent who wouldn't be asked to return next year.

It was in my role as a teaching assistant, leading sections in Introductory Psychology, that I felt most competent. In these seminars I was developing a style that I would call "gently Socratic." Aron Gurwitsch had demonstrated the power of the Socratic method of questioning. But Gurwitsch's style was edgy; he knew the response he wanted and was impatient with students who didn't give it to him. I was learning not to reject answers I didn't like, but to follow the student's answer with a thought-provoking question that might lead the student to an interesting place. The students were responsive, and their continued attendance made it clear that they liked what I was doing.

Ralph had also led sections in Introductory Psychology that fall. We were both scheduled to do it again in the winter quarter, this time assisting Professor Ernest "Jack" Hilgard, who would be teaching the course, assigning his own widely used introductory textbook. At Ralph's urging, we approached Hilgard with the rather impudent proposal that he allow us to coteach an honors seminar instead of the usual cut-and-dried sections. Instead of reading the textbook, our students would read original works of the psychologists being summarized in the textbook—psychologists like John Watson, B. F. Skinner, Sigmund Freud, D. O. Hebb, Abe Maslow, and Kurt Lewin. Hilgard expressed some reservations about the idea, but, after thinking about it for a few days, he decided to give us our head, adding, "Don't blow it."

Ralph and I selected fifteen students from Hilgard's class of some two hundred. In addition to attending Hilgard's lectures, they met with us for three hours one evening per week in Ralph's living room. It was a rich learning experience for the students and for Ralph and me as well. The students read the original works with care; the group discussions were lively and informative. Every single student in that seminar rated it as the best course they had taken at Stanford, and more than half of them went on to graduate school in psychology. The teacher in me found that gratifying, but the scientist in me would not allow me to take much credit. I was well aware that our students could hardly be considered a random sample of the Stanford student body. The group was a highly select one; each student had volunteered with the full knowledge that the seminar would require extra work.

So I already owed a lot to Ralph, because it was through his initiative and persuasiveness that I had such a wonderful teaching experience. And then, a year later, he saved my life. At Christmastime, Vera, Lili, the kids, and I piled into our little VW and drove to Los Angeles to visit relatives. On the way home, as I was driving at night in the rain through the Pacheco Pass, a twisting mountain road with steep drops on either side of the highway, we came around a curve and got hit with a ferocious blast of wind. I cut the wheel sharply to the left, and the car skidded across both lanes of the highway and off the precipice on the opposite side. We were airborne, and I heard Vera say, "Oh, no." And in that moment, I thought, "Is this how it ends?" The car rolled over and over and came to rest on its roof. Incredibly, none of us was seriously injured. Vera suffered a mild concussion, I tore up a knee, and Lili and the babies were unhurt. I pulled everyone out of the car as fast as possible, climbed back up the steep hill, and tried to flag down a passing car. No one wanted to help a disheveled guy on the roadside at night, so I finally stood in the middle of the road waving my arms so that the next car had to stop. I explained what happened, and the driver agreed to call for an ambulance at the next station. He did, and we were all taken to the nearest hospital, where we spent the night.

The next morning I called John Wright, a fellow graduate student, who came to collect us and drive us back to Palo Alto. John and I stopped at the accident scene and walked down the hill. The Volkswagen was totaled. The driver's door had been ripped off when the car had begun rolling and lay halfway between us and the car. "My God," said John. "How come you weren't thrown from your seat? The car would have rolled over you and crushed you. How come you're still here?"

"Ralph Haber," I said. "He had been nagging me for ages to get seat belts. He'd read *Consumer Reports* or something. I thought they were a pain in the neck. They're expensive, and you have to go to a shop and get holes drilled in the floor of your car to have the damned things installed. But I finally did it, just to get him to stop pestering."

Dick Alpert also saved my life, but in a far less literal way. During the break between the winter and spring quarters of my first year, Dick dropped in to our cottage at dinnertime, bearing a cheesecake and a bottle of Courvoisier. He held up the bottle and said, with a self-deprecating smile, "After all, it's the brandy of Napoleon," and asked Vera if she would mind putting a little extra water into the soup so that he could join us for dinner. Vera and I had grown increasingly fond of Dick and loved his frequent, unannounced dinnertime visits. Dick had more style than anyone we had ever met. We were amused and charmed by his refined taste in such niceties as wine and brandy, which, needless to say, was hardly typical of professors, let alone of acting instructors who did not quite have a Ph.D. The Courvoisier was one of his hallmarks, as was the flashy Mercedes that he drove. Dick was to the manor born. His father was George Alpert, a wealthy and powerful corporation lawyer who was also president of the New Haven Railroad, chairman of the board of trustees at Brandeis University, and God only knows what else.

Over dessert, Dick asked me if I had met Leon Festinger, the professor who had joined the Stanford Psychology Department that fall. I didn't know him, but I had heard a lot about him. Although he was only thirty-six, he was a star, perhaps the hottest theorist and researcher in social psychology. He was rumored to be hard at work on developing a new theory on something called "cognitive dissonance." In our stat course we learned that he had invented a widely used nonparametric statistical technique—in his spare time, I guess. He sounded too good to be true. But, alas, "good" is not an adjective I would have used to describe him, for he also had earned a reputation for toughness bordering on cruelty.

Since September the psychology building had been reverberating with stories from his previous academic positions—stories of graduate students having been so humiliated by his overbearing personality and relentless sarcastic wit that they had left the social psychology program and decided to become forest rangers, real estate brokers, or even psychotherapists, in order to get as far away from him as possible. I had not gravitated toward an adviser yet; I was thinking of working with Sears, or Hilgard, or perhaps Al Bandura, who was doing some interesting research on children's imitation of aggression. I wasn't sure who it would be, but I was sure it was not going to be Leon Festinger.

"Well," said Dick, "this Festinger guy is apparently an extraordinary scholar. Some say he is a genius. He has to be good because he is one of the most highly paid professors on campus." (Dick was the kind of person who would know.) "He is so special that Bob Sears gave him the first two quarters off so that he could settle in and set up his lab without bothering with students. Now in the spring quarter he will be teaching a seminar, and only three students have signed up for it. That's a waste of a very expensive resource. The faculty thinks that the graduate students are keeping away because they are afraid of him. By the way, I notice that you haven't signed up for his seminar. How come?"

I wasn't sure whether that was a suggestion, a challenge, or a taunt. But whatever it was, it worked. I wasn't going to let Dick think (know!) that I was a coward. "Well, actually, as it happens, I was thinking of signing up for it," I said. "I will check it out."

And I did, but not right away. As the spring quarter was about to begin, I sought out Judson Mills. Jud was a second-year graduate student who had spent a year studying with Festinger at the University of Minnesota and had come to Stanford as his research assistant. I told Jud the rumors I had heard about Festinger and asked him if they were true. Jud smiled wryly and said, "Well, not entirely. At Minnesota, none of the students ever became forest rangers." Funny, but not helpful. I realized that I had better talk with the man himself.

It was with some trepidation that I stepped into Festinger's office, introduced myself, and told him that I was thinking of enrolling in his seminar. I explained that I didn't know anything about social psychology, and I asked him if there was something I might read that might help me decide whether I wanted to take his course. He leaned back in his chair and slowly looked me up and down. Then he grunted, rolled his eyes toward the ceiling (as if to say, "Just look at the idiots they're sending me these days"), and, with some reluctance, reached into a desk drawer and handed me the carbon copy of a book-length manuscript.

He said, "I hear you have little kids. Is that true?" I was flattered that he seemed to know something about me. I thought he was trying to be friendly, so I relaxed a little. "Only one so far—a little boy; he just had his first birthday," I gushed. It was a mistake. Festinger was not making small talk. He didn't smile. He grunted again, pointed to the manuscript, and informed me that it was a book he had just written, that he had sent the original to the publisher, and that this carbon was the only copy he had left. He made me promise, under the pain of death or dismemberment (whichever I preferred), not to let my toddler get blueberry jam all over it. So much for small talk.

I left his office thinking, "What a prick! Do I really want to spend ten weeks in a small seminar room with that guy?" That evening I told Vera about my encounter with Festinger and asked her opinion. She said, "He sounds nasty. What are your options?" I told her that the best alternative was Jack Hilgard, who was offering a seminar that sounded interesting. I reminded her that Jack and I had a good working relationship based on my teaching the honors seminar the previous quarter.

She said, "Taking Jack's course sounds reasonable—and safe. But since when do you go for what is safe? Why don't you at least take a look at Festinger's book and see if you like it? I will hide the blueberry jam."

After dinner that evening and after Hal was safely in bed for the night, I glanced at Festinger's manuscript. It was called *A Theory of Cognitive Dissonance*. I casually read the first few pages, just to get an idea of what it was about. I had no intention of reading beyond that. But I got hooked, and the next thing I knew it was three in the morning. I had read the damn book in one sitting. It was the most exciting thing I had ever read in psychology. That was more than fifty years ago; it's *still* the most exciting thing I've ever read in psychology.

Festinger started with a simple proposition: If individuals held two cognitions that were psychologically inconsistent, they would experience dissonance, a negative drive like hunger or thirst. Unlike hunger or thirst, it is a cognitive drive, but just as unpleasant. Accordingly, they would be motivated to reduce dissonance as much as they would attempt to reduce hunger or thirst, in this case by trying to change one or both of the dissonant cognitions to bring them into consonance, or harmony. Festinger's defining example was that of the lifelong cigarette smoker who discovers that smoking cigarettes causes cancer. The smoker experiences dissonance. The cognition "I smoke cigarettes" is dissonant with the cognition "cigarette smoking produces cancer." Clearly, the most efficient way for a person to reduce dissonance in such a situation is to give up smoking. The cognition "cigarette smoking produces cancer" is consonant with the cognition "I do not smoke." But most smokers find it difficult to give up the habit; many try and fail, repeatedly. What might they do to reduce dissonance? In all probability they will work on adjusting the other cognition, that "cigarette smoking produces cancer." They might minimize the evidence linking cigarette smoking to cancer, trying to convince themselves that the science is inconclusive. They might seek out intelligent people who smoke and, by so doing, convince themselves that if *those* guys do it, it can't be all that dangerous. They might switch to a filter-tipped brand and delude themselves into believing that the filter traps the cancer-producing materials. And they might add cognitions that are consonant with smoking in an attempt to make the behavior less absurd in spite of its danger: "I may lead a shorter life, but it will be a more enjoyable one"; "I'm just the kind of bold person who enjoys taking risks."

What Festinger did was forge a marriage between the cognitive and the motivational. As he stated it, dissonance theory is essentially a theory about sense-making: why and how people try to make sense out of their environment and their behavior, resolve discrepancies, and thus try to lead lives that are (at least in their own minds) sensible and meaningful. The book contained very little original experimentation, but it contained rich ideas, as well as the seeds of some fascinating research that was to percolate through the professional journals for the next twenty years and revolutionize social psychology. Of course, I did not know that at the time. What I did know was that the theory was new, interesting, and provocative. At least it interested me and provoked me to think in ways that I never thought before.

So I enrolled in the seminar. I figured, "He is a prick, all right, but a smart and interesting prick." There were only six of us in the seminar. In addition to Jud Mills and myself, there were two fourth-year graduate students in psychology, a graduate student who had wandered over from the Sociology Department, and an exceptionally brilliant undergraduate junior named Merrill Carlsmith.

The seminar was lively and tense. Festinger's style was to assign a number of books, most of which had little or no direct relevance to social psychology, and cross-examine us about the content of each book and what ramifications we thought it might have for dissonance theory. For the most part, Festinger did not have a clear, preconceived notion of what those ramifications might be. Unlike Gurwitsch, he wasn't trying to lead us to a specific answer; rather, we were all exploring together. Still, exactly as advertised, he was brilliant and scary. His questions were razor sharp, and he made it clear that we had better answer knowledgeably and not leave any loose ends. It was like having a tiger in the classroom. He could pounce on you at any time without warning, often for reasons that were baffling or trivial to us. Even Jud was not exempt; far from it. One day he gave a report on a book he'd read, and Leon asked him to elaborate on what seemed to me to be a minor detail. Jud couldn't do it, and Leon said, in exasperation, "How could you possibly have missed the point?" Jud stammered some reply, but Leon continued his harassment until the class ended. As Jud and I were walking out of the room together, he was visibly shaking. Then he turned to me and said, "You know, I do think that Leon likes me."

Festinger could be savage and harsh, all right, but he also exuded a warmth, joy, and playfulness. At times he was a cross-examining attorney, trying to trip us up. At other times he was Sherlock Holmes to our Doctor Watson, treating us as colleagues in pursuit of an elusive solution to a complex problem. And he would also break us up with a quick and spontaneous display of humor, occasionally at his own expense. I looked forward to the seminar meetings with excitement and anxiety, and was learning not to worry too much about the anxiety.

Halfway through the quarter, Festinger assigned a term paper in which he asked for an analysis of the Salem witch trials. I read the material, wrote the paper, and handed it in. A couple of days later, I was walking past his office toward the TA room where I had a desk. He saw me go by, yelled out my name, and beckoned me to come in. He picked up my paper from a short pile on his desk, held it disdainfully at arm's length between his thumb and forefinger, turned his face away from it, as if it were a particularly smelly piece of garbage, and said, "I believe this is yours." I was devastated, but I tried to put on a brave front. I said, "I guess you didn't like it very much." He glared at me for what seemed like a very long time. Then he turned his hands palms up, shrugged his shoulders, and a look came into his eyes that anyone who ever worked with him would instantly recognize. It was a mixture of contempt and pity. The reason for the contempt part of that look was obvious: I was wasting his time. The pity part of that look seemed to imply that he felt sorry for me because I had been born brain-damaged. He said, "That's right, I didn't like it very much."

I took my paper and slunk down the corridor to my desk in the TA room. I sat there for about ten minutes before I could gather the courage to open it and read the terrible words I expected to find scrawled in the margins. When I did, I was astounded to discover that there wasn't a mark on it. What was I to make of this? I gathered my courage, marched back to Festinger's office, and said, "Hey, Leon, you forgot to write any criticisms in the margins. How am I supposed to know what I got wrong?" He stared at me for several seconds. Then he turned his hands palms up, shrugged his shoulders, and that awful look of contempt and pity came into his eyes again. He said, "What? You don't have enough respect for your own work and your own thinking to go the extra mile, to follow your own reasoning to its logical conclusions, and you expect me to do that for you? This is graduate school, not kindergarten. You're supposed to tell *me* what's wrong with it."

I walked back to my desk and sat there fuming. I had just come off of a quarter where I was being hailed by the students in my honors seminar as a great teacher, and a month later I was being treated like an idiot by the most interesting professor in the Psychology Department. I was confused and furious. I didn't need this kind of humiliation, and I certainly didn't need to deal with this son of a bitch. I could simply get through this course and ignore him for the rest of my time in grad school.

Yet during those weeks in his seminar I had seen that he was an extraordinary thinker and a great scientist. I knew that I could learn a lot from him if I had the guts to hang in there. With a sigh, I picked up the paper and began to read it carefully, trying to see it through Festinger's eyes. And when I did I found it poorly reasoned, incompletely analyzed, imperfectly argued. The son of a bitch was right! What now? If I rewrote the paper, would he even bother to read it? "Fuck that," I said to myself. "You are thinking like an undergraduate. Rewrite the damn thing for yourself. You owe it to yourself to do it right. Who cares what that bastard thinks?" The truth is, I did. I cared a lot what that bastard thought.

For the next two or three days (it seemed like seventy-two consecutive hours), I worked and reworked that paper until I was satisfied with it. I walked over to Leon's office. As usual the door was open, but he had his nose buried in a book. I didn't want to interrupt him, so I waited at the threshold. He raised his head and looked intently out the window; he seemed to be staring at his own thoughts. I hesitated for a moment or two, strode into his office, plunked my paper on his desk, and said, "Maybe you'll like this one better." I turned on my heel and walked out. To his credit, he must have dropped what he had been doing and read my paper immediately, because twenty minutes later, he came into the TA room carrying my paper. He placed it gently in front of me, sat down on the corner of my desk, put his hand on my shoulder, and said, "Now, this is worth criticizing."

This incident turned out to be a gift of incalculable value. Naturally, I would have preferred it if the gift had come wrapped in a gentler, kinder package. Leon showed me, in the most vivid manner possible, that he was not going to accept anything that fell short of my best effort. By declaring that my revised paper was worth criticizing, he was telling me that I was worth his time and energy.

What I got a glimpse of, at that moment, was confirmed during the rest of my time in graduate school as I got closer to Leon and watched him in action. He put a high premium on his own time and energy. If a student did not go all out, Leon was not going to waste any effort on him. But on those surprisingly rare occasions when a student did give him everything he had, Leon would give that student everything *he* had and, most valuable of all, his criticism, which was always sharp and always on target. Ironically, his taking the trouble to give you his criticism was just about the highest praise he could provide.

———————

From that moment on, for me, Stanford *became* Leon Festinger. Stanford had a great Psychology Department with several first-rate professors, but none had his combination of skill, brilliance, and meticulousness. Leon would not allow us to draw conclusions that were unsupported by evidence. "If you want to go beyond the data," he would exhort us, "that's speculation—a hypothesis for your next experiment." He thought drawing unwarranted conclusions was not only sloppy thinking but bordered on the unethical; he called it "hanky-panky." Leon's favorite joke reveals, to me, his love of precise thinking and precise communication: An old Jewish couple is lying in bed when the wife says, "Saul, close the window. It's cold outside." With a groan, Saul gets up out of bed, closes the window, turns to his wife, and says, "So now it's *warm* outside?"

After the incident with the term paper, I continued to find Leon's seminar exhilarating, but I was no longer intimidated by his style. Whenever he gave me one of those looks, which he did more than a few times, I found it challenging rather than daunting. The six of us in the seminar felt like we were part of something important. The theory of cognitive dissonance was changing the way we thought about the human mind and social influence, and we were contributing to the development of an idea that would permanently change social psychology.

Dissonance theory taught me the great lesson of social influence that was to guide my thinking for the next fifty years as a researcher and writer: Although it's true that changing people's attitudes sometimes changes their behavior, if you want a more powerful change to take place, you will try to evoke a change in behavior first; attitudes will follow. This way of seeing things was completely counterintuitive for laypeople and even for most social psychologists at the time. The idea was that if, for example, you want someone to do you a favor, you must first persuade him that you are a nice person. This is not wrong; it is merely inefficient. As my students would later demonstrate, you can produce a much more powerful effect by first getting him to do you a favor; he will then convince himself that you *deserved* his doing you that favor, and that therefore you are a nice person. And, as a result, he is apt to do you a much bigger favor in the future.

Dissonance theory was a breath of fresh air at a time when radical behaviorism dominated all of psychology. In the 1950s almost all behavior was explained by rewards and punishments. People like food, golf, and their mothers, behaviorists said, because of rewards associated with food, golf, and their mothers. Therefore, if a rat, pigeon, or person kept doing something for no obvious reward, behaviorists would claim we weren't looking hard enough—the reward has to be around here, *somewhere*, or else the rat, pigeon, or person would stop behaving that way. Dissonance theory did not deny the importance of principles of reinforcement; rather, it showed us that the mind is much more complex than principles of reward and punishment would lead us to predict. Of course, Abraham Maslow had also railed against the limitations of behaviorism, but his ideas were vague and untestable. (When Leon learned that it was Maslow who had first gotten me excited about psychology, he said, "*Maslow?* That guy's ideas are so bad they aren't even wrong.") Dissonance theory was pregnant with testable ideas, some of which had far-reaching ramifications. During the second half of the seminar, we began generating these testable hypotheses.

I happened to be reading John Whiting's work on initiations as rites of passage among indigenous tribes of Africa and South America; Whiting was describing the differences, not theorizing about their origins or purpose. But in Festinger's seminar it dawned on me that perhaps one function of those initiations was to create a more cohesive group, just as people who go through extreme basic training required to join the marines develop a strong commitment to the corps, and just as pledges develop attachment to their fraternities after weeks of horrible hazing, and, for that matter, just as I came to love Brandeis after a semester of sleeping in cars.

The prediction from dissonance theory is that the cognition "I went through hell and high water to get into this group" would be dissonant with " . . . only to discover that the group is worthless and its members are insipid." To reduce dissonance, most people would minimize the importance of any negative aspects of the group and focus primarily on the positive ones. But people who voluntarily join the marines (or who work hard to stay at Brandeis) are self-selected; they might have joined the marines or chosen Brandeis because they liked it prior to the initiation. For this reason, correlational data are inadequate to test the hypothesis. I needed to design an experiment so that I could randomly assign participants to either a severe-initiation condition or a mild one and see whether the former came to like an unappealing group more than the latter.

And so one day, as Jud and I were leaving Leon's seminar, I floated my hypothesis by him. Jud responded enthusiastically, and the two of us spent the next several days designing an experiment. Our hypothesis required us to set up a situation where people would volunteer to try out for membership in a group. We would randomly assign one-third of them to a severe-initiation condition, one-third to a mild-initiation condition, and one-third to a no-initiation condition. Afterward, we would ask them how much they liked the group they had joined.

We immediately had two problems. What kind of group would sound so interesting that college students would be willing to undergo a severe initiation to get into it? And what kind of severe initiation could we do, since hazing was out of the question? Jud and I hit on the idea of sex. We figured that almost all young adults are interested in talking about sex. Once we determined the topic of the group discussion, the rest of the procedure fell into place.

We advertised that we were forming groups of students to meet for several discussions on the psychology of sex. (As it turned out, most of the volunteers were women, so we decided to use women only.) We phoned them and arranged an appointment for each participant to come into the lab, one at a time, for a one-hour interview. I greeted each woman and explained that I was a social psychology graduate student who was studying the dynamics of the group-discussion process. I added that the actual topic of the discussion was not important to me; I had selected the topic of sex to guarantee plenty of volunteers. "But that presented me with a major drawback," I would say. "Specifically, shy students find it difficult to discuss sex in a group setting. Because any impediment to the free flow of the discussion could invalidate my research, I need to know if you have any hesitation about entering a discussion about sex." When the participants heard this, each and every one said that she would have no difficulty at all.

Up to this point, the instructions were the same for all participants. If the subject had been preassigned to the no-initiation condition, I simply told her that she was now a member of the group. For women assigned to the severe-and mild-initiation conditions, however, I said that because I needed to be absolutely certain that everyone could discuss sex openly, I had developed a screening device—a test for embarrassment—that I asked them to take. This test constituted the initiation. For the severe-initiation condition, the test was highly embarrassing. The young woman had to recite, to me, a list of twelve obscene words, including *fuck, cunt,* and *blow job,* and two particularly steamy passages from *Lady Chatterley's Lover.* (In 1957, trust me, reading this material out loud was *really* embarrassing—for me as well as the students!) The mild-initiation participants had to recite a list of words related to sex that were not obscene, such as *vagina, penis,* and *sexual intercourse.*

Next, each student listened to a tape recording of a discussion of "sexual behavior" that she believed was being held by the group she had just joined. The recording was identical for each volunteer, and the discussion was as slow, boring, and turgid as I could make it. Finally, Jud (who was blind to each student's condition) interviewed each of the students and got her to rate the discussion and the group members on a number of dimensions—how appealing the group was, how intelligent and articulate its members seemed, and so on. The results were just as we had predicted. Subjects who went through the severe initiation thought the group was terrific, while those who went through the mild initiation or no initiation saw it (correctly!) as dull and boring; several wanted to resign immediately.

It was fascinating to see the specific ways that women in the severe initiation reduced their dissonance. For example, one guy on the tape, stammering and muttering, admitted that he hadn't done the required reading on the courtship practices of some rare bird, and the mild-initiation listeners were annoyed by him. What an irresponsible idiot! He didn't even do the basic reading! He let the group down! Who'd want to be in a group with him? But those who had gone through a severe initiation rated the discussion as interesting and exciting and the group members as attractive and sharp. They forgave the irresponsible idiot. His candor was refreshing! Who wouldn't want to be in a group with such an honest guy? It was hard for me to believe that they had listened to the same tape recording.

I can still remember the exhilaration I felt as the data began to fall into place. I was elated by the realization that I had discovered something new and exciting about how the human mind works—

in this case, that going through a difficult experience in order to gain something makes people like that thing better. More generally, I realized that, as complex as human behavior is, it is also lawful. All I had to do was identify the law, hone it into a testable hypothesis, and invent a procedure to get at the essence of that hypothesis. Doing this experiment also showed me that I might have a knack for creating a methodological key to unlock some of the mysteries of human behavior. It was a great revelation. I don't think I have ever been more excited about anything in my entire life. Intellectually speaking, anyway. It was my first experiment, and it became a classic, one of the defining experiments of dissonance theory.

The challenge of this kind of experimentation is to find a way to imbed the participant in a prearranged scenario that is coherent, absorbing, and believable. The experimenter must have the skills of a playwright, a director, and an actor without abandoning scientific rigor. In our experiments the laboratory comes alive; real things are happening to real people. This way of working allows us to transcend the fabled artificiality of more traditional laboratory experiments. We called this approach "high-impact experimentation" because we plunked people into the middle of a situation that was so real for them that they had to respond as they would have responded outside the laboratory. In designing this kind of experiment, I discovered that it is possible—actually, essential—to achieve scientific rigor without artificiality or sterility. That became my mantra as an experimenter.

Previously, much of the research in social psychology consisted either of investigating trivial phenomena ("people will believe an article published in the *New York Times* more than one published in *Pravda*") or of observing how people who scored high or low on some personality test (like achievement motivation, to take a not-so-random example) would behave in a variety of situations. What I picked up from Leon was the audacious belief that, as scientists, we did not need to confine our research to trivial topics or pallid methods. Rather, with sufficient ingenuity, we could find a way to investigate in the laboratory just about any phenomenon. This could free the scientist from an overreliance on personality variables and from accepting a trait as an explanation for the subsequent behavior. We could learn directly what causes people's behavior, because we, the experimenters, have created the "what." It was the severe initiation that produced a liking for the group, and it did so regardless of the subject's early childhood experiences or personality.

The key ingredient in the high-impact experiment is theatricality. If the experiment is going to work, the script must be believable and the experimenter must be a convincing actor. Otherwise, the subject will not get involved, and the experiment will fail. For some reason, perhaps having to do with my stint as a mike man on the Revere Beach Boardwalk, the dramaturgical requirements of an experiment came easily to me. For example, in the initiation experiment, I was able to come up with a scenario that convinced the subjects that it made sense for them to go through an embarrassing initiation to get into that group discussion. In addition, it didn't take me long to grasp the importance of pilot testing; because our procedures are complex, such pretesting can ensure that the procedure is affecting the subjects the way it was intended. It is the scientific equivalent of rehearsing your Broadway-bound play in New Haven first. If the pilot study doesn't work, it is back to the drawing board.

When I was about to run my first pilot subject in the initiation experiment, I invited Leon to observe through a one-way mirror. When I finished I came back to his office and said, "Any suggestions?"

"Nope."

"What do you mean, 'Nope?' How can I improve my performance?"

"It's perfect. You are ready to go."

"But I've got three more pilot subjects scheduled for this afternoon."

"Cancel them. You are ready to go."

Earlier, I said that Leon's praise, if it came at all, usually came in the guise of criticism. But, occasionally, it came in more direct form, as in his noncritique of my laboratory performance. That kind of praise was the gold standard, precisely because I knew it did not stem from his wish to be kind or any need to be liked, which was unimportant to him.

Shortly thereafter, Leon actually asked for my consultation. He had designed an experiment to test the hypothesis that a person telling a lie for a small reward would believe his own lie to a greater extent than someone telling the same lie for a large reward. The latter has an adequate justification: "I told a lie for twenty dollars; it was worth it." The former feels dissonance: "Why would I tell a lie for only a buck? I must believe it." Festinger had asked Merrill Carlsmith, the undergraduate in the seminar, to carry out the experiment, which was as carefully crafted as an Arthur Miller play.

When the subject arrived at the lab, he would be asked to do a few unbearably dull tasks. (The first was to fill a tray with twelve spools, one at a time and using one hand, then take all the spools out, one by one, then put them back in, over and over again for a half hour.) Merrill would watch, taking notes and doing mysterious things with a stopwatch, then tell the subject the experiment was over, and thank him for his help. He would explain that he was testing the hypothesis that people work faster if they are told in advance that the task is incredibly interesting than if they are told nothing and informed, "You were in the control condition. That is why you were told nothing."

At this point Merrill would say that the guy who was supposed to give the ecstatic description to the next subject had just phoned in to say he couldn't make it. Merrill would beg the "control" subject to do him a favor and play the role, offering him a dollar (or twenty dollars) to do it. Once the subject agreed, Merrill was to give him the money and a sheet listing the main things to say praising the experiment and leave him alone for a few minutes to prepare. Then Merrill would bring the guy into the waiting room where an undergraduate woman was waiting (actually a confederate of ours), and leave him to describe the experiment to her in glowing terms.

But it wasn't working, and Merrill was frustrated because the subjects were suspicious. So Leon and I sat behind the one-way mirror as Merrill ran his fifth pilot subject. Merrill was an extraordinarily bright guy, but, as an experimenter, he was wooden. The poor guy was deprived; while I was gaining invaluable training on the boardwalk, Merrill was wasting his time playing lacrosse at Andover. As Leon and I watched him sleepwalk his way through the experiment, it was crystal clear why the subjects weren't buying it: He wasn't selling it. Leon said to me, "Train him."

And I did. I gave Merrill a crash course in acting. "You don't simply *say* that the assistant hasn't shown up," I said. "You fidget, you sweat, you pace up and down, you wring your hands, you convey to the subject that you are in real trouble here. And then, you act as if you just now got an idea. You look at the subject, and you brighten up. '*You!* You can do this for me. I can even pay you.'"

After three days of intense training (I felt like we were in the Actor's Studio), Merrill was ready. The experiment went off without a hitch. Only one out of forty subjects was suspicious. And the hypothesis was confirmed: The subjects who were paid only one dollar for lying convinced themselves that the tasks were fairly interesting, while those who were paid twenty dollars continued to see the tasks as horribly dull, which of course they were.

I loved every part of the process: coming up with the idea, designing the experiment, writing the script, rehearsing the performance, training an assistant, debriefing the participants so they understood why we did what we did, analyzing the data, and writing up the study for publication. It was like the feeling I had, years earlier in Revere, after I had mastered the skill of fielding a ground ball, when I suddenly knew I could do it. Instead of being nervous in tight situations and praying that the batter would hit the ball somewhere else ("Please God, *anywhere* else but not to me!"), I wanted the ball to come bouncing in my direction.

I had discovered the kind of research I wanted to do, and as the poet Pablo Neruda put it, "something ignited in my soul." I had found my calling. But wouldn't it be ironic if the Psychology Department didn't invite me to return next year? If only I had done better in those damned statistics courses. Near the end of the spring quarter, Leon told me that he would like to hire me as a research assistant for the next two years, starting in the summer. I said, "Sure, if I'm still here. I didn't do too well in my statistics courses."

He turned his palms up and shrugged his shoulders. "Statistics?" he said. "No big deal. A guy like you? After you get your degree, you can hire a statistician or even two; they are a dime a dozen." Leon was pretty good at putting things in perspective.

The warmth of his reaction was the first step toward the eventual demolition of the usual student-professor barrier. At that moment I stopped seeing Leon as merely a difficult taskmaster or even as a challenging mentor, and started seeing him as a friend. At the time Vera teased me by observing that my own severe initiation at his hands virtually guaranteed that I'd come to like him. Perhaps it did, at first. But an initiation doesn't explain why a person's liking for a group (or person) might continue to deepen for decades. Thirty-two years later, when I gave the eulogy at Leon's memorial, evoking the hearty laughter of recognition with my stories of his toughness and that famous look of pity and contempt, I felt the sorrow of losing one of the most warm and gratifying friendships of my life.

———————

In 1959 I earned my Ph.D. and accepted an offer from Harvard to be an assistant professor. The previous year we had replaced the totaled Volkswagen with a 1954 Chevrolet station wagon, big enough for our growing family—three-year-old Hal, two-year-old Neal, and eight-month-old Julie. Vera and I set off on another trip across the country, this time from Palo Alto to Cambridge, and this time with enough money for motels and a stop in Chicago to visit Jason and his new wife. I had all but forgotten the humanistic concerns that had initially attracted me to psychology. I was no longer thinking of doing good; I was now thinking of doing good experiments. As we headed toward Cambridge, my car was full of kids and my head was full of ideas, and I could hardly wait to settle in and get started.

CHAPTER SIX

Outside Harvard Yard

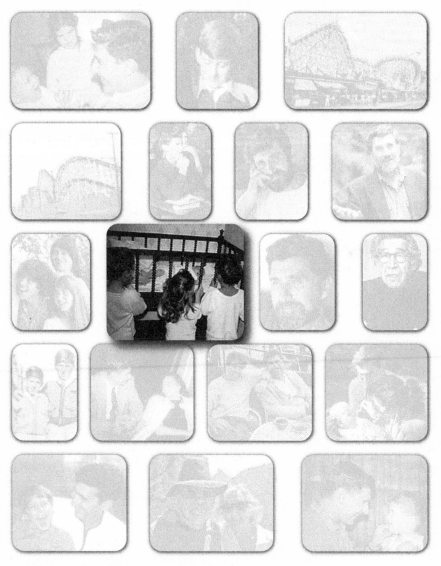

Hal, Julie, and Neal inspecting newborn Josh, 1961.

The distance between my childhood house in Revere and Harvard University is about seven miles, but, for me, the psychological distance was astronomical. Harvard was and is, of course, the pinnacle of American education; Revere was (and, for all I know, still is) among the dregs. While growing up in Revere, I knew no one who was attending or who had ever attended Harvard, even for a week. The year I graduated from high school, even our class valedictorian had been turned down for admission to that hallowed institution. Naturally, when I was a high school senior, I did not bother applying. I imagined that if I had applied, the admissions committee would have taken one look at my high school grades and would have rolled on the floor laughing. And, now, nine years later, here I was, wearing the obligatory tweed jacket and khaki pants, striding through Harvard Yard. Here I was, Harry Aronson's shy little boy, teaching at an institution that would not have wanted him as an undergraduate.

I was feeling a cacophony of emotions. I was feeling proud of myself for having gotten there. I was in awe of the place. It is not only a great university by any criterion but also the place where John Adams, Ralph Waldo Emerson, and Franklin Roosevelt studied. And I was feeling annoyed at myself for being so awestruck; Harvard was the bastion of WASP exclusiveness, where the guarantee of admission was having a father who was a wealthy Protestant alumnus. This was the school that, at that moment, was enforcing a quota limiting the admission of Jews and other minorities. Just three decades earlier, Harvard's president, A. Lawrence Lowell, had had the audacity to insist that sharply decreasing the number of

Jews at Harvard would be good for the Jews because, if a sizable number enrolled, it would fuel the existing anti-Semitism among the Gentile students.

My heart was beating hard as I walked past Widener Library and up the steps of Emerson Hall, which housed the main offices of the Social Relations Department. In those days Harvard psychology was split into two departments. Memorial Hall housed the "hard-science" group who studied animal learning, sensation and perception, physiological psychology, and so on. That department was led by such luminaries as B. F. Skinner and Edwin G. Boring. The "soft sciences" (social psychology, personality, and clinical) had united with sociology and anthropology to form the Social Relations Department. The luminaries of this group were Henry "Harry" Murray, Gordon Allport, and Jerome Bruner. From what I could gather, the main reason for the split was that the luminaries from the soft and hard ends of the continuum could not get along with one another.

Between the tenured senior faculty and the newly arrived, awestruck assistant professors lay the abyss. The abyss was filled with assistant professors in their fourth or fifth year on the faculty. "Harvard is a terrible place to be but a wonderful place to be from," one of those young men informed me. Several others agreed heartily. What they were caviling about was the unwritten law of faculty promotion: Because Harvard was committed to excellence, the institution would not bestow tenure without conclusive evidence that the particular person was the best available scholar in his or her subdiscipline. Because it was unlikely that an assistant professor who had been out of graduate school for only five or six years would meet that criterion, I was warned, tenure was a virtual impossibility. As a result, most of the senior faculty treated the junior faculty in much the same way that native Parisians treat summer tourists, as if we were just passing through on our way somewhere else. Upon hearing this assessment, I shrugged my shoulders and thought, "Too bad, but so what?"

But not all of the assistant professors were ready to throw in the tenure towel. My old pal Dick Alpert had his eye on the prize. Dick had arrived at Harvard as an assistant professor of child development two years earlier and was eager to remain there for the rest of his life. One evening he and I decided to go to dinner and a movie together. After dinner he said that he needed to stop off at his office for a minute on the way to the theater. When we walked in he flicked on the light and then said, "Okay, let's go."

"What the hell was that all about?" I asked.

"Well," he said, "Harry Murray lives just up the street. He often goes for long walks at night. Suppose he comes walking by, sees my light on, and it registers in his mind that I am a hardworking person, worthy of promotion."

I waited for him to start laughing. But he was dead serious.

"I wish you luck," I said.

Although I was appalled by his attitude, Dick was a good friend. He felt at home around Harvard Square and was eager to serve as my guide. "This is the Wurst Haus, a great old-fashioned German delicatessen, excellent beer. This is St. Claire's; you don't want to eat there, but they have a terrific bartender who pours the best martini in town. This is Elsie's: good for a quick lunch; she makes the kind of roast beef sandwich you wish your mother could have made. For Italian food, Simione's in Central Square, but if you want real Italian food, you have to hop on the subway and go to the North End."

Because Dick wanted to be the one to introduce me to what was best about the university, he was eager to accompany me to my first meeting of the full Harvard faculty. The meeting was held in University Hall, a historic building in Harvard Yard, the central quadrangle of the campus. Dick was quick to point out that the building had been designed by Charles Bulfinch. "Class of 1781," he said with a wink, "and you are not to ask which university he graduated from in 1781, wise guy."

The meeting itself was presided over by the dean of faculty, McGeorge Bundy, who was soon to gain worldwide fame as national security adviser to both President Kennedy and President Johnson, and, in that capacity, to become a major proponent of the war in Vietnam. At the moment he was chairing the meeting in an engaging but dominating way. Although he exuded charm, he made it clear that he was in charge. At one point he got into a heated but gentlemanly argument with historian Arthur Schlesinger Jr.

I don't remember anything else about the meeting. I'm sure some business was transacted, but whatever it was, for me, it was the underlying puffery that dominated the proceedings. Almost everyone who spoke seemed to be bathing in his own self-importance. After the meeting, as we emerged from the building, Dick was beaming.

"Didn't you love it?"

"Well, actually, no."

He was aghast. "Why the hell not?"

"A little too . . . a little too . . . "

"A little too what?" He was getting impatient with me.

"Well, I guess a little too Courvoisier for my taste."

Dick burst into laughter. "Oh, my God, you can take the kid out of Revere, but you can't take Revere out of the kid."

"Well, maybe. But, you know, they call Courvoisier 'the brandy of Napoleon,' but they didn't start making the stuff until ten years after Napoleon died. You can look it up."

"So? What's your point?"

I felt awful. I hated ruining it for Dick; he was trying so hard to make me like it the way he did. But I hated the meeting. There was a studied elegance and civility to it that got under my skin. Even the argument between Bundy and Schlesinger seemed unreal. They seemed to be enjoying their own performance rather than disagreeing about anything important. It was the last Harvard faculty meeting I ever attended.

I drove home that evening with a heavy heart. Why did I let that stuff bother me so much? Why did I have to rain on Dick's parade? Why couldn't I have gone along with him or at least kept my mouth shut? Why did I needle him about the "brandy of Napoleon"? That night, after Vera had bathed Julie and put her to bed and I had told the boys some bedtime stories, we retired to the living room for our usual coffee, nightcap, and sharing of the day's events.

"It was eerie," I said. "What Dick saw as admirable pomp, I saw as pomposity."

As usual, Vera saw things more clearly than I did: "You and Dick are on trains heading in opposite directions."

Within a few months of my arrival in Cambridge, I had pretty much concluded that I was not going to get tenure there: not only because tenure was damn near impossible for any of us young guys but also because it wasn't a good fit—either because Harvard (with its elite, gentlemanly anti-Semitism) was not the right place for me or because I (still proudly clinging to some of my blue-collar crudeness) was not the right person for it. I was already working at reducing my own dissonance. I went to that meeting determined to minimize whatever might have been good about it and ready to lampoon anything that could possibly be lampooned ("Bulfinch, class of 1781," indeed). Dick, on the other hand, had decided to go all out for tenure and would do just about anything that would allow him to stay. Therefore, he was motivated to embrace all of it. One of the things I had always loved most about Dick was his uncanny ability to poke fun at himself and his own foibles, including his occasional "little rich boy" antics. But because he was hell-bent on making it there, he could not see the humor in the light-switch gimmick or the pretentiousness in the faculty meeting.

————————

Bulfinch aside, there were many things about Harvard itself that I quickly came to cherish, not the least of which were the intelligence and the motivation of the graduate students. Indeed, during my very first week on campus, while I was still unpacking my books, who should saunter into my office but a young man who was to become my first advisee and the best student I would ever have. It was Merrill Carlsmith, the talented but wooden young undergraduate with whom I had worked at Stanford. After graduating from Stanford in 1958, Merrill began his graduate work at Harvard a year before my arrival. Wooden no more, he embraced me warmly and with excitement as if he had discovered a long-lost older brother. And, in a sense, he had.

"You are a sight for sore eyes," he said. "What took you so long to get here?"

He had been disappointed, complaining that there was no one for him to work with at Harvard; no one on the faculty was doing the kind of high-impact experimentation that he had learned to do at Stanford. I informed him that there were few places in the world where that kind of experimentation was being done. "And," I added with mock bravado, "Harvard is about to become one of them."

"Don't be so sure," he said.

"What do you mean?"

"Well," he said, "I don't quite know how to put this. But what I have picked up is that it is not just a matter of their not knowing how to do our kind of experimental work, it is that some members of the faculty are hostile to it."

"On what grounds?"

"No one has said this to me directly, but, from what I can gather, the general feeling around here is it is ungentlemanly, maybe even unethical, to use a cover story when describing the experiments to our subjects. They don't see it as theater. They see it as lying."

"That's interesting. Well, my friend, are you ready to start doing some ungentlemanly experiments?"

"You bet."

And off we went.

In those days fewer than half of the Social Relations faculty members were housed in its headquarters, Emerson Hall, a venerable ivy-covered building in the center of Harvard Yard. Its most distinguished residents were Gordon Allport and Talcott Parsons; the rest of us had our offices in several cottages scattered outside the central campus. These cottages functioned like fiefdoms, with each of them housing one senior member of the faculty and several junior members. My former mentor from Wesleyan, Dave McClelland, ran the fiefdom at 5 Divinity Avenue.

I had been assigned to 9 Bow Street, a nondescript two-story yellow clapboard house adjacent to a motor-scooter sales and repair garage. My office assignment was no accident. Jerry Bruner, a brilliant, erudite cognitive psychologist, wanted to take me under his wing. The summer before my arrival at Harvard, Jerry had written me a warm welcoming letter, in which he informed me that my office would be near his and inviting me to teach a freshman seminar with him on the human mind. I wrote back telling him that I was happy to be housed at Bow Street but that I didn't think I wanted to teach the freshman seminar. When I arrived in Cambridge I learned that Jerry and I would be coteaching the seminar.

Teaching with Jerry was an interesting experience. In the seminars I had taught with Ralph Haber at Stanford, our aim was to encourage the students to express their ideas in response to pointed questions and encouragement from us. The seminar at Harvard was about Jerry and his breadth of knowledge. I think the students got a lot out of listening to him; I know that I did. I contributed as well, but I missed hearing from the students and getting to know them.

During that first semester Jerry also invited me to attend weekly research meetings with his seven or eight graduate students. I thought the group was doing some interesting research, but their projects were not my cup of tea. So, after attending the first three or four meetings, I skipped one. Jerry came into my office the next day and asked how come I wasn't there. That's when I realized that, as with the invitation to coteach the freshman seminar, an invitation from Jerry was more than an invitation; it was a command. At that point I was reluctant to rock the boat, so I did attend the next meeting. Jerry announced that he needed to fly to London the following day and would miss the next meeting, but that "Elliot will run things in my absence."

I didn't want to let the group down, so I showed up and ran the meeting, but I didn't like what was happening. In effect, Jerry was turning me into his lieutenant, and I did not see that as part of my job description. When he returned from Europe I confronted him. His response was warm and supportive. "Of course I understand," he said. "You have research projects of your own and don't want to get enmeshed in mine."

A few days later I handed a couple of scribbled letters to Mrs. Horan, the secretary whose office was between Jerry's and mine, and asked her to type them for me. She explained that Jerry had told her that she couldn't do that for me anymore because she was being paid from his research grant and I was no longer a member of the team. That administrative decision seemed perfectly reasonable. But it meant I now had to trek a half mile to Emerson Hall, where the department chairman's secretary typed my letters. Having my office at Bow Street had suddenly become a major inconvenience.

Near the end of the semester Jerry came into my office and told me that he was expecting a visiting scholar from Oxford. "Would you mind," he asked, "moving your office up to the attic so as to make space for him?" Again, Jerry's request seemed perfectly reasonable. At first, though, because there was only one office in the attic, I felt isolated. Then Merrill and I managed to clear out a bunch of junk from an adjacent storeroom and commandeered a small table and a few chairs. The room was windowless and unattractive, but it gave Merrill and my other students a place to hang out. All at once my students and I were isolated together. The following September, when two additional graduate students, John Darley and Tony Greenwald, joined us in that cramped little storeroom, we worked in a truly splendid isolation. We had the entire attic to ourselves, and this proved to be an electrifying arrangement. We were forever bouncing ideas off one another, criticizing and sharpening research designs and procedures, and constantly learning from one another.

I was beginning to learn how things were done at Harvard, or at least at 9 Bow Street. But I had yet to teach my first stand-up lecture course, scheduled for the spring semester. The chair of the department, Robert White, had kindly invited me to teach any course I felt comfortable with, so I chose Social Influence and Conformity. But I was anything but comfortable. Although I had had some success teaching seminars and had given guest lectures at Wesleyan and Stanford, I had never been responsible for a whole course. Any idiot can give an effective guest lecture, especially with a week or two to prepare, but to construct a set of coherent lectures that told an accurate and interesting story? *That* was difficult.

One night, shortly before the term began, I woke up in a cold sweat, anxious about what might be in store for me. There I was, a kid who had been educated (so to speak) at Revere High School, intimidated by the idea of lecturing three days a week, exposing my knowledge and ignorance to a roomful of the nation's brightest students. Most had attended elite private schools like Groton, Andover, and Exeter, becoming accustomed to having the finest, most knowledgeable teachers in the country. I wondered what I would talk about at the end of my second lecture, after I had finished telling them everything I knew about social influence. They will discover I am an impostor! They will tear me apart! Worse, they will yawn, stand up, and walk out of my class!

When daylight arrived and my panicky ruminations began to subside, I told myself that although some of these kids might be smarter and more sophisticated than I was, I had something important to teach them and I was passionate about the subject. If I worked hard at preparation, how could I fail to excite them? I crafted each lecture so that it not only went to the core of the theories and research that I knew and loved but also was illustrated by stories—some personal, some historical, some humorous, some touching, some tragic—that illustrated the points I was making in a way that the students would not easily forget. Each of my lectures was a story in and of itself, with a beginning, middle, and end. And each lecture dovetailed into the next, so that, taken together, they formed a series of interlocking chapters that came to a climax in the final class.

Within a few weeks many of the students were bringing their friends and roommates to audit. After each lecture clusters of students hung out asking questions until we were forced to vacate the room by the incoming class. Several walked along with me from Emerson Hall all the way back to Bow Street, asking questions and raising thoughtful objections. They found the course material important and relevant, and many were fascinated by experimental methodology. The student grapevine was the measure of my success: Enrollment jumped from sixteen in my first year to more than sixty my second year to well over a hundred in my third year. I had arrived. I was a teacher.

I was also eager to begin my experimental research, and the first idea I wanted to test stemmed from a running argument that Leon and I had been having during my last year at Stanford. Although the theory of cognitive dissonance had certainly been fruitful, it was still vague around the edges. I had often joked with the younger graduate students, saying that if they really wanted to be certain whether two specific cognitions would produce dissonance, they had better ask Leon. Leon was well aware of the need to establish firm boundaries. Indeed, in his book, he had tried to define the limits of the theory by proposing a hypothetical situation in which a man was driving late at night on a lonely country road and got a flat tire. When the man opened the trunk of his car, he discovered he didn't have a jack. Leon maintained that although the man would experience frustration, disappointment, perhaps even fear, he would not experience dissonance. The example disturbed me. I said, "Of course there is dissonance! What kind of idiot would go driving late at night on a lonely country road without a jack in his car?"

"But," Leon countered, "where are the dissonant cognitions? What is dissonant with what?"

I struggled with that one for several weeks. Finally, it dawned on me that the answer was going to involve the self-concept. In Leon's example, the dissonant cognitions are (a) the driver's cognition that his behavior was idiotic and (b) his self-concept of being a reasonably smart and competent guy. This simple insight led me to the realization that, in previous research, the theory had been producing its clearest, least-ambiguous predictions only when an important element of the self-concept was threatened, typically when an individual behaved in a way that was inconsistent with his or her sense of self.

Back in 1957, when Jud Mills and I had first framed our hypothesis for the initiation experiment, we believed that the dissonance was between the person's cognition "I went through a severe initiation to get into a group" and the cognition "the group is dull, boring, and worthless." But, in 1959, I saw that I could frame the hypothesis in a different way: The cognition "I am a sensible, competent person" is dissonant with the cognition "I went through a severe initiation to get into a worthless group." In the Festinger/Carlsmith experiment, the original hypothesis stated that the dissonance was between "I believe that the task I performed was boring" and "I told a person that it was interesting." Reframed, the dissonant cognitions become "I am an honest, moral person" and "I told a lie."

At the time I thought that what I was proposing was a minor modification. Leon disagreed. He thought the change was huge, and he was not pleased. He believed that my formulation would significantly limit the scope of the theory. "Nonsense," I said. "All I am doing is tightening it a bit." But Leon was right. Actually, we were both partly right. My modification did limit the scope of the theory; but it also made it tighter, and the advantages of that tightness outweighed the loss of generality. Eventually, Leon came to see it my way, but it took him a while (about ten years!) to fully embrace the change and to begin talking about cognitive dissonance in terms of the self.

What I thought, at the time, was a minor adjustment turned out to be a major revision, one that transformed dissonance theory from a theory about attitudes into a theory about the self. Because beliefs about the self are the most important cognitions that people hold, then dissonance is most painful, and therefore most likely to motivate change, when our behavior or attitudes are inconsistent with who we think we are. Moreover, the importance and centrality of cognitions about the self make them resistant to change. Thus, in my self-consistency formulation, the existence of dissonance motivates us to maintain our self-concept by changing our attitudes and subsequent behavior.

I realized that the reason that most of our experiments had worked was because virtually all of our participants had reasonably high self-concepts. Indeed, my thinking about cognitive dissonance in terms of the self-concept uncovered a previously hidden assumption imbedded in the original formulation: namely, that, like the residents of Garrison Keillor's Lake Woebegone, most people think of themselves as above average in just about everything. But what about people who don't think so highly of themselves? By my reasoning, if an individual considers himself to be a schnook, he would expect himself to do schnooky things, such as going through a severe initiation to get into a worthless group or lying to another person for a paltry sum of money. For such individuals, dissonance would not be aroused under the same conditions as for persons with a favorable view of themselves. Rather, dissonance would occur when negative self-expectancies were violated—that is, when the person with a poor self-concept behaved in a way that reflected positively on the self.

That is precisely what Merrill and I set out to investigate. In our experiment we did not want to try to influence a person's entire self-concept, which would have been unethical as well as impossible. But we could test our idea more efficiently. All we would need to do is give people false feedback on some specific ability that they didn't know they had. We constructed a bogus but convincing personality test that we dubbed "The Harvard Social Sensitivity Test." This consisted of a series of twenty cards; each card contained three photographs of young men (which we selected, arbitrarily, from an old Harvard yearbook). Merrill told the subjects that one of the photos on each card was that of a hospitalized schizophrenic, and their task was to guess which one. After choosing the alleged schizophrenic on each of the twenty cards, Merrill recorded the amount of time it took them, pretended to grade their answers against a bogus answer key, and announced their score and the time it took them. The initial test consisted of four sets of twenty cards each. Merrill told half of the subjects that their score on each set was very high (either a sixteen or a seventeen); he told the other half that their scores were consistently low (either a four or a five).

At this point, half of our subjects saw themselves as being socially insensitive and half as being highly sensitive, according to our official-sounding test. Next, to create dissonance, Merrill manipulated the feedback about their performance on a critical fifth and final trial of twenty cards, giving the subjects scores that were either the same as their previous scores or the opposite of their previous scores. Thus, in the crucial experimental conditions, one-half of the participants who expected to do poorly on the fifth and final task received the same low score on the final trial (four correct); this result was consonant with their self-concept of low social sensitivity. The other half received an unexpectedly high score on the final trial (sixteen correct), a result that was dissonant.

How could we get an indication of the degree of discomfort each person felt? After administering the final test, Merrill, who had blossomed into a convincing actor, slapped his forehead in chagrin and confessed that he had forgotten to time their performance on that trial and was not sure what he could do about it. He went into the adjacent room, allegedly, to ask Professor Aronson what he should do. A few minutes later Merrill returned to the room, apologized profusely, and told them that he needed to ask them to take the fifth test again, "so that I can record how long it takes you. Please pretend that you are seeing the final set of photos for the first time."

This ruse gave participants an opportunity to change their answers on retaking the test. We hypothesized that the number of responses a participant changed when allowed to retake the test would be an accurate measure of their degree of discomfort with their score on the aborted trial. And the results clearly supported our prediction of the need for self-consistency: People who expected a low score and received a low score changed few of their answers. But people who expected a low score and received a high score changed many of their answers—thus guaranteeing a lower score. Their success on the final trial created dissonance with their self-concept; to reduce dissonance they intentionally sabotaged their own performance. How could we be sure that our subjects were reducing dissonance rather than, say, having forgotten their correct answers on the aborted test? Easy. Those whom we had randomly assigned to the condition where they expected a high score and got a high score changed almost none of their answers, thereby demonstrating that memory was not an important factor.

After Merrill ran his final subject and I debriefed her, explaining the hypothesis and the reason for the deception, we rushed to the room that held the "MonroeMatic" calculator to analyze our data. I read off the numbers while Merrill punched the keys. The results were highly significant.

"This is a groundbreaking experiment," Merrill said. "Let's celebrate!"

"I'm not sure how groundbreaking it is," I replied, "but we can talk that over during our celebration. Let's go to St. Claire's. I'm told that their bartender makes a great martini."

Thus began a tradition that I continued throughout my career as a mentor. Whenever my students and I completed an experiment, we celebrated with martinis. These celebrations were not merely joyous punctuation marks; more often than not, they produced conversations that were a prelude to our next experiment. And the first of these celebrations was no exception. I told Merrill that I wanted to find a way to teach Hal, now three and a half years old, to behave a bit less aggressively with his two-year-old brother, Neal, and that I was thinking of a variation on the procedure he used in the Festinger/Carlsmith experiment. Merrill said, "You mean whenever Hal hits Neal you will punish him by making him pack a bunch of spools in a tray?"

"Not exactly. But look, your experiment was about insufficient reward, right? I mean, paying a person one dollar for lying was not enough to get him to justify telling the lie. So he needed to add justifications by convincing himself that the spool packing was more interesting than he had thought—therefore making him less of a liar."

"Right."

"Okay, but you cannot offer a small reward to Hal for not hitting Neal because he is almost always not hitting Neal. That means we have to use punishment, or at least the threat of punishment. Suppose I threaten to prevent Hal from watching cartoons on TV for a whole month if he hits Neal. That's a severe punishment, and it might get him to stop beating up on Neal for a while, at least while I am in the room. But that's not what I want. Because he still will like the idea of hitting Neal."

"So you want Hal to convince *himself* that hitting Neal—or any other little kid—is a bad idea."

"You got it. And how do I accomplish that?"

"Of course!" Merrill said. "By threatening him with a very small punishment. You have turned my experiment with Leon inside out: Small rewards for telling a lie gets a person to convince himself that what he said was true. But a threat of small *punishment* for committing a forbidden act will get a person to convince himself that he didn't want to do it in the first place because it is not fun or interesting. How can we test this on several little kids? We can't stand around and wait for them to beat up on each other, can we?"

"No, but we can offer threats of either mild or heavy-duty punishment for some minor activity that little kids do all the time."

And so, right there in St. Claire's bar, Merrill and I worked out the procedure that came to be known as the forbidden-toy experiment.

Merrill and I purchased several attractive toys and brought them to the preschool run by Harvard University. We invited the kids, who were four and five years old, to play with them. We came

back for two hours a day for the next five days, establishing rapport
with the children and encouraging them to play with the toys we
had brought. After a few visits the children would greet us excit-
edly, referring to us as "the toy guys."

On the sixth day we brought each of the children into an ad-
joining small playroom and asked him or her to tell us how much
they liked each of the toys. The next day we brought each of the
children into that playroom again, where they could play alone
with the toys. We pointed to the toy that the child had ranked as
their second most favorite, placed it a few feet from the other toys,
and told the child that it was okay to play with all of the toys except that one. We threatened half of the children with mild punishment for transgression ("I would be a little angry"), and we
threatened the other half with more severe punishment ("I would
be very angry. I would have to take all of the toys and go home
and never come back again. I would think you were just a baby").
Then we left the room and allowed the children twenty minutes
to play with the other toys. We watched through a one-way mirror
to see whether they would resist the temptation of playing with
the forbidden toy. All of them did.

On returning to the room we asked each of the children to rank
the attractiveness of all the toys once again. And now the children
who had gotten our mild threat rated the forbidden toy as being
significantly less appealing than they originally said it was. Because
they lacked much external justification for refraining from playing
with the forbidden toy, they needed to supply some of their own
justification. And that is just what they did. They convinced themselves that they hadn't played with it because they didn't really like
it.

In contrast, the children who had gotten our severe threats did
not change their opinion of the forbidden toy. They continued to

rate it as highly desirable; indeed, some even found it more desirable than they had before we had threatened them for playing with it. They had good external reasons for not playing with the toy and therefore had no need to invent additional reasons, so they continued to like the toy.

Dissonance theory would predict that the children's shift in toy preference would be fairly permanent, and it is, as my friend Jonathan Freedman found when he repeated our experiment at the Stanford preschool. Freedman used as his forbidden toy an extremely appealing battery-powered robot that scurried around hurling objects. Two months later almost all the children who had been mildly threatened were still resisting the temptation to play with the robot, whereas the majority of the children who had been severely threatened went right to it. We had demonstrated a powerful phenomenon: The children did not come to devalue their behavior (playing with the toy) because an adult told them it was undesirable; they convinced *themselves* that it was undesirable. And that new conviction had staying power. This paradigm may well apply beyond toy preference to more basic and important areas in child rearing, such as the control of aggression—which, of course, was the practical problem that had originally piqued my interest. Was I able to get Hal to persuade himself that beating up on Neal was a terrible idea? Not completely. The problem with applying our finding to everyday aggression is that we would need to find exactly the right level of threat: mild enough to induce the child to supply his own justification for refraining to act aggressively, but severe enough to get him to refrain from aggressing in the first place. If the threat is not quite severe enough to induce restraint, it might lead him to justify his aggressive behavior toward his younger brother ("I guess I really like beating up on the little bastard, because I am braving a punishment in order to keep doing it"), which, of course, is the exact opposite of what we would hope to accomplish. I worked hard to fine-tune the level of my admonitions to Hal, and eventually his aggressiveness toward Neal did, indeed, diminish. Whether this small success was due to my intervention or to maturation (Hal's, not mine!), or to countless other possible factors, I cannot be certain. Alas, my little experiment at home, on one child, lacked a control condition.

———————

Near the end of my first year at Harvard, I received a registered letter from the National Science Foundation approving my application for a three-year research grant. So I was in a good mood when I returned home that evening. I walked into our living room and saw Hal sitting on the floor with a sheepish look on his face. He was staring at what had been a ten-inch statuette depicting a ballplayer with his glove raised high over his head, as if he were about to make a catch. It was a chintzy little thing, made out of some nondescript material painted to look like bronze. But bronze it was not. Its flimsiness was apparent, in part because it was lying there in three distinct pieces. "Daddy, I dropped it, and it broke all by itself," Hal said.

The statuette wasn't one of Hal's toys. It was a baseball trophy and a survivor, having remained intact for many years of rough-and-tumble travel. I had managed to pack it and bring it with me whenever I made a major move. For fourteen years it always had a place of prominence on my mantel or dresser as I went from Revere to Waltham, to Middletown, to Palo Alto, to Cambridge. I bent down, picked it up, and looked at it forlornly, wondering if it could be repaired. Was that crummy little trophy that important to me?

Fifteen years earlier I had had my bar mitzvah. I read and sang from the Torah, made a speech to a synagogue overflowing with relatives, friends, and the usual array of *schul-menschen*—old men who spoke little or no English and seemed to spend most of their days in the synagogue. Because of my intense shyness, I hated the whole ordeal. The best thing about my bar mitzvah was that once it was over, I no longer had to attend Hebrew school. And the best thing about no longer attending Hebrew school was that it freed up my late afternoons for baseball. In February the Red Sox went to Sarasota, Florida, for spring training. Around the same time, kids from my neighborhood would head for the nearby diamond to begin impromptu choose-up games of baseball. Revere, Massachusetts, was not Sarasota, Florida. It was usually bitter cold in late February, with patches of sooty snow in the outfield. When the temperature rose above freezing, the turf turned to mud.

Although we didn't need an incentive to play, that winter and spring we had a special reason to hone our baseball skills: The Revere Parks Department had announced that it was planning to initiate a summer league for thirteen and fourteen year olds. The league would consist of eight teams, one from each of the eight baseball diamonds scattered around the city. I desperately wanted to make that team. This was long before the birth of Little League, with its strict adult supervision, tight organization, uniforms, experienced coaches, impartial umpires, and all the trappings of the big leagues. Those of us trying out for our neighborhood team were a ragtag group of kids. Yet, on our own, we managed to self-select a team fairly and sensibly. It was a meritocracy, pure and simple: The most talented nine guys were on the team, regardless of race, creed, or color.

Although anti-Semitism was a powerful force in my neighborhood, it did not intrude on the selection process. Only two Jewish kids tried out for the team, and both of us made the starting lineup. Although I was uncomfortable at first with my Gentile teammates, expecting the worst, after a few games we bonded as a team. A few years later, when my father died and our family was sitting shiva, my aunts and uncles were startled by the frequent visits from the "goyim," my former teammates. The guys managed to overcome their discomfort with this Jewish ritual because they wanted to lend me their support during my time of mourning.

I wanted to play center field. It always struck me as the mountaintop of baseball, commanding, as it did, a 180-degree view of everything that was happening on the field. But I was not a fast runner. By consensus, the position was awarded to Sonny Barnacle, the fastest thirteen year old in the neighborhood. Although I was disappointed, the decision was fair. I was assigned to play second base. Jason had schooled me in the art of fielding grounders on rough terrain. Under his tutelage (and constant nagging), I learned to let go of my fear and get my body in front of all grounders hit in my direction. Moreover, although I was not fast, I was quick; that is, I was adept at taking those first three or four steps in the right direction as soon as the batter hit the ball. This enabled me to get a good jump on most grounders, putting my body in front of them before lowering my glove to field them. If a ball took a bad hop, it would usually carom off my chest, and I was able to pounce on it and throw the runner out.

Uniforms? We wore our ordinary street clothes, usually torn and dirty. Equipment? Most of us owned gloves, but that was about it. Our left fielder patrolled the outfield with a catcher's mitt, because that was the only glove he owned. The Parks Department supplied bats, a chest protector and mask for the catcher, and one ball per game. Often, the game was interrupted for several minutes while we all hunted for a foul ball lost in the tall weeds and assorted rubble bordering the diamond.

Our first season as a team we lost more games than we won. But the next year we were a year older and stronger. Billy Mac-Donald, our pitcher, added a slow curve to an already good fast-ball. Les Hiscoe, our best hitter, had been lifting weights, and now hit for power. And I, thin as a rail, gave up trying to hit home runs and learned to be a contact hitter. I consistently hit soft line drives just over the infield. Kenny Gordy, our shortstop, and I worked for hours on turning double plays and got pretty good at it.

We won the championship that year and were each given a tro-phy in a formal ceremony. It was, as I said, a chintzy little thing, but it assumed great importance for all of us and for me, in par-ticular. It was the first thing I had ever won, the first time my talent at anything had been recognized. I cherished that trophy. Kneeling by my son, I turned its broken pieces around and around in my hands and seriously thought about having it repaired. Then I grinned at Hal, stroked his head, and said, "You are absolutely right. It did break all by itself. It's not your fault." I stood up and, with a sigh, dumped the pieces of the trophy in the trash, realizing, at long last, that I didn't need it anymore.

Early in my second year Gordon Allport invited me to give a guest lecture in his undergraduate personality course. I suspected that he was one of the people Merrill had in mind when he warned me that some of my colleagues had serious reservations about the ethics of high-impact experiments. Gordon, at sixty-three, was the most distinguished professor in the Social Relations Department. Fame and respect had come early in his career; I was charmed by the fact that he had been elected president of the American Psy-chological Association (APA) when I was in the first grade, learn-ing how to read.

I saw Gordon as the instantiation of the best that Harvard had to offer: a wise, kind, scholarly, upright elder statesman. He was always impeccably groomed, his suits always neatly pressed, his shoes always shined. Every aspect of his demeanor was perfectly proper. When I was with him I felt especially rumpled, unkempt, and tousled, and had to fight the urge to check to make sure that my fly was zipped all the way up. I didn't spend a lot of time with Gordon, but his presence was an important part of my sojourn at Harvard. I was very fond of him, and my fondness grew the longer I knew him. I think he liked me a little, too. Not excessively, of course, because, as I suspected, I was not his kind of person.

He confirmed my suspicion in his introduction to my lecture. After showering me with the typical compliments ("brilliant," "creative") that a gentleman scholar gives a visiting lecturer, he concluded by referring to me as "the master of mendacity." I was taken aback. I was not absolutely certain what "mendacity" meant, but I guessed it had something to do with lying; at best it was a backhanded compliment but, more likely, an outright insult. Making such a statement was so out of character for Gordon that it spooked me, causing me to stumble over the first few sentences of my lecture.

Afterward, I walked Gordon back to his office. We paused outside the door, and he reached out and warmly shook my hand with both of his. As he opened his mouth to thank me, I said, "Gordon, what's with this 'master of mendacity'? Were you calling me a good liar, or what?" He turned bright red and invited me into his office.

"No, no, no, of course not. I was primarily complimenting you on your skill in doing those deception experiments that you and Mr. Festinger are so adept at."

"Gordon, forgive me, but I suspect that you think that kind of research is . . . is . . . *schmutzig*." I intentionally used the Yiddish word for "dirty." I knew that Gordon would understand me because it was identical in German, a language he knew well.

He laughed. "Well, I wouldn't say that. Let me just say that I would be unable to do that kind of experiment. I know you think of it as theatrical, but I see it as deceptive."

"Call it what you will," I said, "but you realize, of course, that we do explain everything to each of our subjects at the end of the session, and none of them has ever expressed any unhappiness about the process."

"Fair enough," he said. "But why do it in the first place? Why all the theatrics, the sleight of hand, the deception, the gimmicks?"

"For one reason only: because theatrics or deception, whatever you want to call it, is the only way to test the hypotheses I am most interested in."

"Why don't you just ask people what they would do?"

I did a double take. At first I thought Gordon was pulling my leg, but then I realized that for all his wisdom and sophistication, he had little or no understanding of the basic requirements of an experiment. Nor did he seem to understand one of the most fundamental things about us humans: We don't know what we would do in most hypothetical situations, and even after we have behaved in a certain way, we are often unaware of why we did what we did. Because I had lectured about the initiation experiment in his classroom, I used that as my example. I described to Gordon how, when I was debriefing the subjects at the end of the session, all of the subjects in the severe-initiation condition agreed that my hypothesis was interesting, but most insisted that *their* liking for the group had nothing to do with the initiation. They liked the group, they assured me, because it really, truly was interesting.

Gordon stroked his chin thoughtfully and said, "And you believe they were incorrect because . . . "

"Because we had randomly assigned each subject to different conditions! The only difference between the experimental condition and the control condition was the severity of the initiation. Statistically, the difference between conditions could not have happened by chance. Therefore, I can say, with a high degree of certainty, that most of the people would not have liked the group if they had been in the control condition."

"Your logic is airtight," he said. "Can I buy you lunch?"

And off we went to the Harvard Faculty Club, where we had a most enjoyable meal. To get the conversation off research, I asked him whether he had grown up in New England.

"Oh, no, far from it. I was born in a small town in rural Indiana and grew up in Cleveland. My father was a country doctor. He never made much money and didn't want to. I was able to attend Harvard as an undergraduate only because they offered me a scholarship. You look surprised. Did you think I was born in Harvard Yard?"

Now it was my turn to blush. "Of course not . . . Well, as a matter of fact, just about. You do seem . . . "

"Why, Professor Aronson, I do believe that you have stereotyped me."

I raised my hands over my head in mock surrender. "Guilty as charged," I said.

"A common error," he said, gracefully letting me off the hook.

Grace was one of Gordon's major hallmarks. A decade after his death in 1967, I was invited to write a retrospective review of his 1954 masterpiece, *The Nature of Prejudice*, to mark the twenty-fifth anniversary of its publication. "The conclusions Allport drew are not noticeably different from the conclusions that a reasonable scholar would draw today," I wrote. "This is a tribute to the wisdom, scholarship, and judgment of a graceful mind." To read that book now is to appreciate how far ahead of his times Gordon was in his understanding of prejudice and its bitter consequences.

Shortly after my lunch with Gordon, I was invited to Yale to give a colloquium for the Psychology Department. Afterward, a young assistant professor introduced himself and asked me to his office because he was eager to describe the details of an experiment that he was designing. His name was Stanley Milgram, and the experiment was to be on the topic of obedience to authority. He was inspired by the capture and pending trial of Nazi war criminal Adolf Eichmann and wanted to determine the extent to which ordinary people would obey the commands of an authority figure, even if it meant subjecting an innocent person to severe pain. I told Milgram that I thought it was a great idea and a daring experimental procedure. I had no idea that it was to become one of the most important and controversial experiments ever done in social psychology.

In Milgram's experiment, described to participants as "an experiment on learning," the subject (who was cast in the role of teacher) tested another person (the learner) on a series of paired words that the learner had supposedly memorized. The teacher sat in front of a machine with toggle switches labeled as ranging in intensity from 15 volts to 450 volts (and above that, ominously, XXX) and was told the learner was attached to this shock generator. Every time the learner made an error, the experimenter, dressed in a white lab coat, told the subject to administer an electric shock and to increase the shock level after each incorrect answer. Milgram's question was: How far would a person go in blind obedience to an authority figure, in this case the white-coated experimenter? In actuality, of course, no one got any shocks. The learner was an accomplice, and his responses were scripted.

Two years later Milgram's published results electrified (so to speak) the psychological world. Earlier, he had asked several psychiatrists, as well as his colleagues and students, to predict what percentage of people would continue delivering shocks to the very end. They all were certain that no more than 2 or 3 percent, a few sadists, would go beyond 300 volts. Yet nearly two-thirds of the subjects continued to administer shock all the way, up to the highest levels, simply because the experimenter said, "The experiment requires that you continue." Many were uncomfortable, many sweated and protested and complained, yet they obeyed. In subsequent replications the results were almost identical. It mattered not whether the subjects were students, salespeople, or carpenters; men or women; Americans, Europeans, or Middle Easterners.

Milgram had answered Gordon's question—why couldn't you "just ask people" what they would do?—far more convincingly than I did. His experiment demonstrated unequivocally that "just asking people" what they think they would do if an authority ordered them to harm another person would yield completely unreliable answers.

Nonetheless, the experiment evoked a firestorm of criticism on ethical grounds. Psychologists, ethicists, and many general readers were outraged by the intense discomfort Milgram's procedures caused the participants. To take just one example, Diana Baumrind, a developmental psychologist, claimed that the procedures had caused "loss of dignity, self-esteem and trust in rational authority," and thus would be "harmful in the long run." I do not deny the ethical problems raised by the experiment, and in the main I think it is good that procedures this extreme are no longer possible. But most of the critics overlooked the sturdiness and resilience of the average participant; even those who felt miserable about going all the way to the maximum level of shock later said they had learned a lesson of incalculable value. Not one of Milgram's subjects complained, and none reported having suffered any harm. Indeed, when polled a few weeks later, 84 percent said they were glad to have participated, and the rest were neutral, a record of satisfaction that exceeds that of most innocuous psychological experiments. Gordon Allport was not among Milgram's critics. He was not happy with the ethical problems embedded in the procedure, but he felt that the data Milgram gathered were of great consequence. A few years later Milgram joined the faculty at Harvard. He would not have been hired without Gordon's endorsement. Apparently, Gordon had overcome his distaste for high-impact experimentation.

In spite of our differing approaches to the Harvard scene, Dick Alpert and I remained close friends. He was a frequent visitor to our home in Arlington, just northwest of Cambridge, and Vera and I spent weekends with him in his rustic family retreat in the White Mountains of New Hampshire. We hiked, swam, and played music together, all with far more enthusiasm than talent.

I had also served as an adviser on his research grant to study early childhood education. So it was no surprise when Dick phoned and asked if I could join him and Timothy Leary for an informal lunch and consultation on a research project they were planning. Tim Leary, a close friend of Dick's, was a personality psychologist who had taught for several years at Berkeley and had joined the Harvard faculty about the same time I had. I didn't know Tim well, but I liked what I knew; he was smart, energetic, and interesting, exuding charisma and a touch of mystery. Undergraduates passed along juicy rumors about him, most of which were flat-out wrong, greatly exaggerated, or maliciously distorted.

One rumor that was definitely true, however, was that Tim had been experimenting with mind-altering drugs. On a visit to Mexico he had ingested some hallucinogenic mushrooms that he claimed had expanded his consciousness in powerful and positive ways. The hallucinogenic effects may have been temporary, but his excitement about the experience was permanent. He believed the mushrooms had the potential to improve humanity and change the world, and that was what Tim and Dick wanted to discuss with me over lunch that day. Tim said that the psychoactive ingredients of the mushroom had recently been synthesized into a drug called psilocybin, and he and Dick wanted to conduct some experiments with it. They thought they might begin with graduate students at divinity schools in the Boston area.

"This drug will give them a religious experience beyond their wildest dreams," Dick said.

"And," Tim added, "just imagine what will happen when we feed psilocybin to hard-core convicts! In a matter of months, we may be able to virtually empty our prisons!"

"All this from a little mushroom?" I asked.

Tim's eyes flashed with anger. "It's a little mushroom that opens the heart as well as the mind. It's a little mushroom that usually makes people feel their connection to other people. It's a little mushroom that I'm convinced will reduce violence and stands a chance of making war obsolete."

My question may have been glib, but it had struck Tim as sacrilegious. I was taken aback by their fervor, which was messianic to say the least. I couldn't decide whether their ideas were grand or grandiose.

After an awkward pause Dick said, "We want to be as scientifically correct as we can possibly be with this research. You know a lot about how to do experiments. How can we design this one so that it is tight enough to be published in *JASP*?"

I told them what it would take to get published in the *Journal of Abnormal and Social Psychology*, our field's most eminent journal. I told them about experimental design and procedure, including the importance of a placebo condition, the elegance of the double-blind procedure, and why it would be essential to test one person at a time (to eliminate the possibility of social influence and emotional contagion). I saw Tim and Dick exchange a look that conveyed "Boy, is this guy square!" They then patiently explained to me why most of my suggestions would be impossible for them to implement. Their primary reason was the overriding importance of what they called "set and setting"—mental set being a person's expectations about the drug and setting being the immediate environment in which the person is taking the drug.

"For example," said Tim, "if you put on a white coat and administer this stuff in the confines of a mental hospital, people are likely to have scary hallucinations; they'll think they are losing their minds. But if a group of friends is sitting around in a comfortable living room with a fire blazing in a fireplace, their hallucinations are likely to be exciting rather than scary."

"Besides," said Dick, "if we administer psilocybin on several occasions to convicts about to be released on parole from Concord Prison, and then we compare their recidivism rate to a group on parole who didn't get psilocybin, isn't that good enough?"

"Well, if you can have truly random assignment of convicts to the two conditions, and if you can control for everything except the drug, then it just might pass muster."

"What do you mean by *everything*?"

"I mean everything. For example, all that sitting around by the fireplace with a congenial group of people might contribute to their wanting to stay out of prison. If that setting is in the experimental condition, it also needs to be in the control condition."

Dick and Tim nodded. There was a long silence. Then Dick said, "Well, there goes *JASP*."

In retrospect, one thing about my behavior during that meeting puzzles me. At no time did I raise any concerns about possible harm that the ingestion of psilocybin might cause participants in their research. In 1961 psychedelic drugs like LSD and psilocybin were perfectly legal, and social scientists were well aware of the anthropological studies of cultures that used peyote, coca leaves, marijuana, and other mind-altering substances the way we in the West drank alcohol, with no adverse effects. But the synthesized drugs, in which the active ingredients were extracted and distilled, were so new that nothing was known about possible long-term effects on the brain. So, at that time, it was not unreasonable for a cautious person to have some concerns about possible decrements in thinking and memory. Fortunately, a half century later, it is known that the occasional ingestion of psychedelics has no discernible harmful effects. At least I cannot remember any!

Did Tim and Dick succeed in emptying our prisons? Obviously not. They did manage to complete their experiment, such as it was, with parolees, although, as predicted, their procedure was too loose to be accepted for publication in a refereed journal. But the Harvard administration was not pleased with their activities. Two years after our lunch conversation, both men were summarily fired: Dick for involving undergraduates in the project, against the terms of their agreement with the administration, and Tim for failing to meet his teaching obligations.

I had no idea that Tim and Dick were heralding the dawning of the Age of Aquarius and that they would become its major spokesmen, though, after they left Harvard, they would go in different directions: One would seek world peace and mind-altering experiences through drugs, the other through spirituality. Tim Leary took the drug route. He was soon to become a cultural icon, exhorting students and other young adults to "turn on, tune in, and drop out." President Richard Nixon would call him "the most dangerous man in America," and the government would eventually imprison him for the possession of a few ounces of marijuana. Dick Alpert was to live and study in India for several years, returning to America as Baba Ram Dass, a spiritual leader who sought to expand people's consciousness without the aid of chemicals. In 1980 I invited him to give a guest lecture to my social psychology class at the University of California at Santa Cruz. Sporting a long gray beard and flowing white robes, he sat cross-legged on a table and held three hundred students spellbound for ninety minutes. Afterward, my dear friend the holy man and I spent several hours reminiscing about the old days at Harvard. I reminded him of the night that, in his quest for tenure, he had flicked on the lights in his office, hoping Harry Murray would notice. He beamed at me beatifically and said that although his dismissal from Harvard had been a bitter pill at the time, he had achieved a different and a far richer kind of tenure.

———————

Early in the spring of 1961, at a faculty cocktail party, Dave McClelland came over to me. After a few minutes of chitchat, he drew closer, lowered his voice, and said, "You and I haven't had a chance to talk much this year. Are you happy here at Harvard?"

"Well," I said, "I have great students, and we are doing some research that is exciting the hell out of me."

"Yes, I've heard. I'm proud of you, of course. But I hope you realize that you didn't answer my question."

Dave was astute. Although I was happy with my courses, with my students, and with the research my students and I were doing, I felt there was something missing.

"The truth is," I said, "I can't get over feeling like an outsider."

"Is that all? Hell, everybody at Harvard feels like an outsider."

"Really? Even Gordon Allport?" I was kidding, but Dave wasn't.

"Especially Gordon Allport," he replied.

Up until that moment, I thought that my vague discontent was only my problem and that it would eventually fade. But even if Dave was only partly right, I knew my feeling was likely to stay with me for as long as I remained in Cambridge. I wondered briefly if that was how I wanted to live for the next few years.

But Dave had set the stage. Several weeks later Stan Schachter phoned and asked me if I would consider taking a job at the University of Minnesota. Stan had been Leon Festinger's first and most distinguished student. Although he and I had barely met, I liked him a lot and thought of him as my intellectual uncle, so I did not reject the idea out of hand. Besides, Minnesota had a strong social psychology program. Leon had taught there before going to Stanford, and Harold Kelley, a first-rate social psychologist, had taught there for several years before leaving for UCLA in 1960. I liked the idea of being in the same department with Stan, and I told him so.

"Well, actually," Stan said, "last week I accepted a professorship at Columbia. We were thinking of you as my replacement."

"What's going on at Minnesota? Why is everybody leaving? Is there something you aren't telling me?"

Stan assured me that there was nothing wrong. It was just that as a native New Yorker, he missed the city terribly and yearned to get back there, and that Hal Kelley had always wanted to live in California. "Believe me, the University of Minnesota is a great place," he said, "especially for a social psychologist. It's just that losing both of us within two years puts the social psychology program in jeopardy. That's why I am coming to you. You are the young guy who can hit the ground running and scoop up the baton without missing a step. I predict that in two years it will be your program, and nobody will even remember that Hal and I were ever here."

"Yeah, fat chance!"

"Okay, a slight exaggeration. Do me a favor. Come and visit us. Give a colloquium. Meet the faculty. See for yourself. I guarantee that you will like it."

Stan was right. The atmosphere was relaxed, and the faculty, though no less distinguished than the scholars at Harvard, were charming and warm, immediately making me feel like a valuable person and a grown-up—a sharp contrast to my experience in Cambridge. Minnesota also had another attraction: the Laboratory for Research in Social Relations, with its own research budget. It had several rooms, beautifully outfitted with all the equipment you could want—one-way mirrors, tape recorders, sound systems—and such a contrast to the one research room I had at 9 Bow Street. On the final day of my visit Stan accompanied me into the office of the department chair, Kenneth MacCorquodale. Kenneth was a fastidious guy whose office was immaculate; Stan was a famous slob, whose office accumulated anything he happened to deposit there. As usual, Stan had a cigarette dangling from his mouth, and as usual he was oblivious to the growing length of ash, which eventually fell, as it often did, onto Kenneth's office rug. Kenneth complained, and Stan said, "Come on, Corky, don't be such an old lady." Kenneth turned to me and told me about the trip the two friends had taken together through Europe the previous summer, a cheer-up trip for Stan, who was recently divorced.

"Every time we stopped at a hotel," he said, "Stan would empty his pockets onto the dresser: in addition to the loose change, there was all kinds of debris—a couple of old cigarette butts, a half of a movie ticket, two empty matchbook covers, some lint. Then the next morning, Stan would sweep them up carefully into his hand and put them all back into his pocket."

And then, while I was still laughing, Kenneth turned to me and said, "The job is yours if you want it. What would it take to bring you here?"

I was taken aback. I was not accustomed to that kind of directness, or to faculty who combined joking and storytelling with serious job matters. That was sure not the way they did things at Harvard. I didn't know what to say. So I said, "I don't know what to say. Why don't you make me the best offer you can? I will discuss it with Vera and give you an answer within a few weeks."

Shortly after I got home I received a formal letter from Kenneth informing me that the university was offering me an associate professorship, with tenure, plus the directorship of the Laboratory for Research in Social Relations. It was an incredible offer, given that I was only twenty-nine years old and had held a Ph.D. for only two years. The only thing I didn't like about it was the directorship. So I phoned Stan and told him my qualms about accepting an administrative job. He was reassuring. "Don't be a schmuck!" he shouted. "The only thing being director means is that you get to decide how the money gets spent. I did it for years, and I'll bet you a million dollars that I hate administrative work even more than you do. Take the fucking job, I implore you, if for no other reason than to relieve my guilt at walking out on them."

I phoned Leon to chat about it. "What are your misgivings?" he asked.

"Well, the main thing is that Harvard attracts some of the best students in the world. Will they be that good at Minnesota?"

"You don't need Harvard; you will attract great students wherever you teach."

"Me?"

"You! Take the job. That's an order."

Vera and I discussed the issue up, down, and sideways. On a personal level Boston was home for me—the Red Sox, the Revere Beach Boardwalk—and it had become a real home for Vera. Both of our families were there: my mother, who still lived in the house where I had grown up; my sister, Paula; Vera's sister, Lili, who had followed us to Cambridge; and their parents. Vera's mother and father, who had come to the United States via Israel, were living with us in Arlington. They were an enormous help, caring for our three children and Vera, who was then pregnant with our fourth, and they were not about to uproot themselves again to move to Minnesota. My own mother was doing well; after my father's death, she had slowly begun to enjoy her independence. She was proud of my being a professor at Harvard, though she was never quite clear on the concept of what a "professor" did, let alone what kind of psychologist didn't have patients. One afternoon in the middle of the week I went to see her. Her sister called, and my mother told her she couldn't talk just then as I was visiting. My aunt had obviously asked, "How could Elliot get time off from his job to do that?" I heard my mother respond, "You know how it is in the professor business. They don't pay much, but you can't beat the hours."

So Vera and I had many personal reasons to stay. But we both knew that I would be forced to leave Harvard in two or three years anyway; why postpone the inevitable? Why not do it now when I could go to a great job? I called MacCorquodale and accepted the offer. He wanted me to come that September, but I said that would be impossible. First, our baby was due in August; we did not want to move with a newborn, and Vera would need some recovery time. Second, I was reluctant to leave my three graduate advisees high and dry. In academia there are two kinds of professors: the trees, who stay rooted to one spot forever, and the nomads, who change universities with some regularity, either for personal reasons or for professional opportunities. If I was going to become a nomad, I did not want to be one of those who could heartlessly abandon their students.

Kenneth and I struck a compromise: I would come midyear. Within a few months I had gotten Merrill started on his dissertation and had helped him secure an assistant professorship at Yale, Tony Greenwald had begun working with Walter Mischel and Gordon Allport, and John Darley had agreed to join me as my chief research assistant. By January, when baby Joshua was five months old, Vera and I were ready to pull up stakes once more and move with our four children to the icy upper Midwest.

One night that August, just before Joshua was born, the phone rang at ten o'clock. In our family, whenever the phone rang after eight, it portended bad news, and this was no exception. It was

Jason, calling to tell me he had been diagnosed with cancer in his right shoulder and that he was about to undergo surgery to amputate his shoulder and arm. I went straight to the airport and caught a night flight to Chicago. On the plane I kept picturing Jason without his shoulder and wishing it weren't true, hoping that there had been some horrible mistaken diagnosis. Five days later, on my return flight home, I wished it were only the shoulder he would lose.

A few days after the surgery an intern had told Jason's wife, Erica, and me, in confidence, that the cancer had metastasized throughout Jason's body and that my brother would not have long to live. Jason didn't know. In those days doctors rarely told patients the truth, if the truth was bad news. I hated concealing it from him. I knew that Jason was the kind of person who deserved to know the truth, no matter how grim. But his physician and Erica decided that it would be better if he didn't know. I figured it was their call, so I went along with the conspiracy of silence and allowed Jason to believe that the surgery had been a success.

In September Jason came to Boston. He wanted to visit our mother and sister and meet his newest nephew. I invited him to give a guest lecture in my social psychology course, to talk about social influence from his perspective as a political scientist. He eagerly accepted: "I thought you'd never ask!" (As a Revere kid like me, he held Harvard in the highest esteem.) Jason gave a great lecture, keeping the students enthralled with examples of political influence and chicanery from ancient Athens to contemporary Chicago. He frequently dashed to the blackboard, writing with his left hand, as effortlessly as though he been a lefty from birth. The students loved him. As we walked out of the classroom, he put his arm around my shoulder and said, "You see? My dream came true. We did get to teach at the same college."

During his visit he complained of shortness of breath and wondered aloud what could be causing it. I suspected that the cancer had spread to his lungs, and in that moment I could no longer continue the charade of silence. He had a right to know, a right to decide how he wanted to spend whatever time was allowed to him. And so I told him. He sighed deeply and was quiet for several minutes. The first words out of his mouth were not about him but about me. He thanked me for having the guts to tell him. "It must have been a heavy burden for you," he said, "to have carried that secret all these weeks."

When Jason and I were growing up in Revere, baseball and poker were more than games; like working on the boardwalk, they provided constant lessons in what it is to be a mensch. Once, when we were in our early teens, we were in the stands, watching a high school baseball game. The batter struck out swinging hard on three straight pitches. As he walked toward the bench he looked disdainfully at the barrel of his bat, as if it had let him down. Jason yelled out, "It's not the bat, asshole!" I laughed. Jason's crack was funny, but it was also a lesson in taking responsibility. It echoed his admonition when he was teaching me how to play poker. I had been dealt three terrible hands in a row and, at the fourth, had whined, "Another crappy hand!" Jason shot me a stern look and said, "Never, ever complain about the hand you are dealt. It's the law of averages; good hands, fair hands, terrible hands, they will even out in the long run. Any idiot can win when he is dealt a full house. The trick to poker is to play the hand you are dealt in the best possible way. You can win with a lousy hand, if you play it right."

Jason died four months after his last visit to Boston, having just turned thirty-two. He spent those months surrounded by the people he loved most. Because Jason's friends were uncommonly bright, sophisticated, and articulate, his apartment was the closest thing to a literary-philosophical salon I had ever seen. I wanted to hang out with my brother as much as I could without shortchanging my family or my students, so I spent that fall commuting almost every weekend between Cambridge and Chicago.

Late one night, asleep on Jason and Erica's living room couch, I heard a sound coming from the kitchen. It was about three o'clock, and Jason was fussing with the teakettle. As we sat together drinking a cup of tea, he said, "Look how life takes care of things. I always thought that I would be afraid of death, but at the end, because the pain is so intense, I can feel myself getting ready to let go." My brother was dealt the lousiest hand imaginable, and he played it right, to the end.

CHAPTER SEVEN

The Warmth of Minnesota

"I wanted to be the best husband and father I could be."

J ason and I are in a huge, cavernous railroad station, something like Grand Central Terminal. We know that the train is about to leave, but we don't have tickets and we don't know which of the multilevel tracks our train will be departing from. We are racing around but cannot find the ticket window. Finally, we spot one in the far end of the station. "Wait here," Jason says. "I'll take care of it." Wallet in hand, he dashes to the ticket window. When he returns, he is gasping for breath; he hands me a ticket and, pointing, says, "You'd better hurry; the train is about to leave on that track over there."

"Aren't you coming?"

"I'm afraid I can't join you. You'll have to go it alone from here on. Don't worry, and don't look back. You will be fine."

Somehow, I am not surprised to hear him say that. And, in the dream, I am surprised at not being surprised. We hug, I take a deep breath, and I hop on the train just as it is beginning to move. I look back; Jason waves to me in a sad salute.

No need for Sigmund Freud to interpret this one. When I was seventeen years old, my brother, in defiance of our uncles, guided me to the right track, put me on a fast train, and, then, when my own family and career were secure, he died. He remained behind, forever at the station.

I missed Jason terribly. Next to Vera, he had been my closest friend and confidant. Once the initial shock of his death began to subside,

I found myself turning inward, focusing on my own mortality. It was suddenly obvious to me that the Aronson family was cursed with a genetic defect that made us more cancer prone than the average family. Not only had that dreaded disease struck down my father and brother in their prime, but it had also killed two of my father's siblings in their thirties. My first reaction, worried about financial security for Vera and the kids, was to take out a huge life insurance policy. If I was going to die young, I would not leave my wife and kids destitute. The Prudential Insurance Company was only too happy to sell a large policy to a twenty-nine-year-old professor in perfect health.

I began joking to my friends and colleagues about "shortgevity" running in my family. I believe I did that, ad nauseam, as a kind of memento mori; that lighthearted statement did for me what the skull on the desk did for a medieval scholar—serve as a reminder that life is too short and unpredictable to waste much time on unimportant or uninteresting things. So, I told myself, I had damn well better make use of whatever time I had left. I said to myself, "Okay, schmuck, stop wallowing in grief and self-pity. Let's suppose, seriously, that you have only four or five years left to live; how do you want to spend your time?"

I wanted to spend more time with Vera and the kids. More than spending time, I wanted to be the best husband and father I could be; Hal, Neal, and Julie were now six, five, and three, and Joshua was an easy, happy baby. I also wanted to be the best teacher, the best researcher, and the best colleague I could possibly be. I always had those ambitions, but now my focus was sharper and more immediate. I figured out ways to spend more time with my family without taking anything away from the work I loved doing. I concentrated on being fully present, actively making plans with and for Vera and the kids.

I was amazed to learn how much time there is for everything if one doesn't waste a good deal of it on trivia. I worked hard and well at the university, but almost all evenings and weekend days became sacrosanct family time. I refused to let course preparation, the writing up of research articles, colloquium invitations, or other business intrude on Saturdays and Sundays during the day. When I was home, I was really there. Although I fiercely guarded weekend days as a time to enjoy the children, weekend evenings were something else. Vera and I frequently hired babysitters so that after we tucked the kids in, we could step out, going to movies, theaters, or restaurants, or to one of the faculty parties that my sociable colleagues were forever throwing. Vera and I made a conscious decision to be more than the parents of four children. It was important to us to continue to think of ourselves as young lovers. On weekend nights when we did stay home, we conspired to keep our romance alive. After putting the kids to bed, we prepared simple but elegant late-night dinners with candlelight and wine.

Not all the changes I went through as a result of Jason's death were positive and rational. I began drinking far more heavily. In the past I had enjoyed nightcaps with Vera as well as a martini or two with my graduate students whenever there was something to celebrate. But in Minnesota my drinking became more intense and more frequent. At parties I often got drunk. Vera and my friends told me that I was an affectionate drunk, not a belligerent one, but the fact is that they (usually Vera) had to *tell* me because, the morning after, my memory of my behavior was cloudy at best.

Vera also kept cautioning me that I was driving too fast and taking crazy risks. As I look back, I see what an irrational thing that was for me to do, given how hell-bent I was, at least consciously, on being present (and alive!) for my family for as long as possible. Many years later I learned that the three most common manifestations of grief among men are heavy drinking, reckless driving, . . . and singing sad, sentimental songs in the shower. Bingo: I was three for three. Fortunately, the intensity of my grief and my irrational behavior subsided within two years and did not result in any wrecked cars or strained friendships. Yet my dream of Jason at the train station has recurred all my life, serving as a reminder to keep things in focus and in perspective.

When Vera and I first arrived in Minneapolis, we rented a house some distance from the campus. The following September, when our lease was about to expire, we decided to buy a home of our own, though we didn't have much money. After searching for a few months, we found only two houses that were large enough and in our price range that we both liked. They could not have been more different. One was a charming old Victorian, within walking distance of the campus. I liked it a lot, primarily because it meant that my colleagues and graduate students could casually drop in on us to discuss research or just schmooze. But that house was adjacent to an industrial area, without much space for our children to play. The other choice was a tract house in the suburbs, newer but without distinction, a thirty-minute drive from campus. It had two advantages: It had a large yard and was only a mile from Lake Owasso. Eventually, that was the house we chose, because we agreed it was better for the kids.

Not long after we moved in, I saw an ad for a used canoe and immediately bought it as a surprise for Vera and the children. When I arrived home on that freezing, bleak December day with the canoe lashed to the roof of my car, Vera burst into laughter.

"What's so funny?" I asked.

"Ask Leon!" she said.

Of course! I had felt so much dissonance about buying the house in the suburbs that I needed to do something right away to justify that purchase. I somehow managed to ignore the obvious fact that it was the beginning of the long winter season in Minneapolis and would be another five months before the frozen lake would thaw out enough for the canoe to be usable. During the winter Minnesotans frequently take shortcuts by driving across lakes; they joke that the unofficial arrival of spring is the first car that falls through the ice. So, for five months, my canoe sat lazily in our garage. But it did more than take up space; it helped me come to terms with giving up my dream of living close to campus.

When I first moved into my office at the Laboratory for Research in Social Relations, I found, to my astonishment, that the lab was not the beehive of activity that it had been when I visited the previous spring. Indeed, things looked bleak. For one thing, the secretary, the very person whom Stan Schachter had assured me would know all the ropes and would relieve me of the onerous administrative work, was seven months pregnant and had one foot out the door. In addition, there were only a few graduate students. When Hal Kelley and Stan Schachter moved on, they had taken their favorite students with them, and those who remained were busily working on their dissertations or already committed to working with either Dana Bramel or Ben Willerman, my two colleagues at the lab. What to do? I needed a research assistant, and no one was available. Dana and Ben informed me that there was a wealth of talent in the Twin Cities and suggested that I advertise in the *Minneapolis Tribune*.

It seemed a strange way to hire a research assistant, but it turned out to be a great idea. I received a flood of responses and interviewed the eleven who seemed most qualified. Most of them could have done the job, but one interviewee struck me as being uncommonly bright. Her name was Ellen Berscheid. Ellen had earned a master's degree from the University of Nevada and was working for Pillsbury Mills in marketing, "exploring," as she put it, "ways to persuade housewives to buy cake mix." Her behavior during the interview puzzled me. She told me she really wanted this job, yet she was not going out of her way to make a good impression. Far from it. From the moment she walked in the door, her demeanor was feisty and contentious; she seemed primed to argue with me about ideas great and small. I had the feeling that if I had said, "It's a sunny day" (which it was), she would have replied sharply, "Nonsense. It is about to snow."

But she was clearly the most qualified candidate, so I offered her the job. After a few months I was so impressed with her that I urged her to take some graduate courses and work toward a Ph.D., which she did, finishing in record time. Thirty-five years later, when Ellen was given the APA's highest honor, the Distinguished Scientific Contribution Award, she wrote a brief professional memoir. On reading it, I was charmed to learn that she regarded our interview as having been a major turning point in her life. Because she had suffered from the pervasive sexist attitudes and treatment in her previous job, she wrote, she had walked into my office expecting more of the same. She was surprised and delighted that I had selected her on the basis of her qualifications alone, in spite of what she referred to as her "wrong gender and undeniably bad attitude."

The new students were a smart and lively group. Dana, Ben, and I had recruited and selected them carefully, and by October the lab was humming with exciting research. The new graduate students included a brilliant Jesuit priest (Eugene Gerard) and a gifted mountain climber (Darwyn Linder). John Darley, having completed his course work at Harvard, now joined me at Minnesota as my majordomo and role model for the newer students. On a postdoctoral level, our greatest acquisition came out of the blue. One day I received a call from Leon Festinger, who told me that he had a first-rate new Ph.D., Elaine Hatfield Walster, who was having trouble getting an academic position, given the bias against hiring women at most universities at that time. Leon asked me if there was any way we could find a job for her at Minnesota.

"How good is she?" I asked.

"You know Stan Schachter?"

"Of course," I said.

"You know Elliot Aronson?"

"A little bit," I said.

"Well," Leon said, "she is in that class."

There was, however, no position open in our department for another social psychologist, so I thought that was the end of it. But a few weeks later, when I learned that the Student Activities Bureau was advertising for a research specialist to arrange freshmen orientation dances, I called the dean of students.

"This is a golden opportunity for you and for us," I said. "Why hire a hack researcher to collect data on who goes to the dances and whether or not they had a good time? Why not hire a skillful experimental social psychologist who will make something interesting out of this opportunity and who will do the job right— maybe even discover something of scientific importance? If you hire the right person, we in the lab will work with him or her as well. You get a capable scientist with built-in consultants, and we get a good colleague."

"Terrific idea," the dean said. "Do you have anyone in mind?"

"It just so happens . . . ," I said, and so Elaine came to Minnesota. She in fact did use this assignment as a vehicle for a groundbreaking study on dating preferences among college students, which was published in our leading journal. We gave her an office in the lab, where, just as I had hoped, she spent most of her time working and interacting with the grad students, who treated her as if she were a regular faculty member. She proved to be an excellent, intuitive researcher and became one of my all-time favorite colleagues. Because she had no teaching responsibilities, for Elaine the job was like having a high-paid postdoctoral fellowship. After two years she was offered and accepted an official position as an assistant professor in the Psychology Department. Eventually, Elaine and Ellen Berscheid teamed up to form what proved to be a highly productive research partnership that lasted for more than two decades.

The weather in Minnesota was frigid, but the social climate was warm and could not have been more different from the one I experienced at Harvard. There were no barriers between faculty members as a function of rank or tenure. Newly hatched assistant professors joked freely with their most distinguished colleagues, who included Starke Hathaway (the inventor of the Minnesota Multiphasic Personality Inventory, the single most important personality test of that era and since), David Lykken (a national expert on the physiology of lie detection), Norman Garmezy (a clinical psychologist ahead of his time in studying children's resilience), and Gardner Lindzey (editor of the monumental two-volume *Handbook of Social Psychology*). There wasn't any antagonism between the clinicians and the experimental psychologists, as was true in most departments at that time, with each side feeling that *they* were doing the important work—the clinicians in the study of real people, the experimentalists in the rigor of their science. I am convinced that the primary force underlying this atmosphere of respect was Paul Meehl. Meehl was extraordinarily smart, an excellent experimentalist, a masterful psychotherapist, a brilliant philosopher of science, and a first-rate psychometrician. When the acknowledged superstar of the department bridges all subdisciplines, how can any of the lesser stars quarrel with each other?

I believe that Meehl's stature and ideas contributed to one other major difference between Harvard and Minnesota: While Harvard maintained its excellence by being extremely conservative when making a tenure decision, Minnesota maintained its excellence by making shrewd guesses about the future productivity of the young people on the faculty. I recall chatting with Meehl during my first year, telling him how pleased and surprised I was that they had taken a chance on me by offering me a tenured position when I was only two years out of graduate school. He said this was no gamble at all.

"Really?" I said. "Why?"

"Passion," he said.

"Passion?"

"Past productivity is a good predictor of future productivity," he said, "but the surefire predictor is passion. Anyone reading your work can easily see the joy you take in doing it."

Meehl also saw no reason to follow any set rule in the timing of promotions. "When people are doing good research," he said, "they should be promoted rapidly." One year later he came bounding into my office with a big grin on his face and announced that the senior faculty had unanimously voted to promote me to full professor. This promotion came as a bolt from the blue. I had not asked for it, nor was it made in response to an offer from another university. They promoted me simply because they felt I deserved it. It took me many more years in academia to realize just how rare an attitude that was.

If the social and intellectual atmosphere in the department as a whole was warm and congenial, the atmosphere in our lab would have to be described as downright cozy. We all enjoyed working together, teaching together, collaborating, and just hanging out. Because I was finally working with a critical mass of like-minded experimental social psychologists, I was able to institute Tuesday-night research meetings for all of the social psychology faculty and graduate students. We would meet at one of our homes and, over beer and pretzels, serve as informal consultants on one another's research ideas, experimental procedures, data analysis, and so on. We even organized a faculty-student softball team that was talented enough to challenge the fraternity jocks for the intramural championship. We never missed an opportunity for a party.

Vera and I treated the grad students like members of the family. The students got to know our kids, and hung out a lot at our house. At one of the Tuesday-night meetings, Josh, who was not quite three at the time, was playing around with some of the students. It was way past his bedtime, but he was having so much fun that he refused to heed Vera's calls. Finally, Vera came into the living room and scooped him up. Trying to wriggle out of her grasp, he extended his arms toward Darwyn Linder and cried, "Darwee, help! Help me!" For months after that, the other students greeted Darwyn with Josh's plea.

At the University of Minnesota I discovered that the architectural design of a building can have a profound effect on the productivity and creativity of the people in it. The layout of the lab was ideal. We occupied about half of the fourth floor of Ford Hall. The faculty offices and experimental rooms were clustered together, and all were adjacent to the most important place in the lab—a huge room at the end of the hall, where all of the social psychology graduate students had their desks. That room had three or four blackboards and two coffeepots, one of which was always kept brewing as the other was being emptied. We called that room the "bullpen" because it was the place to hang out and shoot the bull. Our conversations ranged from the trivial (gossip and sports) to the vital. We constantly threw out research ideas, and from them, experiments took shape.

One afternoon I came into the bullpen to find Gene Gerard and Darwyn Linder doubled up with laughter. Gene was reading passages aloud from a book by British civil servant C. Northcote Parkinson. It was Parkinson's tongue-in-cheek thesis that, in a government bureaucracy, work will always expand to fill the time available, and he had hilarious examples to bolster his case.

After listening for a few minutes, I said, "You know, Gene, that's not simply funny. It's also interesting."

"Uh-oh," Darwyn said. "Be careful, Gene. I know that look. You are about to get roped into doing an experiment."

"I'll ignore that crack," I said. "But it happens you're right. Look, it's true that, in a bureaucratic organization, people mark time a lot; they pretend to be working so that the work does expand to fill the time available. They are doing this because they are simply sitting around doing boring stuff and watching the clock. But what if a person is given a task to do—and because of an accidental occurrence, he has all day in which to do it. So he goes over it a few times, polishes it, hones it, and so on. Then, a short time later, he is given a similar task but is allowed to leave the office and go home as soon as he finishes it. I'm thinking that his first experience might lead him to define the task as one that *requires* a great deal of time—and therefore, he might spend more time on it than it deserves even though he is now wasting his own time and not the bureaucracy's time."

"You mean," Gene said, "once the time expands, it stays expanded in that person's mind?"

"You got it."

And so Gene and I did the experiment; it was a simple, straightforward procedure, pretty much as we outlined it in the bullpen. While a subject was working on a tedious task, the experimenter (Gene) was abruptly called out of the room to take an urgent long-distance phone call. We simply varied the amount of time he was allegedly on the phone. In one condition, he was gone for far longer than the participant needed to finish the task. In the other condition, he was gone for a shorter time, but just adequate for the participant to finish comfortably. In the next phase, Gene gave the subject a similar task, told him that he was free to leave as soon as he finished, thanked him for his participation, and went back to his office. The subjects who had been in the "excess time" condition took far longer to complete the second task than those in the "adequate time" condition. We had gone beyond Parkinson's law! We had shown not only that a task expands to fill the time available but also that the person doing it will then define the task as one that *requires* extra time.

The bullpen members loved this experiment, and we kept applying it to our own lives. For example, the first time I was invited to present a special address at an APA symposium, the invitation arrived in July, when I had plenty of leisure time; I spent five days preparing my presentation. A couple of years later I received a similar invitation, but this time I had other obligations and had only two days to prepare. At first I panicked and almost declined the invitation. After all, writing a speech takes five days! Then I realized, after some mental effort, that maybe it didn't always take five days. I did it in two.

––––––––––

One of the fundamental questions in social psychology is: Why do people like or dislike each other? In the early 1960s virtually all of the answers that psychologists offered were inspired by a simplistic application of behaviorism: We like people who reward us in one way or another. We like those who are physically attractive because it is aesthetically rewarding to gaze upon beauty. We like people who are competent and smart because, if they are doing things for us, we can trust them to get the job done. We like people who share our beliefs and values and, most important, who seem to like us—who shower us with praise and express interest in us and our activities. Conversely, we certainly don't like people who cause us pain, embarrassment, or discomfort.

These explanations were what any layperson would refer to as "just common sense." As my grandmother would have said, "You had to get a whole entire Ph.D. to learn this? I could have told you that when you were still in diapers." (In fact, my colleagues and I jokingly referred to this kind of research as "bubba psychology," *bubba* being Yiddish for grandmother.) It's not that the guiding principle is wrong; it's that it is incomplete and grossly oversimplified. One of the reasons I was so excited about the initiation experiment was that no one's grandmother could have predicted our results.

And so, when I decided to plunge further into the area of attraction, I wondered about other exceptions to behavioral predictions. For example, if the presence of a competent person is rewarding to us, then it follows that the more competent a person is, the more we should like him or her. But another person's competence might present some cognitive complications that are unique to human beings. What if a person is *too* competent, coming across as unapproachable and superhuman? His very competence might make us uncomfortable in his presence. We might like that person more were he to show some evidence of fallibility. Hypothetically, if Herb is a brilliant mathematician as well as a great basketball player and a fastidious dresser, I might like him better if, every once in a while, he added a column of numbers incorrectly, blew an easy layup, or appeared in public with a gravy stain on his tie.

My musings were further reinforced (dare I say) by an incident that had taken place about a year earlier. In the spring of 1961 the American military believed that invading Cuba at the Bay of Pigs would lead to the overthrow of Fidel Castro. The invasion was a fiasco and a huge embarrassment to our nation and to President Kennedy in particular, as he had authorized it. Yet immediately after that fiasco, the Gallup Poll showed that Kennedy's popularity had actually increased. How could this be? One reason might have been the desire to support our president in time of crisis, another the fact that Kennedy took full responsibility for the blunder. But a third possibility struck me: Kennedy was an extremely attractive man. He was young, handsome, smart, and witty. He was a war hero, had written a Pulitzer Prize–winning book, was the youngest president in our nation's history, and had a beautiful, talented wife and two cute kids (one boy, one girl). In short, he seemed damned near perfect. Perhaps, I thought, committing that blunder increased his attractiveness by making him seem more human—more like the rest of us.

To test this idea I designed a simple experiment with Ben Willerman and Joanne Floyd. The participants were students at the university. We told them that we were auditioning candidates to represent Minnesota on *The College Quiz Bowl*, a popular show in which students from different universities competed against each other. We explained that we wanted them to help us select the team by giving us their frank impression of one of the candidates. Each student then listened to an audiotape in which Ben interviewed one of four stimulus persons, all played by a willing grad student: a nearly perfect candidate, a nearly perfect candidate who commits a clumsy blunder, a mediocre candidate, and a mediocre candidate who commits a clumsy blunder. On each tape Ben asked the candidate a set of extremely difficult questions like those on *College Bowl*. The grad student, using the same tone of voice, played each stimulus person, differing only in his answers.

Thus, the "nearly perfect" candidate answered 92 percent of the questions correctly, and when Ben asked him about his activities in high school, he modestly admitted he had been an honor student, the editor of the yearbook, and a member of the track team. The mediocre candidate answered only 30 percent of the questions correctly, and during the interview revealed that he had received average grades in high school, had been a proofreader on the yearbook staff, and had tried out for the track team but had failed to make it. On the other two recordings, the stimulus person committed an embarrassing pratfall, clumsily spilling a cup of coffee all over himself. The audiotape included sounds of commotion and clatter and the anguished voice of the candidate saying, "Oh, my goodness, I've spilled coffee all over my new suit."

And in fact our participants rated the nearly perfect person who committed a blunder as the most likable and the mediocre person who committed the same blunder as least likable. (The blunderless perfect person came second in attractiveness, and the blunderless mediocre person finished third.) Clearly, there was nothing inherently attractive about the simple act of spilling a cup of coffee. The same action that added an endearing dimension to the perfect person, making him more likable, made the mediocre person appear that much more mediocre and, hence, less likable.

Our findings became widely known among social psychologists as "the pratfall effect." And, from that moment on, around the lab, every time one of our graduate students screwed up in some way, he or she would claim, "I did it on purpose, so that you would like me more!" To which I would reply, "All well and good, but before you blunder, you had better be sure that you are nearly perfect to begin with."

In those days the most famous popularizer of behaviorism was the supersalesman Dale Carnegie. His book *How to Win Friends and Influence People*, written in 1936 and translated into thirty-one languages, remains one of the most widely read self-help books of all time. If you want to get people to like you, to buy your product, or to change their behavior in any way, Carnegie advised, you should "dole out praise lavishly," that is, reward people by acting as though you sincerely like and appreciate them and are interested in the things they are interested in. The more attractive you seem to find a person and the more attractive your own characteristics, the more that person will like you.

Carnegie's salesmanship ran contrary to my own experience. If a person I hardly knew showered me with praise, I would suspect an ulterior motive: Is he trying to sell me something? But even if he or she doled out praise in a manner that was above suspicion, it might not be as valuable to me as someone who showed a bit more discernment in doling. Imagine that you're a young man at a cocktail party, and you meet a woman, Peggy, for the first time and have a pleasant conversation with her. After a while you excuse yourself to refill your glass. As you are returning, Peggy has her back to you and is engrossed in conversation with another person. You hear her talking about you, so, naturally, you pause to listen. She has no ulterior motive in what she is saying; she doesn't even know you are eavesdropping. Thus, if she tells her friend that she was impressed by you, that she likes you, that she finds you bright, witty, charming, gracious, honest, and exciting, you will probably like her. What a smart, perceptive person she is! If you hear her tell her friend that she dislikes you, that she finds you dull, boring, dishonest, stupid, and vulgar, you will probably like her less. What an insensitive clod she is, to draw conclusions about you after one five-minute chat!

So far, nothing unusual. Now, however, imagine that you attend seven cocktail parties on seven consecutive nights, and, miraculously, the same thing happens. You chat with Peggy for several minutes, you leave, and when you return, you overhear her talking about you. Her comments might be uniformly positive, uniformly negative, or varied—they might start negative and become positive, or start positive and go south. Which of these four possibilities would lead you to like Peggy most? Least?

According to reward-reinforcement theorists (and Dale Carnegie), you should like Peggy the most in the first situation, where she is doling out praise lavishly, and you should like her least in the second situation, in which she is saying only negative things about you. Because positive statements are rewarding, the more of them the better, and because negative statements are punishing, the more of them the worse. But I had a different idea. Because human beings are cognitive animals who are forever trying to figure things out, we pay close attention to *changes* in a person's feelings toward us. Thus, if Peggy begins by disliking me, but the more she gets to know me the more her liking increases, this will have greater positive impact on my feelings about her than if she had been uniformly positive—because it constitutes a gain. In contrast, if she liked me at first but the more she got to know me the less she liked me, this would be painful because it constitutes a loss—and therefore I would like her least of all. I called this the gain-loss theory of attraction.

In physics, Albert Einstein constructed some brilliant thought experiments that were definitive. Alas, in social psychology, our thought experiments are never definitive. However, they can be good starting points; then we have to bring them into the laboratory. But how could we invent a credible scenario that captured the essence of the seven cocktail parties, given that the whole shebang had to unfold in less than an hour? We needed to invent a situation in which the subject interacts with a preprogrammed confederate, eavesdrops while the confederate evaluates him or her to a third party, has another conversation with the confederate, eavesdrops again, converses again, eavesdrops again, and so on through seven pairs of trials. What sensible cover story could we concoct? But Darwyn Linder and I came up with one.

When the subject (a female college student) arrived at the lab, Darwyn greeted her and led her to an observation room connected to the main experimental room by a one-way window and an audio-amplification system. Darwyn told her that two women were scheduled for that hour: One would be the subject, and the other would help perform the experiment, and because she had arrived first, she would be the helper. Darwyn asked her to wait while he left the room to see if the other woman had arrived. A few minutes later, through the one-way window, the subject was able to see Darwyn enter the experimental room with another female student (Darcy Oman, an undergraduate, who served as our confederate). Darwyn asked Darcy to be seated and said that he would return shortly to explain the experiment to her. He then reentered the observation room and began the instructions to the real subject, who believed herself to be the helpful confederate.

Darwyn told her she was going to assist him in performing a verbal conditioning experiment on the other student (Darcy); that is, he was going to reward Darcy every time she used a plural noun in conversation. He told the subject these rewards would increase the frequency with which Darcy would say plural nouns, but his interest lay in whether the use of plural nouns generalizes to a new situation. That is, will people continue to use more plural nouns when they are talking to a different person, someone who has not rewarded them for doing it? Darwyn explained that he would try to condition Darcy by subtly rewarding her with a nod, a smile, and an "mmmm hmmm" every time she said a plural noun. "Will she continue to use an abundance of plural nouns when she talks to you," he asked the subject, "even though you will not be rewarding her?" He added that our volunteer's tasks were to listen in and record the number of plural nouns Darcy used while talking to Darwyn and then to engage Darcy in a series of conversations in which the use of plural nouns would not be rewarded—so that Darwyn could listen and determine whether generalization had taken place. Darwyn then told the subject they would alternate in talking to Darcy until each had spent seven sessions with her.

Darwyn made it clear to the subject that Darcy must not know the purpose of the experiment, lest the results be contaminated. He explained that he would tell Darcy that the experiment was about attraction, and ask her to carry on a series of seven short conversations with the subject. Between each of these conversations, both she and the subject would be interviewed—Darcy by Darwyn and the subject by an assistant in another room—to find out what impressions they had formed. During the seven meetings

Darwyn had with Darcy, the subject was in the observation room, listening to the conversation and dutifully counting the number of plural nouns used by Darcy. Because she had been led to believe that Darcy thought that the experiment had to do with people's impressions of one another, it was understandable for Darwyn to ask Darcy to express her feelings about the subject. Thus, the subject heard herself being evaluated by a fellow student on seven successive occasions. This setup is more complicated in the telling than the doing. To the participants who were embedded in the experiment, it was completely believable: Only four of the eighty-four subjects were suspicious of our procedure.

There were four major experimental conditions: (1) positive—the successive evaluations of the subject made by the confederate were all highly positive; (2) negative—the successive evaluations were all highly negative; (3) gain—the first few evaluations were negative, but they gradually became more positive; and (4) loss—the first few evaluations were positive, but they gradually became negative. The results confirmed our predictions: The subjects in the gain condition liked Darcy significantly better than those in the positive condition. (So much for Dale Carnegie's advice to dole out praise lavishly.) Similarly, the subjects in the loss condition disliked Darcy more than those in the negative condition.

Just as the layout of the lab and the bullpen facilitated creative conversations and generated friendships among grad students and faculty, the layout of the Minnesota faculty club did the same for instructors at all levels, from new assistant professors to the most eminent. It was another stark contrast with Harvard, whose faculty club was elegant: starched tablecloths, excellent food, and waiters who served us. Yet I ate there just a few times and only when invited by a senior professor. The faculty club at Minnesota was informal, with mediocre food served cafeteria style, on plastic trays. Most of us in the Psychology Department ate lunch there almost every day, and what our lunches lacked in ambience they gained in the fun and intellectual stimulation of our conversations. We brought our trays to a large round table at the far end of the dining hall, which was known as "the psychology corner." But it was hardly exclusive; we were often joined by colleagues from other departments, such as philosopher of science Herbert Feigl and novelist Jack Ludwig.

It was at these lunches that I got to know Gardner Lindzey, who was to become one of the closest friends I have ever had. At first I was in awe of him; he was twelve years my senior and had written or edited two of the most important books in social psychology. Gardner was the star of the round table, an entertaining storyteller and a catalyst of conversation. And he seemed to know everything about everyone's research. At one moment he would be asking Kenneth MacCorquodale detailed questions about some of the animal learning experiments he was doing, and the next he would be probing David Lykken to tell more about the lie-detection experiments that he had begun. But he would always find a way to make each person's research relevant to the interests of the other people at the table. He knew everything I had ever published, asking detailed questions about how it was that I had decided on this or that specific procedure.

Gardner was a broadly educated scholar who was not only a fountainhead of information; he was also an accomplished gossip. He knew everything that was going on in the profession (say, who was leaving which university to teach somewhere else, who was promoted, who had been denied tenure) and also who was about to get a divorce and who was sleeping with whom. When I asked him one day why we hadn't seen Jack Ludwig at the table for a while, he looked at me in astonishment. "Haven't you read *Herzog* yet?" he said. "It's been out for two months! You must read it immediately. It's about people you know." *Herzog*, of course, was written by Saul Bellow, who, a few years earlier, had been a visiting professor at Minnesota. None of us (except Gardner, apparently) knew that during that time, Bellow's wife had had an affair with Jack, who had been one of Bellow's close friends. Bellow was furious, and although he and his wife had gone to a psychotherapist for counseling, it didn't help and they divorced. Bellow got his revenge the writer's way, by writing a novel in which he barely disguised the characters. He is Herzog, and Jack is Valentine Gersbach, who has an affair with Herzog's wife. (Jack had a clubfoot; Valentine has a wooden leg.) Herzog goes to a psychiatrist, Dr. Edvig, who seems so matter-of-fact about his patient's situation that Herzog accuses Dr. Edvig of being in love with his wife himself. The psychotherapist Bellow had gone to see, Gardner told me, was . . . Paul Meehl. Later I asked Paul about the way Bellow had characterized him. "Oh, these novelists," he said.

After a few of these stories, I started to tease Gardner by calling him the Hedda Hopper of American psychology. Paul chastised me for that. "You are underestimating our friend," he said. "Gardner's gossip is not limited to the U.S. It is international in scope."

One morning Gardner phoned and asked me if I wanted to join him for a "businessman's lunch."

"What's that?" I asked.

"There are some great restaurants in downtown Minneapolis. The faculty club is pleasant, but you don't want to ruin your palate by eating there *all* the time, do you?"

"Certainly not," I replied.

"Be outside your building at 11:30. I'll swing by and pick you up."

In that first lunch Gardner and I reminisced about our days at Harvard. He had gotten his doctorate with Gordon Allport in the late 1940s and had taught there for a few years thereafter. He asked me who my favorite Harvard people were. I named a few.

"You were at 9 Bow Street, weren't you?" he asked.

"Yes, I was."

"That's funny. I notice that you didn't mention Jerry Bruner as one of your favorite people."

"To tell you the truth, Jerry and I didn't get along very well."

"I hated the bastard too," said Gardner gleefully.

"I didn't say that."

"I heard what you said. And, like I said, I hated him too."

There are many reasons that Gardner and I became close friends, but that got us off to a flying start.

This was the beginning of a number of businessman's lunches Gardner and I had, usually once or twice a week, occasionally with David Lykken or Paul Meehl. I quickly learned that Gardner's major criterion for a good restaurant was not the food but the quality of the bar. Our lunches lasted for well over two hours and were always preceded by two or three martinis and followed by a cognac. Amazingly, each of us was able to work hard and well in the afternoons. Since our friendship began while I was in my heavy-drinking period, Gardner's style fitted my needs at the time, but the lunches and the friendship continued even after I cut back to one martini. As for Gardner, well, I never knew anyone who enjoyed drinking more and who could hold his liquor so well and with such grace. He was capable of abstaining for weeks at a time without a craving, and in a close friendship of almost fifty years, I never saw him out of control.

For the next few years Gardner and I had many provocative conversations and strenuous arguments about research and theory in social psychology. Once he proclaimed that Solomon Asch's experiment on conformity was the single most important experiment in the field. I said, "Nonsense! There was no theory behind it, no control group—it was just a demonstration that people conform more than we imagined. Now, the Festinger/Carlsmith one-dollar to twenty-dollar experiment was *really* important—it had theory; it was counterintuitive; it changed the field! Who would have guessed that people who told a lie for one dollar rather than twenty dollars would come to believe that lie?"

After one of these exchanges Gardner invited me to coedit the second edition of the *Handbook of Social Psychology*. Because I had always considered the *Handbook* to be the bible of our field, this offer was like, well, being asked to edit the next edition of the Bible. The *Handbook* contained up-to-date thinking, research, and theorizing by the world's most eminent social psychologists. I agreed, figuring that I would learn a great deal from working with Gardner (as indeed I did).

A few weeks later, while I was still in a glow over the honor of being an editor, Gardner announced that he expected me to contribute a chapter as well. This time I demurred. "There are a few areas where I could do a decent job of writing a chapter," I said. "But as an editor I would want to recruit the best scholar working on a topic, and the best scholar ain't me."

"How about writing a chapter on experimental methodology?" he asked.

"I'm no methodologist," I said.

"But you did teach a seminar on that at Harvard."

"Well, yes, but that was mostly a hands-on course, where I helped students find the best way to test a given hypothesis."

"Precisely the kind of thing that would be great for the *Handbook*," said Gardner. "All you need to do is take a good hard look at your own experiments and try to make explicit the wealth of tacit knowledge that you have, so that others can understand why you did what you did."

"But teaching people how to do experiments is in the doing, not in the reading," I protested. "It is part of a master-apprentice relationship. You learn to be a great chef by working with one, not by reading a cookbook. This may even be truer in social psychology than in cooking. We don't have standardized procedures because, most of the time, each new hypothesis requires the invention of a new procedure tailored to test it. Leon had to invent the 'one-dollar, twenty-dollar' procedure, Jud and I had to invent the initiation procedure, and so on. We are always flying by the seat of our pants. It's an exciting way to work, but it makes it impossible for anyone to write a chapter called 'How to Do Experiments in Social Psychology' that will be of any use to the student who is just starting out."

"Don't be so damn rigid," said Gardner. "Nobody has ever tried to do it before. This could be a unique contribution. Think of it not as something that would replace working with a master experimentalist but as a set of ideas that might serve as an adjunct to the apprenticeship. Why not give it a try? After you write the chapter, if you don't like the way it turns out, as editor, you can simply reject it."

Although I was not convinced, I decided to plunge in—but not by myself. I recruited my favorite former graduate student, Merrill Carlsmith, who was more excited about the challenge than I was. As Gardner had suggested, we started by looking at our own experiments, to articulate the thinking that went into the design and implementation of each one. We were trying to write a cookbook without recipes. It wasn't easy.

We began by tackling the central criticism directed against experimental social psychology at that time: The mere fact that experiments were taking place in a laboratory setting made them "unrealistic." Merrill and I asked what proved to be an important question—what does "realism" mean? And the answer led us to clarify the difference between what we called "mundane" realism from what we called "experimental" realism. For example, several critics had claimed that Stanley Milgram's obedience experiment was unrealistic. After all, how often in our day-to-day lives are we asked to inflict a series of electric shocks on an innocent stranger? But that criticism missed the point: Milgram's study was unrealistic only in the mundane sense. In terms of experimental realism, the procedure was real as hell to the people participating. They sweated real sweat. Merrill and I concluded that in some situations, mundane realism is necessary; if you ask people to read a communication that you planted in a dummy newspaper, the newspaper had better look real. Usually, however, mundane realism is of no importance as long as what is happening in the laboratory has real consequences for the subjects.

Merrill and I then tackled the nuts and bolts of constructing high-impact experiments. We spelled out the experimenter's most important challenge: How to take a compelling conceptual variable, the thing you want to understand, and translate it into a concrete set of empirical steps. The trick is to achieve a high degree of scientific rigor without losing, in the translation, the essential, complex beauty of the idea. This is harder than it sounds; many a grand, important topic gets boiled down into something trivial or simplistic by the time it has been operationalized into a precise sequence of experimental events.

The next problem is to determine how to measure the effect of your intervention. In social psychology the most frequently used measure is a rating scale of some sort, usually in the context of an interview. For example, in the initiation experiment, we asked subjects to rate how much they liked the group they had joined; in the one-dollar or twenty-dollar experiment, Merrill asked subjects to rate how much they had enjoyed the boring task of packing spools. Such measures are the easiest to administer and are often the only feasible way you can get the information you want. The experimenter must not forget, however, that a rating scale is only a stand-in for behavior. Whenever possible, it is preferable to observe what people actually do rather than to ask them what they think or how they feel. In the forbidden-toy experiment, if we want to determine whether we have succeeded in reducing a toy's appeal, it is better to watch and see whether the kids resist the temptation to play with the forbidden toy than to ask them to tell us how much they like the toy. That's why Jonathan Freedman's replication of our experiment was an improvement on the original. He used the behavioral measure; he observed what the children did.

Writing this chapter turned Merrill and me into better experimenters, because it made us confront our shortcomings as well as our skills in the laboratory. Moreover, it forced us to think creatively about solutions to the problems we had posed. Getting a behavioral measure is ideal, but what if doing so is impossible, either ethically or practically? Is there a better alternative than going back to the familiar rating scale? Merrill and I invented a compromise that we dubbed "the behavioroid" measure. Suppose you want to know if watching a poignant film depicting hunger in urban America will make people more altruistic. Showing the film is easy, but you can't very easily follow the audience around for the next few weeks to see if they become more helpful to others. However, you *can* ask the subjects whether they are willing to sign an official-looking contract committing themselves to a specific altruistic action, such as volunteering to work in a soup kitchen. Of course, getting a person's "behavioroid" commitment is not quite the same as seeing whether he or she actually turns up for duty in a soup kitchen. But it is far preferable to simply asking people to rate their feelings about the poor or about the value of soup kitchens.

Finally, we gave considerable attention to the postexperimental interview—the debriefing of the subjects. Because so many experiments in social psychology require deception, Merrill and I argued that it is of the utmost importance for experimenters to disclose everything that took place and to explain why we had done what we had done. Full disclosure is a vital part of our implicit contract with our subjects. Because no one enjoys being told that he has been duped, the disclosure must be done with tact and sensitivity, or the subject will feel that he or she has been a gullible fool. The experimenter can explain that because the cover story was so carefully crafted, just about *everyone* accepted it; far from being "gullible," the subjects behaved perfectly normally and reasonably. And then we explain the goal of the research—why deception was necessary and what we hope to have learned about human nature as a result of our methods. We make sure that each and every one of our subjects leaves the experimental room with her self-esteem intact, in at least as good a shape as she was when she first came in, with the bonus of having learned something interesting. I often spent as much time chatting with my subjects after the experiment as I did during the experiment itself.

When we were colleagues at Harvard, my old mentor David McClelland once told me that he had run only one social psychology experiment in his whole life, when he was a grad student at Yale. He was observing a young man through the one-way mirror when the guy suddenly stood up, unzipped his fly, and began to examine his penis in the mirror, apparently looking for a rash or abrasion. I asked Dave how he dealt with it in the debriefing.

"I didn't debrief him," he said. "It would have been too embarrassing. For both of us."

I clucked my tongue. "Dave," I said, "in this business, you *always* debrief. There are no exceptions. If the subject were ever to learn, perhaps from a friend who was in the experiment, that the mirror was one-way, he would have been mortified. It is always up to the experimenter to find a gentle, perhaps in this case even a humorous, way of telling him what happened."

And so we finished our chapter, and I, in my role as coeditor of the handbook, accepted it. Much to our own surprise, Merrill and I had done just what Gardner had hoped we would. By forcing ourselves to make our tacit knowledge explicit, we produced a document that graduate students in social psychology have been relying on for almost five decades. That methodology chapter of the *Handbook* underwent its most recent revision in 2010. My newest coauthor is Kevin Carlsmith, Merrill's son, who was a toddler when Merrill and I were writing the original. I admit I enjoy the irony. A project that I had initially rejected, thinking it impossible, became one of my most enduring contributions to the field. As my grandmother would have said, "Go figure!"

———————

In 1964 Gardner left the University of Minnesota to become chair of the Psychology Department at the University of Texas at Austin, with the mandate to make it into one of the strongest departments in the country. A year later he urged me to join him and become head of the social psychology program. I had been at Minnesota only three and a half years and was reluctant to leave. True, all of the graduate students I had supervised now had good job offers, so I had no ongoing mentoring obligations.

I talked it over with Vera, who said she could go either way. On the one hand, she had developed strong friendships in Minneapolis and was hesitant to pull up stakes yet again. On the other hand, as a young mother with four small children, she found the severity and length of the winters particularly difficult. The kids would look through the windows at a bright and sunny winter day and scream to go outside to play. Then, after ten minutes, frozen to the bone, they would scream to be let back in. (Imagine the time it takes to get one little kid into and out of a snowsuit, hat, boots, and mittens and multiply that times four, and you have some idea of what Vera was up against.) And so she left the decision to me.

A reasonable person would have stayed put. I loved everything about the Psychology Department, and I had no desire to move at all; even if I had, Texas would not have been near the top of my list. I'm embarrassed to confess that I held a negative stereotype about the state, and my impression of Texas as a raw and wild place had been exacerbated by the 1963 assassination of President Kennedy in Dallas. But, in the end, my friendship with Gardner trumped both my rational judgment and my prejudice. We moved to Austin.

CHAPTER EIGHT

Becoming a Texan

Elliot at the National Training Laboratory in Bethel, Maine, 1971 (top).

Neal, Julie, and Hal: "Can we have your permission to sneak out at night?"

The decade I spent in Austin, 1965 to 1974, was arguably the most tumultuous era of the twentieth century. It was an exciting time to be alive, and a particularly exciting time to be a social psychologist. The Vietnam War was raging, and the antiwar movement was gaining momentum. Students across the country were staging sit-ins, love-ins, and protests of all kinds. "Make love, not war!" protesters shouted, and many of them were practicing what they preached (sometimes in public). The civil rights movement and the women's liberation movement were constantly in the news, raising consciousness—a term that was exactly right—not only of obvious and blatant forms of prejudice and discrimination but also of the more subtle forms of which even good liberals were oblivious. After all, when Gordon Allport and I had had our lunch at the Harvard Faculty Club, freely discussing anti-Semitism and racial prejudice, it did not occur to us to be equally outraged that female faculty had to enter the club through the back door.

These social changes seemed attainable to some, utopian to others, and dangerously anarchic to many. When, in 1970, the Ohio National Guard fired on students at Kent State who were peacefully demonstrating against the war—killing four, wounding nine, and paralyzing one for life—many Americans were outraged, while many more thought that the students got what was coming to them. In that atmosphere, especially at a university, nobody remained neutral. In the aftermath of the Kent State shootings, thousands of University of Texas students decided to march to the capitol in downtown Austin to stage an antiwar demonstration. In response, the Texas Rangers, a tough, conservative corps of lawmen,

197

announced that they would be there in force to "maintain order," and everyone knew what that meant. Several Rangers had openly expressed hostility to what they regarded as the unpatriotic excesses of student demonstrations against the war, announcing that they would be only too happy to break some heads in the interest of keeping the peace. For their part, most of the student leaders were defiant and talked as if they were determined to provoke the Rangers. The situation was a tinderbox; the major TV networks sent their top reporters down to cover what they were sure would be a photogenic riot. Although I endorsed the students' protest, I worried about their safety, so, along with a handful of other faculty members, I offered to help out as an organizer and marshal.

We went to the students' meeting the night before the march. It was a mob scene, with hotheads exciting the crowd with cries of "Fuck the pigs!" and the crowd shouting back "Yeah! Right on!" A few of my colleagues and I spoke, cautioning the students against giving the Rangers any ammunition (as it were) for turning the peace march into a violent melee. We exhorted them to make their protest in a clear and forceful way but without doing anything blatantly provocative that might put their lives at risk. Our words were received with a smattering of polite applause but not so much as a single "Right on." When I left the meeting, I was not sure which way the students would go. The next day I set off for the demonstration with trepidation and a heavy heart, but it went off peacefully, without incident. Although vociferous, the students did nothing to give the lawmen reason to use their batons. Or guns. The TV crews packed up and left, apparently concluding that the nonriot was not newsworthy.

The social changes erupting across America made many of us aware of problems in the university, which, in a sense, is a microcosm of the larger society. The University of Texas was a first-rate institution with amazingly low tuition rates for residents of the state; any Texas high school graduate with decent grades could come to Austin and obtain an excellent education virtually without charge. Yet when I arrived there, the student body was almost completely lily-white; even the football team, with aspirations to a national championship, had only one black player. When I talked with a few of the black and Latino students in my classes about this, they told me that minority students were reluctant to apply to UT because they saw Austin as an unfriendly place. And they were right; it was unfriendly, primarily because blacks and Latinos had difficulty finding housing near campus. There were plenty of available rooms, but most landlords refused to rent to minorities.

Clearly, the first step toward a solution was to make it illegal for landlords to discriminate against black and Mexican American students. Thus, when the Austin City Council decided to discuss a fair-housing proposal, my colleague Bob Helmreich and I attended their meeting and addressed the council members, endorsing the proposal from the standpoint of equal educational opportunities at the university. To bolster our argument, a week before the meeting I conducted a simple field experiment: I sent students to answer ads for housing near campus. Time after time, when a well-dressed, well-spoken African American or Mexican American student asked to see one of the listed apartments, he or she was informed that it had already been rented. An hour later I would send an Anglo student to the same location, and he or she would immediately be shown the apartment. The large discrepancy in responses to these students could only have been due to the landlords' prejudices, and that was the evidence I presented to the Austin City Council. That night the council passed the ordinance by a slim margin. It was the first fair-housing ordinance in any major city south of the Mason-Dixon line.

The local bigots were furious. One night at two o'clock our phone rang. On the other end of the line was a man with a gravelly voice who called me a "nigger lover" and said, "We know where you live, and we know you have four kids. Make sure, if your doorbell rings at night, that you're the one who answers the door, because one of us will be there with a double-barreled shotgun and we don't want any of your kids to get hurt." When I reported this threat to the Austin Police Department, the desk sergeant informed me that there was nothing they could do about it.

"Besides," he said, "the guy on the phone is probably just trying to scare you."

"He is succeeding," I replied.

Our family lived in fear for several weeks, but gradually we realized that the sergeant had guessed right; the gravelly voiced guy did not show up, and we resumed breathing. Nonetheless, it was our first close encounter with the rage and resistance that bigots freely express. But our intervention study, which may have contributed to the fair-housing law, was worth it. The number of minority students at the university increased sharply the following year.

My experience at the city council and with the gravelly voiced guy reawakened in me a need that had been lying dormant for fifteen years: finding ways that I could combine doing good research with doing good. I didn't have to wait long. In 1971 the Austin public schools were finally desegregated, and all hell broke loose. African American, Anglo, and Mexican American youngsters were in open conflict; fistfights were breaking out among these groups in corridors and school yards throughout the city.

Austin's effort to desegregate its schools was a delayed response to the landmark 1954 Supreme Court decision in *Brown v. Board of Education*. In that decision the Court overruled the prevailing law that segregation of blacks and whites was acceptable as long as their educational facilities were "equal." The Court decreed that "separate but equal" was inherently unconstitutional because even if white schools and black schools were the same, the mere act of being segregated had a negative effect on the self-esteem of minority children that "might never be undone." I remember the exhilaration that so many of us felt at the time. Abe Maslow was practically dancing around his office. "This is the beginning of the end of prejudice!" he exclaimed. The reasoning seemed self-evident: If segregation lowers self-esteem, then integration should raise it; once the self-esteem of minority children was raised, their academic achievement would improve. Moreover, given the assumption that prejudice is based largely on ignorance and unflattering stereotypes, bringing minority kids and white kids together should decrease their reciprocal animosity.

Before long it became clear that desegregation was not going to be easy and was not automatically going to produce the hoped-for results. In most places it was typically followed by turmoil in the community and hostility in the classroom. Prejudice in the schools was actually increasing, and the self-esteem and performance of minority kids were not improving. The situation in Austin was typical, albeit more dramatic, of what was happening across the country.

In the midst of this uproar, the assistant superintendent of schools called me to ask if I had any ideas about what could be done. He wanted an end to the violence; I wanted to know why desegregation was not producing the benefits we had anticipated. Our interests dovetailed, and I accepted the challenge.

The first step was to find out what the hell was going on in those classrooms. I sent my graduate students to systematically observe fifth- and sixth-grade classes in two elementary schools. "Sit in the back of the classroom and say nothing," I instructed them. "After a while, the kids will forget you are there. As you observe, take nothing for granted. Some things are so common that it is easy to miss their importance. A good way to avoid that mistake is to imagine that you are a visitor from Mars and have never been in a classroom before; you are observing everything these earthlings do for the first time. Write every observation down. Then rank-order your list in terms of the frequency of each behavior."

When they brought me their observations, one thing leaped out at us, something that anyone who has ever attended traditional public schools takes for granted. The typical classroom is a highly competitive place in which students vie with one another for the attention and praise of the teacher. In Austin, as in most communities, in this competition the minority kids were virtually guaranteed to lose. The previous law, "separate but equal," had been separate all right, but things had never been equal. The schools that the black and Latino kids had been attending prior to desegregation were substandard; as a result, their reading skills were approximately one full grade level behind those of the Anglo kids. So when the teacher would call for the answer to a question, it was the white kids who raised their hands, hoping to be called on, and the minority kids who squirmed in their seats, trying to look invisible. The competitive structure of the classroom, coupled with the uneven playing field, confirmed and magnified the children's existing stereotypes of each other. The Anglo kids saw the minority kids as stupid and lazy; the minority kids saw the Anglo kids as arrogant and pushy.

Our intervention was a simple one, consisting of restructuring the dynamics of the classroom from competitive to cooperative. We invented a technique that created small interdependent groups, designed to place students of different ethnic backgrounds in a situation where they needed to cooperate with one another in order to understand the material. We called it the jigsaw classroom, because the process was like assembling a jigsaw puzzle, with each student contributing a vital piece to the total picture. For example, if the topic was "The Life of Eleanor Roosevelt," each child in the small group was assigned a paragraph describing a phase of Mrs. Roosevelt's life. Each child's task was to study that paragraph alone, and then rejoin the group and report its contents to the others. The only access each child had to all the paragraphs and information, therefore, was by paying close attention to what each of the other children in the group had to say. Immediately after the jigsaw session, the teacher gave a written exam on the life of Eleanor Roosevelt.

As we were setting up this design, I worried about what would happen if one kid, perhaps one who couldn't read very well, really did screw up. Then everyone in his jigsaw group would hate him even more. I remembered how I felt as a boy when the least-talented baseball player, the one chosen last for the team, would be put in deep right field. The poor kid stands there praying no one will hit the ball to him, and then he's suddenly sent an easy fly ball with the bases loaded—and drops it. Every kid's nightmare! I immediately thought of a way of ensuring against such a calamity in our classroom: After the students read their own paragraph a few times and learned it pretty well, they would join an "expert" group. This expert group would consist of one member from each of the jigsaw groups, all of whom had been assigned the identical paragraph. They would then rehearse their selection together, allowing the slower students to get up to speed, before rejoining their original team. The expert group made it difficult for a child to screw up completely by simply not understanding the assignment. Of course, it didn't make each child's performance flawless, nor did it eradicate a child's nervousness, but it did protect every child from being a drag on his or her classmates.

And so we began our pilot study, comparing a sixth-grade classroom divided into jigsaw groups with a control classroom structured as usual. At first the children simply repeated their competitive strategies, but in a few days they realized that their competitive behavior had abruptly become dysfunctional. Take the example of a Mexican American boy whom I will call Carlos. English was his second language, and, although he was fluent, he spoke with an accent that often evoked taunting or derisive laughter among the Anglo kids. So he usually kept quiet in class. But when we introduced jigsaw, he could no longer avoid talking; he was required to present the paragraph he had learned.

When Carlos began to recite his piece of the puzzle (Eleanor Roosevelt's middle years), he had learned the paragraph well, but he was nervous and frequently stumbled and mumbled. Initially, some of the other children sighed audibly or looked away; one called him stupid. In a competitive classroom this kind of behavior often succeeds in throwing your opponent off balance. But in a jigsaw classroom the kids soon understood that their disparaging remarks and gestures would keep them from learning the piece of the puzzle that Carlos was struggling to give them—and would thus prevent them from getting a high grade on the exam. They had to learn to be patient, to listen carefully, and to prompt Carlos by asking the kinds of questions that would help him articulate the information he had. In the process they learned that Carlos was smarter and nicer than they had previously thought.

Within a week of instituting jigsaw, there was a discernible positive change in the classroom atmosphere. Visiting teachers in specialties such as art and music were among the first to notice it; they would spontaneously ask the classroom teacher what it was that he or she had been doing differently. After six weeks we documented the changes empirically. We asked the children to rate how much they liked their classmates—all of them, not just those in their jigsaw group. We also asked them how much they liked school, and we validated their responses against their attendance records.

The formal data confirmed our casual observations: Compared to students in traditional classrooms, students of all ethnicities liked school more (absenteeism significantly declined) and liked each other more—across and within ethnic lines. For white students self-esteem and test performance remained constant. But the minority students in jigsaw classrooms showed a significant increase in self-esteem, and their test performance averaged nine percentage points higher than those of minority students in traditional classrooms. This difference was highly significant both statistically and meaningfully. A black sixth grader might be earning a score of 72 on an exam in a traditional classroom, but his counterpart in a jigsaw classroom would earn an 81.

One of my graduate students, Diane Bridgeman, subsequently found that children in jigsaw classrooms also develop a greater ability to empathize with others than children in traditional classrooms do. Why? In a jigsaw classroom students must pay close attention to their teammates so that they can ask good, helpful questions; as a side effect of this process, they learn to put themselves in the other children's shoes. I was excited by this finding because learning to empathize is at least as important as learning geography or history.

The jigsaw method proved to be teacher-proof. In replicating this study we used a stringent test, and we stacked the cards against jigsaw: We assigned to the control condition those teachers whom their principals had designated as being the best in each of the schools. Thus, the improved performance of children in the jigsaw classrooms could not be attributed to superior teaching but only attributed to the method itself. Over the years, as we continued to implement the jigsaw technique, the findings remained the same. Moreover, the schools that adopted this approach became more truly integrated. We had taken photos of the playgrounds during recess, so we had clear evidence of who was hanging out with whom. Whenever they had free time, students in traditional schools were clustering in groups according to race or ethnicity. Students in jigsaw schools were more likely to mingle interracially.

I was elated. At long last, I had produced a scientifically sound answer to the question I had asked myself when I was nine years old, sitting on that curbstone in Revere, nursing my bloody nose and my split lip. I had shown that prejudice *can* be overcome, and that children of different ethnic backgrounds can learn to like one another. What it takes is not simply *increased* contact but the right *kind* of contact. As Gordon Allport had written in *The Nature of Prejudice*, "While it may help somewhat to place members of different ethnic groups side by side on a job, the gain is greater if these members regard themselves as part of a team." I knew the truth of this observation personally, given my experience with my baseball teammates in Revere. Most of those guys had regarded Jews with suspicion and distrust. Once we began to cooperate as a team, however, those feelings dissolved. We came to understand and like one another, developing an affection and respect that persisted long after the baseball season ended.

My students and I published our results in a peer-reviewed scientific journal, but I wanted our technique to be known not just to other psychologists but also to the general public, especially teachers and parents. So I wrote up our findings in a nontechnical way and submitted the article to the popular magazine *Psychology*

Today, where it was featured prominently, complete with full-color photos. I made a few hundred copies, sent them to school superintendents all over the country, and offered to train teachers free of charge. Then I sat back and waited for the requests to come pouring in.

How naive! You can't give something away if nobody wants it, and not many wanted it. When I followed up with phone calls, most of the superintendents and principals explained that they were doing just fine and didn't need an outsider to come into their schools and set up some new method. One of them was unusually candid. "Do you know what would happen if we instituted your technique?" he said. "My phone would be ringing off the hook with complaints from parents. 'Do you mean to tell me that my child is being taught by some black kid? What are we paying the teachers for?'" It dawned on me that I had been invited to intervene in Austin only because the schools were in crisis. In most school systems anything short of crisis was doing just fine by their standards.

I felt I was riding a roller coaster, elation followed by a disillusioning plummet. I had found a reliable, virtually foolproof technique for reducing prejudice and raising academic achievement in our schools, and I couldn't give it away. My friends and colleagues tried to reassure me. "That's the way bureaucracies are," they said. "There is nothing you can do about it." Somehow, I did not find their words reassuring.

And so the jigsaw technique languished for nearly fourteen years. Then, in 1984, in commemoration of the thirtieth anniversary of *Brown v. Board of Education*, the United States Civil Rights Commission singled out Austin as a model city in which school desegregation had worked in the manner intended. The commission gave much of the credit to the jigsaw classroom, and I began getting requests from all over the country to train teachers.

Although, over the next several years, I trained hundreds of teachers in dozens of school districts, jigsaw has not entered the mainstream of American education; it remains a small drop in a very large bucket. How come? Here we have an easy-to-use, cost-effective, empirically based intervention that works and that teachers enjoy using. Why is it that jigsaw failed to capture the attention of Congress or the Department of Education? My best guess is that it did not fit either a right-wing or a left-wing political agenda. The Left is committed to the idea that only massive and expensive systemic changes can make a difference in the lives of most disadvantaged children. The Right believes that it is futile to expend resources of any kind on children whose poor academic performance stems either from genetic inferiority or from deficient parenting. As a citizen I was deeply disappointed and regret that I was not a more effective advocate for jigsaw. As a social psychologist, however, perhaps I should not have been surprised that useful empirical findings often fall by the wayside if they run counter to the prevailing political ideologies.

The course I most enjoyed teaching was Introductory Social Psychology. I got a great kick out of being the first person to awaken college freshmen and sophomores to the excitement and promise of this discipline. But at Texas I was becoming increasingly impatient with the existing textbooks. It's not that they weren't scholarly enough, or that they were inaccurate, or that they didn't have enough graphs, tables, charts, or references. If anything, they had too much of that stuff. But these books were simply not addressing the problems that our students were most concerned about—the war in Vietnam, the racial divide, political assassinations, and other major events affecting their lives. No wonder that most of my students found the texts dull and irrelevant.

I did a fair amount of complaining about the limitations of existing textbooks. One day one of my teaching assistants, having grown weary of my constant kvetching, said, "Why don't you write one of your own?" I dismissed the idea out of hand. I'm afraid that my response was somewhat snobbish. "I'm a scientist," I said. "We scientists shouldn't be wasting our time writing textbooks." Instead, I prepared a few rough essays on my favorite topics, linking experimental research to contemporary social problems in a personal way and telling stories from my own life, and I assigned these readings as a supplement to the formal textbook we were using. Before I knew it, I had a rough draft of a brief but punchy textbook in social psychology. I called it *The Social Animal*.

Because I didn't know I was writing a textbook, I got to do one of the things I loved most in writing: speaking in my own voice, using the first-person singular, as if I were talking directly to students. In the first chapter I enunciated what I rather grandly referred to as "Aronson's First Law: People who do crazy things are not necessarily crazy." (That's just one of my many First Laws; there never was a second.) Of course, I was mocking myself by assigning it the status of a First Law, but the statement itself was dead serious, reflecting what I regard as the essence of social psychology, namely, that the social situation can exert a powerful impact on human behavior. Situations can make sane people do crazy things, moral people do immoral things, smart people do stupid things, and brave people do cowardly things. If we, the observers, are unaware of the social circumstances that evoke those actions, we are tempted to conclude that they are caused by some deficiency in the character or sanity of the person doing them.

The book was published in 1972, and much to my delight, it was an immediate success. It is now in its eleventh edition, has been translated into fourteen foreign languages, and has received many awards. Naturally, I loved the praise and the response of my colleagues, but most gratifying of all is the number of people who have written to tell me that it was because of reading *The Social Animal* as an undergraduate that they decided to become a social psychologist.

———

It was exhilarating to be part of a psychology department that was growing in excellence and achieving national prominence. Gardner Lindzey proved to be an excellent chair with an impeccable eye for talent. Among the many dynamic faculty members he hired was Michael Kahn, whom Gardner lured from Yale to take over the huge introductory psychology course. Michael and I had originally met at Harvard, when he was a graduate student in clinical psychology, and we became close friends. By the time he came to Texas, he was not only a superb teacher but also a trained T-group leader. (The T in T-group means "training," short for "sensitivity training.") T-groups were invented by Kurt Lewin, who is generally considered to be the father of experimental social psychology. (I always referred to him as my "intellectual grandfather" because he was Leon Festinger's mentor.)

Actually, Lewin had invented the T-group by accident. He wanted to know whether small-group discussions might lead to creative solutions to social problems, so he assembled about fifty educators and divided them into small groups. To assess the groups' success, Lewin asked several of his graduate students to observe the groups during the day and then, in the evening, to interpret and discuss the dynamics occurring in each one. One evening a few of the educators asked if they could sit in and listen to the graduate students' observations. One of the educators, upon hearing an observer's interpretation that she had been angry during a discussion that morning with one of her colleagues, protested vigorously. She hadn't been angry at all, she said, merely energized by the topic. The observer held his ground—"You sure looked angry to me!"—and the ensuing discussion was lively and illuminating. The next night all fifty of the educators showed up and gleefully joined the discussion, frequently disagreeing with the interpretations of the trained observers.

Lewin was quick to grasp the significance of this event. A group that forms to discuss how to solve a problem can benefit enormously by taking time out to discuss its own feelings and intentions, and the members do not need training in group dynamics to do this. Indeed, the participants themselves are much better observers of their own process because each is privy to his or her own intentions. This information is not easily available to outside observers, no matter how astute and well trained they are. Over time, what evolved was the agenda-less group—a group that met with no formal plan and no problems to discuss other than its own dynamics, with the goal of helping members communicate with each other more effectively and learn how they are perceived by others. The T-group quickly became the vanguard of the human potential movement.

Lewin thus produced not only many of the nation's most eminent experimental social psychologists but also the first generation of T-group leaders. Over the years the two camps parted company. When, as a graduate student, I had asked Leon for his opinion of T-groups, he greeted my question with a sneer. He was contemptuous of them because he saw them as having dubious value and little or nothing to do with social psychology. When I expressed my own skepticism about T-groups to Michael Kahn, he said, "Hey, you're a scientist. Why not find out for yourself? I'm about to start a T-group in Austin. Join us. Afterward you can tell me what's wrong with it." It was an invitation I couldn't refuse. I went, I participated, I loved it. I decided to learn more, and the place to learn more was the National Training Laboratory founded by Lewin's students in Bethel, Maine. In 1967 I spent a summer there as a participant, the following summer as an intern, and one summer later I was a leader.

But Festinger's skepticism was not entirely unfounded. During the 1960s and 1970s encounter groups (as they were commonly called on the West Coast) attracted a lot of thrill-seeking participants and plenty of goofy practitioners. Many groups were based on dubious theorizing and bad psychology, led by self-appointed tin-pot gurus. Some of their methods were foolish, others coercive. But at their best, when conducted by competent leaders well trained in group dynamics, T-groups provided participants with illuminating exercises and insights that they could take away with them. These skills made them better friends to their friends, better teachers to their students, better bosses to their employees, better parents to their children, better spouses.

What I loved most about the T-group was its emphasis on straight talk: helping members identify the difference between their feelings and their opinions and judgments of others and to be clear in their expression of those feelings rather than disguising them as insults, blame, or false flattery. There was no agenda; there was no focus on past experiences or childhood traumas. The emphasis was on the "here and now." In one T-group I led, a middle-aged man I'll call Tim confronted a slightly younger man, whom

I'll call Peter, and said, "I've been listening to you and watching you for three days, and I think you're a phony."

What's wrong with that observation? Isn't Tim simply stating his honest feeling about Peter? Well, no. The key to our understanding of this encounter rests on the term "feeling"; Tim was not expressing a feeling, he was expressing a judgment. By "feelings" I do not mean a hunch or hypothesis, as in "I feel it's going to rain today"; I mean anger, joy, sadness, happiness, annoyance, fear, discomfort, warmth, hurt, envy, excitement, and the like. So I asked Tim what his *feelings* were about Peter.

"Well, I feel that Peter is a phony," he said.

"And what does that do to you?"

"It annoys the hell out of me."

Now another member of the group intervened and asked, "What kinds of things has Peter done that annoy you?" After some probing by the group, Tim admitted he got annoyed whenever Peter showed affection to any of the women in the group. On further probing it turned out Tim was "annoyed" by Peter's attractiveness to women. Eventually, Tim owned up to feelings of envy: Tim wished he had Peter's charm and popularity with women. But, as many people do, Tim had initially masked this feeling of envy, transforming it in his mind into disdain. He was protecting his ego; Tim had learned over the years that if he admitted to feeling envious of another man, it would have made him vulnerable and appear weak. By expressing disdain, however, Tim put himself one up. Although his behavior was successful in protecting his ego, it blocked his ability to understand his authentic feelings and their cause. And it was blocking his ability to communicate directly and effectively.

In this society most of us glide through life protecting ourselves; in effect, each of us wears a suit of behavioral armor, to minimize how much other people can hurt us. But sometimes we become so successful at hiding our true feelings from others that we hide our feelings from ourselves as well. The group leader makes it possible for members to remove that armor by creating a climate of safety. Group members feel free to express their vulnerabilities without fear of being attacked or mocked.

But what if Tim hates Peter; should he express his hatred? What if Tim believes that Peter is an evil person; should he express that belief?

> TIM: "I hate you, Peter; you are evil."
>
> PETER: "No, I'm not."
>
> TIM: "Well, that is the way I see it. I'm just giving you feedback like we're supposed to do in here."
>
> PETER: "That's your problem—besides, you're not so great yourself."

By calling Peter names, Tim sets up the situation in a way that invites Peter to defend himself and to counterattack rather than to listen. But if Tim were to lead with his feelings ("I am hurt and angry"), he would be inviting Peter into a discussion about what he (Peter) might have done to hurt and anger Tim.

Speaking straight about feelings, and separating them from judgments, is effective for two reasons. First, a person's opinions and judgments about another person are purely conjecture. Tim's opinions about Peter's being a phony and an evil person may reflect reality, or just as likely, they may not. They are merely Tim's theories about Peter. Only Peter knows for sure whether he's being a phony; Tim is guessing. But Tim's statement that he is feeling envious or angry is an absolute fact. Tim is not guessing about his feelings; he knows them. Indeed, he is the only person in the world who knows them for sure. Peter may or may not care about Tim's theories or judgments, but if he wants to have a friendship with Tim, he is probably interested in knowing Tim's true feelings and what role he (Peter) plays in triggering them. Second, when Tim states an opinion or a judgment about Peter, he is saying something about Peter only, but when he states a *feeling* evoked by Peter's behavior, he is revealing something about himself as well. Thus, the statement of feeling is a gift of sorts. Metaphorically, it is Tim opening the door to his home and letting Peter in. When Tim states a judgment about Peter, however, he is storming Peter's barricades and making attributions about Peter's motives or personality. Peter has good reason to resist this, because Tim has no right to be in his home without an invitation.

We all enjoy receiving positive feedback. One of the great insights of T-groups is they teach participants the benefits of negative feedback as well—to see such feedback as valuable information rather than as an attack on the ego. For example, what can Tim and Peter do with the information their exchange in the group has given them? The leader will prod other members of the group to state whether they share Tim's discomfort with Peter's behavior. If Tim learns that he is alone in his reaction—"You mean I'm the only one who is feeling envious and hostile about this guy?"—he realizes that he has a problem with men whom women find attractive. But if other men in the group agree with Tim, then Peter has valuable information: There is something about his behavior with women that provokes envy and hostility. Now it is Peter who needs to make a decision about how to behave outside the group: whether to continue as he always has and let other men continue to be envious and perhaps express their envy in hostile ways; or modify his behavior to cause other people (and ultimately himself) less difficulty. *The decision is his.* Should he decide that his "enviable" behavior is too important to give up, he has still learned the impact it has on other men. In the future he will not be surprised by their responses and less likely to overreact to them.

T-groups taught me many lessons that I took into my personal and family life and carried with me ever after. For one, my T-group experience made me finally ready to "hear" the wise words Abe Maslow had offered me so many years earlier, when he told me that my sarcastic qualities and sharp edge, while not "venomous," were keeping people at arm's length. At the time, I felt I needed that sharp edge for self-protection and to disguise the pain of shyness. In T-groups, some fifteen years later, I realized I was ready to give it up, and I did . . . most of the time. Needless to say, I did not become a saint. I still enjoy using sarcasm and locker-room humor on occasion, but I do it for fun or to defuse a tense situation. I try to use my "sharp-edged humor" judiciously and with mindful awareness of its possible effects on others.

At home the lessons of T-groups helped me become better at communicating my feelings and solving problems. In the early years of our marriage, Vera let me know she could not abide my raising my voice when angry, much less my storming out of the house. Not having a good alternative to that way of expressing anger, I tried to stifle it. In the T-group I learned to talk about feelings of anger in a calm but forceful tone and in a nonblaming, nonhostile manner, in a way that Vera could hear without getting upset. When couples who have been married many years are asked "What is the secret? How do you do it?" they often reply with some banality, such as "We never went to bed mad." That's not terrible advice, but it is unrealistic, to say the least. After fifty-five years of marriage, I can attest to the fact that Vera and I went to bed mad on occasion, but we learned never to let a quarrel stew for very long without resolution—talking about what caused it and how to avert it in the future. Our experience in T-groups taught us the benefits not only of expressing anger constructively but also of expressing warmth and affection when we felt it, with a look, a word, or a touch. It taught us how to listen to what the other person was really saying and feeling and to take responsibility for our own words and deeds.

Early in our marriage Vera had decided not to pursue a career because she wanted to be a full-time wife and mother, and, indeed, raising four children with the skill and attention she put into it was a full-time endeavor. But in the mid-1960s, with the women's movement gaining momentum and *The Feminine Mystique* on people's minds, she often felt uncomfortable when, at dinner parties or meetings, people would ask her what she did. When she answered that she was a mother and housewife (that was before "homemaker" entered the lexicon), they seemed to lose interest in her, as if being a stay-at-home mom automatically meant that she had nothing interesting to say. Their disdain infuriated me. To anyone who knew Vera, she had plenty to say. But when she decided to become a T-group leader, she was able to expand her considerable talents and intelligence into a new domain. At first we led groups together, which was enormous fun. She was skillful; her presence injected into the group that quality of serenity I had always admired in her. She created an aura that allowed members of the group to feel perfectly secure, even when they were in the throes of anxiety, despair, and other powerful emotions. Later, she went on to lead groups on her own, an experience that put to rest any niggling feelings she had about being "just a mother."

Vera and I even brought T-groups into our family. Every Friday evening, after dinner, we'd spend an hour going over the events of the week. We encouraged the children to bring up any unfinished business, unresolved conflicts, or unhappy feelings (and even happy feelings!) about one another or with us. They loved having this chance to speak up, and we loved discovering some of the things that had been going on behind our backs. Misunderstandings were aired and potential feuds averted. Once eight-year-old Josh said to twelve-year-old Julie that something she'd said had hurt his feelings, and she responded, "Oh, Josh, don't be silly. I didn't mean anything by it." Vera said gently, "Julie, take Josh seriously. Listen to what he is telling you. The fact that you didn't intend to hurt him doesn't mean he wasn't hurt." What could have been a rift between the two siblings, or Josh's withdrawal into sulking, ended in greater understanding and, as it did this time, a hug.

I want to say a word about hugs. T-groups are frequently caricatured as places where participants believe that hugging is a panacea for whatever ails them and where, as a consequence, people run around dispensing insincere hugs at the drop of a hat. The caricature has some merit. Occasionally, a participant would turn to me and announce that he or she "needed a hug." As leader, my usual response was to gently remind the person that I was not a vending machine and did not see the value of dispensing hugs as if they were candy bars. I would then try to help the person discover what it was that he or she was feeling that might be making them insecure or anxious, and what they wanted to do about it.

Yet the greatest lesson I drew from T-groups was how to become the kind of affectionate, expressive man that my own father never was. "My father never hugged me" is a common lament in our culture nowadays, one that some men use to justify their coldness toward their own children. For me, the fact that my father was inept at expressing affection physically served to strengthen my resolve to be a different kind of father—to give my children and wife what he could not give to his. But I had a lot to learn. When hugging and touching are appropriate, for me there is no better way to convey affection, offer comfort, provide solace. The recent research on the physiological benefits of touch—it lowers blood pressure, reduces pain, and soothes tensions—comes as no surprise to me. As social creatures we crave touch; we need touch. I will remember all my life how deeply moved I felt when my philosophy professor, Aron Gurwitsch, put his hand on my head and said, "Good boy," or when Leon Festinger squeezed my shoulder and announced that my term paper was worth criticizing. These warm gestures, the first from adult men I admired, helped me realize that real men do touch, and my work in T-groups showed me further its emotional benefits. I felt freed at last from my father's physical coldness. Since the time my kids were infants to the present day, I love hugging them. And when I watch them unself-consciously showing their affection to Vera and me, to their own kids, to their nieces and nephews, and to their friends, I feel that Vera and I have given them the best of lessons.

The family T-groups also helped teach the kids the value of straight talk. Late one night, as we were about to go to bed, Hal and Neal, then ages sixteen and fifteen, approached us with an odd request. They asked permission to sneak out of the house and go roaming with their friends.

"What's roaming?" we asked.

"Well," said Hal, "when their parents go to bed, some friends of ours sneak out of the house, and just wander around the city— from about midnight to three o'clock. We were going to sneak out tonight to meet up with them, but then we worried that you might wake up in the middle of the night, see that we were gone, and get scared."

I smiled. "So you are asking our permission to sneak out unnoticed?"

"I know it sounds stupid," Neal said, "but that's about it."

"Your friends don't do anything illegal like vandalism or anything, do they?"

"No, I promise," said Hal.

Vera and I looked at each other and gave them the okay.

The next morning they told us what had happened. At about
two thirty, while on their way home, they were stopped by a patrol
car. "Do your parents know you're out?" the cop had asked them.
When they said yes, naturally he didn't believe them, so he drove
them home and walked them to our front door, fully expecting
them to be shaking in fear of our reaction. But Hal and Neal were
so calm that he asked them again, "Are you *sure* your parents know
you are out?" He guessed they were telling the truth and walked
away, probably thinking that we were terrible parents. Hal and
Neal never had the desire to go roaming again. "It just isn't as
much fun as we thought it might be," they said.

As for me, I was leading something of a double life. During the
week I would be conducting rigorous laboratory experiments at the
university; on weekends Vera and I would lead intensive T-groups
in the community. All kinds of people attended—ministers, doctors, homemakers, lawyers, contractors, professors, and business-
people. My scientific colleagues thought I had lost my mind, and
possibly my brain, and could not understand why I was wasting
my time leading encounter groups. (They even invited me to give
a keynote lecture at a scientific convention with the title: "Whatever Became of Elliot Aronson?") My newfound humanist colleagues, however, could not believe that I was wasting my time
conducting sterile laboratory experiments. I myself saw no discon-
nect. In the course of leading T-groups I was learning about attraction, competition, social influence, and effective communication—
central themes in social psychology, after all. Conversely, my ability
to bring my training as an experimental social psychologist into

the T-group enhanced my ability, I felt, to cut through bullshit to get to the core of an issue and to expose some of the psychological processes that were facilitating or impeding group discussion.

At the invitation of the Texas Classroom Teachers Association, I began traveling all over Texas, to large cities and small rural towns, with two of my T-group trainees, Jev Sikes and Matt Snapp, leading workshops for teachers. These workshops were the essence of T-groups, focusing on how to communicate effectively to students and how to listen actively to their anxieties and difficulties. The three of us were quite a culture shock for most of these teachers. They would come to the first session, neatly and professionally dressed, and meet us—bearded, casual, informal, looking like those dreaded California hippies. One teacher later told us that when we walked into the lobby of the hotel where the session was to be held, she said to her friend, "Oh, my God, I hope those three guys aren't going to be in our group." Ten minutes later she found to her dismay that "those three guys" were the leaders. Yet the teachers listened, participated, and learned. Two years later the TCTA singled out our work for its annual award, a recognition that was particularly gratifying to me. It meant that the teachers in this socially conservative state had come to appreciate the value of humanistic psychology and its promotion of what almost all of them had previously regarded as a "touchy-feely," even subversive, approach to public education.

———

Despite our deep involvement in community and political activities, Vera and I did not succeed in becoming authentic Texans. Although we liked Austin and the university, we never quite believed that this was the place where we wanted to spend the rest of our lives. So when Hal entered his senior year in high school and began applying to colleges, Vera and I realized that it was time to make a conscious decision. We had always been a close-knit family, and soon our kids would be scattering. Where could we find a place to live that would be so attractive that when our kids were grown, they would like to settle nearby? The short answer was "not Texas."

The long answer was more complicated. Ideally, we wanted to move to an attractive city, near an ocean, with a temperate climate. That meant the Pacific Coast. One of the universities that I found particularly appealing was the University of California at Santa Cruz, which, though only ten years old, had already achieved a reputation for excellence. Hal liked the sound of it, too; he applied and was accepted. UCSC had been founded on an innovative approach to undergraduate education. It was divided into eight separate colleges, each college contained a few faculty members from each of the academic departments, and each college had a specific theme. Michael Kahn had moved to UCSC a few years earlier, where he joined the faculty of Kresge College as it was about to open its doors. Kresge's theme was creating a "living learning" community, where students would blend their academic learning with experiential learning in T-groups. It was a natural for Michael, and for me.

In 1974 the founding chancellor of UCSC, Dean McHenry, offered me the position of professor of psychology and provost (administrative head) of Kresge College. The entire Psychology Department, he said, was very enthusiastic about the possibility of my joining them. It was a great offer, except that I did not want to be an administrator. While I was agonizing over the decision, McHenry called me back. "I feel compelled to tell you," he said, "that several of the women on the Kresge faculty are demanding that we hire a woman as provost. Although they have nothing against you personally, they see this as their opportunity to have the first woman provost, and there are already two good candidates on the short list. But because the great majority of the Kresge faculty voted for you, the job is yours if you want it." For me, that tipped the balance, and I declined the offer. As appealing as Kresge looked, I thought the women had a reasonable demand, and, besides, I had no desire to begin my career at UCSC by causing a controversy. Two weeks later McHenry phoned to say that they had appointed a woman as provost, and would I entertain an offer to join the Kresge faculty solely as a professor of psychology? I would and I did.

As an added bonus, the city of Santa Cruz had a thriving boardwalk with a rare bona fide wooden roller coaster, very much like the one I grew up with in Revere. My life was coming around full circle.

CHAPTER NINE

The Winds of Change

Courtesy Jon Kersey

Lecturing, 1994 (top).

Budding social psychologist Josh and his first mentor at their favorite coffeehouse, 1989.

When we moved to Santa Cruz from Texas, I felt I was in paradise. The weather was heavenly. I was near an ocean again. And I was at a liberal institution with a liberal student body. As a place to live, Santa Cruz was everything Vera and I had hoped it would be for ourselves and our family, then and now; three of our four children still live in or near Santa Cruz. At the university the highs were higher than at any place I had ever taught; however, the lows were also lower.

During my first three years on campus, my office was next to a philosopher on one side and a physicist on the other; across the corridor was a historian, and two doors down, a poet. One result of this happy proximity was that the philosopher next door to me, Ellen Suckiel, and I developed a course we called Philosophical and Psychological Foundations of the Life Cycle that, year after year, received the highest student evaluations on campus. In practice the college system at UCSC was a wonderful way to teach undergraduates because it combined the best aspects of a small private college, like Swarthmore or Reed, with the facilities of a large state university. Hal blossomed there; his excitement (and mine) inspired Neal, Julie, and Josh to follow him to UCSC.

Initially, the living-learning community at Kresge College worked beautifully. As in all of the colleges, students could take standard university courses in traditional subjects, such as history, psychology, or biology, as well as special interdisciplinary seminars. At Kresge the seminars added a level of intensity to the usual academic discussion, because they were often run as T-groups. The students were required to learn the course material, and professors

retained their authority to make intellectual demands, set requirements, and evaluate the students' performance. But students also
learned about themselves, their relationship to their peers, and
ways to communicate clearly and effectively. The T-groups I had
been conducting in Bethel, Maine, had a finite duration, about
two weeks, and when they were over, participants dispersed to
their home cities—Boston, New York, Chicago, Montreal—saying
fond good-byes to their groupmates and taking whatever they had
learned back home. At Kresge, however, participants remained
right there. The result was the emergence of a close-knit community where the traditional academic barrier between "living" and
"learning" was obliterated.

In 1970 Carl Rogers, the leading clinical psychologist of his
time, had called the encounter group "the single most important
social invention of the 20th century." Yet this great social invention
flourished for only about two decades. The T-group was doomed
by the return of the Puritan influence on our society—an influence
entrenched in American culture, one that ebbs and flows but never
quits. When I was at Harvard I had thought that Tim Leary and
Dick Alpert's glowing hope for the power of psilocybin to empty
our prisons was naive, but I also found their optimism thrilling
and contagious. I was excited by the decade of antiwar protests
and movements for equality and the rosy future these events pre-
saged. And I loved the work we were doing in encounter groups,
promoting the notions that barriers between people could be lowered, that warmth and understanding could overcome suspicion
and prejudice. My own naïveté rested on the assumption that
progress toward these goals would be linear. "If things are this good
now," I thought, "just imagine how they will be in ten years!"

What I did not anticipate was that many people outside the college would come to view the goings-on at Kresge with suspicion,

others with envy, and a good number with outright hostility. "Hey! Those people are having *fun* over there! If it's that much fun, it can't be educational!" Once, one of our students told a professor that he was headed over to Kresge for an appointment with Michael Kahn, and the professor said, in all seriousness, "Be careful—he might hug you." It was easy to lampoon T-groups as being nests of touchy-feely self-absorption and pseudopsychology. The campus had a new chancellor and Kresge had a new provost; neither supported the living-learning experiment. The younger faculty members, sensing the opposition of the administration and wider community, were reluctant to participate. Thus, within three years of my arrival at Kresge, the living-learning community collapsed, a harbinger of the demise of T-groups across the country. The students were disappointed. I was heartbroken.

The Kresge experiment having failed, I moved to Adlai Stevenson College, one of the more traditional UCSC colleges, where I devoted most of my energy toward strengthening the graduate program in psychology. When I had first arrived there was no graduate program to speak of, and none of my colleagues in social psychology were actively engaged in experimental research. I urged the department to hire Tom Pettigrew and, later, Anthony Pratkanis, two superb social psychologists with active research agendas, and soon Tom, Anthony, and I had developed a graduate program in applied social psychology that was attracting good students. Yet the very factors that made our university a great environment for undergraduates militated against graduate training. Because the members of the Psychology Department were scattered in all corners of the campus, there was no way for graduate students to interact easily with us. After my experiences at Harvard, Minnesota, and Texas, where my graduate students were in offices adjacent to mine and we could interact freely and easily throughout the day, I felt that student-faculty proximity was crucial to a good graduate program. I convinced the chancellor to provide us with a trailer and place it on the edge of Stevenson College; the trailer provided space for experiments as well as offices for the graduate research assistants. Not luxurious, but neither was that attic at 9 Bow Street.

In 1977, against my better judgment, I agreed to serve as interim department chair until we could find someone to take the job on a permanent basis. That year, the graduate student colloquium committee decided to invite Arthur Jensen to give a talk to the psychology faculty and graduate students. Jensen was a controversial figure. His research on intelligence had led him to the conclusion that there was a genetic component to the average racial differences in IQ. This was, of course, volatile stuff, and coming as it did in the midst of the civil rights movement, it was inflammatory.

I had read one of Jensen's key papers and was persuaded that he was a serious scholar and not a bigot. As a social psychologist, however, I thought Jensen was overlooking environmental and situational explanations for racial differences. I was reluctant to invite him to give a colloquium not because he was controversial but because, given our limited departmental budget, I would have preferred to invite psychologists who I thought were doing far more interesting research. But the graduate student committee argued that it would be exciting for them to have the opportunity to challenge Jensen's conclusions in a face-to-face, friendly confrontation. As chair, I was not looking to foment controversy, nor was I looking to avoid it. I agreed to invite him.

On the phone Jensen accepted my invitation and then astonished me by demanding protection; he explained that, during the preceding few months at several universities, students had shouted him down, spat on him, and jostled him. I assured him that would not happen at Santa Cruz because we had an open-minded student body and, even more important, our colloquia had always consisted of small gatherings of about ten graduate students and seven or eight faculty members, sitting around a table in a seminar room. I joked that our graduate students hardly ever spat on our guests. Jensen was not amused.

Then, much to my surprise and disappointment, the night before his arrival, a few hundred students staged a rally at which they burned one of his books and some of his research publications and announced that they intended to storm the colloquium the next evening. In Texas I had become all too familiar with the intolerance of right-wingers, so it was a shock to encounter the intolerance of liberals—people whose values I shared but whose tactics could be just as undemocratic as those I had encountered in Austin.

The anger and potential violence of the students posed a dilemma for me. I had guaranteed Jensen safety; the prospect of two hundred students "storming" a seminar room that held twenty was alarming. Should I have the cops come out to protect him? Should I call off the meeting? Neither choice was acceptable. I did not want to create the conditions for a student-police confrontation, but neither did I want to capitulate to undemocratic rowdiness. After a good deal of thought, I arrived at what I considered to be a judicious solution: I decided to hold the seminar at a professor's home and posted a notice on the seminar door announcing that the meeting had been moved off campus. When a horde of undergraduates arrived at the seminar room and found no one there, they were furious.

The next day I was vilified in the student newspaper, which called me a racist for inviting Jensen and a coward for not letting the students get at him. The irony was not lost on me. Ten years earlier, in Austin, I had been called a "nigger lover." Now, in Santa Cruz, I found myself accused of being a racist. Indeed, in a bizarre echo of Austin, that night I received an unpleasant phone call at home. It was from an angry student rather than a gravelly voiced man, and it came at eight at night rather than two in the morning, but it was disquieting nonetheless.

"Are you going to be keeping your office hours in the patio outside the Kresge coffeehouse tomorrow, as usual?"

"Of course," I responded.

He said, ominously, "You better be there."

When I arrived at the patio and approached my usual table, there were three students waiting for me: Hal, Neal, and Julie Aronson. (Josh was still in high school.) Vera had told them about the phone call and the possibility of trouble, and they showed up to offer their dad moral support and, if needed, physical protection. Ten minutes later a few dozen students, some carrying torches and all chanting "Aronson's a racist," marched up the hill to the patio and surrounded my table. They activated a tape recorder and recited into the microphone a list of their grievances against me. Then they thrust the microphone in my face and said, "What do you have to say to that?"

I did what almost any liberal professor would have done: I gave them a five-minute lecture extolling the beauty of the First Amendment. I told them that I regretted shutting students out of Jensen's talk, but the book burning and rowdiness of the previous evening had left me no choice. I told them that the point of education is not simply to confirm what we believe but to hear and discuss the ideas of serious scholars who hold a wide range of opinions—some of which we will disagree with, some of which we may even find offensive. At a university, learning often emerges from

argument, but the argument must be civil. The students listened.
A few even applauded. They dispersed quietly.

I looked over at my kids. They were grinning.

"Not bad, Dad," said Hal.

"Very good," said Julie.

"Let's get some coffee," said Neal.

It took me a while to overcome the distress I had felt, but I came
to see the Jensen incident as reflecting a combination of student
qualities that I cherish: being feisty *and* teachable. I'd never encountered that combination before, not even at Harvard. In the
main, Harvard undergrads were more sophisticated and knowledgeable than UCSC students, but in my experience they also
seemed more conventional. I admired and enjoyed the UCSC students' willingness to speak their minds, ruffle feathers, and listen,
and they repaid me by flocking to my introductory social psychology course. In 1979, when the Alumnae Association decided to
establish an annual Distinguished Teaching Award, they honored
me as their first recipient.

———

In the late 1970s and early 1980s another transformative change
in American society was gathering steam. Whereas T-groups were
all about lowering self-imposed barriers between people ("touching
others is good, healthy, humane"), society, spurred by the women's
movement, was moving toward respecting boundaries ("touching
others is disrespectful, inappropriate, and patronizing"). I had
learned to value the importance of expressing positive feelings toward other people, verbally and physically. Of course, I understood
and accepted the feminist critique of inappropriate touching for
the purpose of demonstrating power or dominance. Needless to

say, uninvited touching is wrong, and it is as wrong in an encounter group as it is in the larger world. But before long few
people were making the distinction between appropriate and inappropriate touches; all touches were being viewed with suspicion.
I felt caught between these two conflicting social philosophies.

One semester I had four graduate teaching assistants for my
large introductory social psychology course: Erica and Suzanne,
third-year students who had been working with me since their arrival and had become personal friends of Vera's and mine; Alex, a
second-year student who was just beginning to work with me; and
a young woman I'll call Lois, a first-year student I hardly knew.
At the end of the term, as we were reviewing what had happened
in the course, Lois turned to me and said, in an accusatory tone,
"I have a bone to pick with you. I couldn't help noticing that when
you interact with your teaching assistants, you touch the women
far more frequently than you touch Alex. I find that to be sexist
and demeaning."

Puzzled, I replied, "Yes, I agree with your observation. Suzanne,
Erica, and I, when we converse, do frequently reach out and touch
each other on the arm or shoulder; but have I ever touched you?"

"No," she said.

"And I don't touch Alex, right?"

"Right," she said.

"Erica, Suzanne, and I have known one another for years. Isn't
it a more parsimonious explanation," I suggested, "that I touch
friends more frequently than people I don't know well?"

"Maybe," she said. But she made it clear that she was not
convinced.

Suzanne and Erica recounted the incident to Vera with much
amusement, but I wasn't sure whether to laugh or cry. Where have

you gone, Aron Gurwitsch? In 1953, when my fine old philosophy professor placed his hand on top of my head and said, "Good boy," I saw it for what it was: an expression of warmth and affection, a gesture of intellectual camaraderie. In today's climate of suspicion, would students see that as demeaning or even as a sexual pass? That exchange with Lois epitomized the atmosphere that was developing at UCSC and most other colleges across the country.

One morning a representative of the recently formed sexual harassment office came to the psychology faculty meeting to lay out the guidelines for faculty-student deportment. I found almost all of these guidelines sensible and reasonable and agreed with most of what she said. She spoke not only of the obvious ethical wrongdoing of abusing professorial power for sexual advantage but also of more subtle violations. Students, she said, often have crushes on their professors, but that doesn't mean they want a sexual affair; indeed, they often don't know what they want. But then she said something that didn't sound so reasonable. Under the new policy, male faculty members were urged to refrain from inviting female graduate students to research conferences. Steve Wright, a young social psychologist, immediately spoke up. Some conferences, he said, like the meeting of the Society of Experimental Social Psychology, attract the best researchers and the leaders of our field. Attending these meetings presented a great opportunity for our graduate students to become acquainted with the very people who might one day offer them teaching positions. He added, correctly, that this new policy would put our female graduate students at a disadvantage in the job market.

The sexual harassment official shrugged. She had no answer to Steve's concerns and went on to her next rule: All professors were thenceforth obliged to inform her office of anything they might hear about a possible sexual relationship between a teacher and a student. This sounded so strange that I thought I might have misunderstood her. I raised my hand.

"Let me get this straight," I said. "If a student tells me that she thinks that professor X might be sleeping with student Y, I am supposed to report this rumor to your office?"

"That's right," she said.

I was incredulous. I looked around the room at my colleagues, but no one flinched. I had no way of knowing whether they thought that reporting rumors was a good idea, were too frightened to object, or were simply complacent. Or perhaps, like me, they thought the rule was bizarre and had no intention of complying but saw no reason to speak up.

My mind wandered. I remembered walking across campus one sunny spring day when a beautiful young woman suddenly leaped out from behind a tree and flung herself into my arms. We hugged. The woman was my daughter, Julie, a sophomore at the time. A few weeks later one of Julie's housemates casually mentioned that her boyfriend, Ron, had asked if Julie was still having an affair with Professor Aronson—a friend of his had actually seen them necking on campus. She laughed and informed Ron that Julie's last name was Aronson. That's how rumors work, of course, transforming a hug into necking, and necking into an affair. But what if Julie's last name had not been Aronson and the student who had hugged me was doing so out of playful affection? Would all bystanders be required to report it to the sexual harassment office? What was becoming of our community? After a long pause, I spoke up. "I'm not going to report rumors," I said.

The meeting was acquiring a Kafkaesque quality. I thought about my baseball buddies, Billy and Al, and how, back in 1951, they had mocked me for coming out against Joseph McCarthy and his political fishing expeditions. "Do they teach you that stuff up there at the college?" they had asked. Now, some four decades later, hearing echoes of that time, I felt my head was spinning. As a liberal I agreed with the goals of the sexual harassment official. But as a social psychologist I knew that the recommended methods were likely to backfire and possibly become dangerous. Asking people to report idle rumors is a totalitarian tactic that spreads fear, suppresses dissent, and can sweep the innocent into the net of the guilty.

I took another look around the room at my colleagues. Three of them were married to women who had been their students. Would the new rules make these marriages retroactively "inappropriate"? The university's rules were designed to protect young women who, as the official had told us, "don't know what they want," but what about mature, capable women who do know what they want? Did the university really want to put itself into the business of making that discrimination—this love affair is good, but this other one is bad?

A few days later my friend Dane Archer, a sociologist, strode into my office fresh from his own departmental meeting with a sexual harassment official. Like me, Dane was appalled by the demand to report rumors, but he was amused by the clash between the new rules and the fact that some of our colleagues were married to their former students. He had just read a tongue-in-cheek essay in the Harvard alumni magazine in which John Kenneth Galbraith, the distinguished economist, had offered to turn in his marriage license because his beloved wife of some sixty years had been his student when they married. "But I think Galbraith got it wrong," Dane said. "The way I interpret the current regulations, we professors *are* allowed to marry our students. We just aren't allowed to date them."

Several weeks later a few unsigned fliers were posted on trees and bulletin boards across the campus. They were cleverly worded—simply a request for information about a couple of popular male professors. Neither man was actually accused of sexual harassment. I shook my head in dismay. I didn't take it seriously; I thought it was a childish prank. Then, one morning, several of these handwritten fliers appeared with *my* name on them, and suddenly the prank wasn't funny. They read:

If you have had any personal experience with

ELLIOT ARONSON

in regard to sexual harassment, please call the
sexual harassment office at *[number given]*.
Complaints can be anonymous/confidential.

In smaller print at the bottom, it said that the sexual harassment office "had no prior knowledge of this flier."

I had a sick feeling in the pit of my stomach. Rumor and innuendo, even if proved wrong, often stick, and it is nearly impossible to prove one's innocence, especially when one has not actually been accused of anything. But I came close to getting that proof. Weeks later, at my request, Ray Gibbs, then chair of the Psychology Department, spoke with the sexual harassment official and learned that although anyone could have phoned her office under the cloak of anonymity, not a single call had come in. A few days later, my own office phone rang. It was a student, who was sobbing.

"Dr. Aronson," she began hesitantly, "I am calling to apologize. I took your social psychology course, and I thought you were wonderful, so when the group asked me to help them put up fliers about you, I protested. 'He's not as wonderful as you think,' they said. 'You'll see.' So I went along with them, and then, after all that time went by and no one called the office, well, I felt so bad . . . "

"Thank you," I said. "I really appreciate you telling me. But how do you know that no one called?" She hung up abruptly.

The incident was over. Well, not quite. I suspected that some students and faculty who had seen the fliers might leap to the conclusion that I ran around campus harassing students. For the next few weeks I felt uneasy; every time I walked down a corridor or along a sidewalk on campus and a young woman walking toward me avoided making eye contact (as most of us normally do), I felt some anxiety. Was she averting her eyes because she thought I was a harasser? One voice inside me said, "What the hell do you care what other people think of you?" But a second voice kept replying, "I guess I care more than I'd like to."

Several weeks later my old friend Ralph Haber arrived for one of his frequent weekend visits. During Sunday brunch, as if to test which of my voices was the stronger, he asked, "What's this I hear about you sexually molesting students?" A close family friend of his, a UCSC student, had passed along the gossip. Ralph said, "I told her that, knowing you as I do, any such allegations had to be false. But she insisted that her information was accurate and that you had been hauled before some committee."

I found that my anguish and annoyance had faded, and I was able to joke about it. "No," I told him, "there was no committee because there was no accusation. And besides, it's not sexual molestation that I am innocent of; it is sexual harassment that I am innocent of."

Meanwhile, my research was flourishing. Tom Pettigrew, Dane Archer, Marti Hope Gonzales, and I spent several years doing research on energy conservation, which had come to public attention with a jolt in the 1970s; Diane Bridgeman and I were extending our experiments on the jigsaw classroom. Then, in the 1980s, our campus, like so many others, was abuzz about the emergence and rise of a horrible new disease called AIDS. Because there was no cure in sight, the challenge was to prevent it. And because almost all AIDS infections were occurring through voluntary sexual behavior, it immediately made prevention a social-psychological problem rather than a medical one: how to persuade sexually active people to use condoms.

Scary ads proved to be utterly ineffective. Our Health Center conducted a vigorous campaign, handing out pamphlets and presenting illustrated lectures and demonstrations, but still only about 17 percent of sexually active students were using condoms regularly. The Health Center asked me to assist them in beefing up their campaign.

First, my graduate students and I conducted a survey to determine *why* most undergrads weren't using condoms. No surprise: They considered condoms inconvenient and unromantic, antiseptic rather than exciting. To counteract that common belief, we produced and directed a brief video depicting an attractive young couple using condoms in a romantic and sexy way. In the video the woman puts the condom on the man as an integral part of foreplay. I hasten to add that our video would have been R-rated rather than X-rated. There was almost no nudity involved, and putting on the condom, though accompanied by erotic moaning and groaning, took place under the blanket. Nonetheless, our talented volunteer actors portrayed sexual pleasure convincingly. This procedure might have been considered risky, or even foolhardy, given the existing political climate at UCSC. But I felt that the problem we were addressing was too important to shy away from, and the university's Internal Review Board agreed. They unanimously approved of the experimental procedure.

The video proved to be effective, but only for a short time. Condom use increased for a few weeks and then declined sharply. Follow-up interviews revealed that the video had opened the students' minds to the erotic possibilities of condom use, but once they tried it a few times, they realized that they were not having nearly as much fun as the couple in the video, so they stopped using them.

Undaunted, I tried a different tack. I knew from my years of research on cognitive-dissonance theory that change is greater and lasts longer when behavior precedes attitude, when people are not simply admonished to change but placed in a situation that induces them to convince themselves to change. For example, in our initiation experiment, we didn't try to convince students that the boring group they had joined was interesting. That strategy would have failed, just as the condom ad campaigns and the R-rated video had failed. Rather, we put people through a severe initiation that induced them to persuade *themselves* that the group was interesting.

So how could we induce people to persuade themselves to use condoms? My first thought was to try to apply the Festinger/Carlsmith paradigm, where they induced people to tell a lie ("Packing spools into a box is really interesting!") for only a small amount of money, thereby creating dissonance; the participants could reduce dissonance by convincing themselves that the task really *was* interesting. But the paradigm would not work in this situation because, in effect, there was nothing to lie about. Sexually active students were fully aware that AIDS was a serious problem and that condoms were a smart way to avoid contracting the virus. They knew all that and still weren't using them.

In an attempt to figure it out, I created a thought experiment. Suppose you are a sexually active college student who doesn't use condoms. On going home for Christmas, your seventeen-year-old brother, who has just discovered sex, boasts to you about his sexual encounters. Being a responsible older sibling, you warn him about the dangers of AIDS and other sexually transmitted diseases and urge him to use condoms. Suppose I overheard this exchange and said to you, "That was good advice you gave your kid brother. By the way, how often do *you* use condoms?" This challenge forces you to become mindful of the dissonance between your self-concept as a person of integrity and the fact that you are behaving hypocritically. How might you reduce dissonance? You could agree that you are a hypocrite, or you could start to practice what you have just finished preaching. You could use condoms yourself.

And that is how, in 1989, I came to invent the hypocrisy paradigm. In a series of experiments with my graduate students Jeff Stone and Carrie Fried, we invited sexually active students to deliver a speech about the dangers of AIDS and the importance of using condoms. We videotaped each speech and informed the speakers that their video would be shown to high school students as part of a sex-education class. In the crucial condition, after they made the videotape, we got them to talk about the situations where they had not used condoms themselves, making them mindful of their own hypocrisy. And it worked.

Naturally, we could not follow them into their bedrooms, but we did get a secondary behavioral measure: their actual purchase of condoms. Students in the "hypocrisy" condition bought more condoms than students in the control condition who made the same videotaped speech but were not made mindful of the fact that their own behavior contradicted their stated beliefs. And we had reason to believe that they were not only buying condoms but also using them. Several months later we conducted a follow-up survey, disguised as an assessment of sexual behavior on campus, by hiring undergraduates to telephone all the students who had participated in the study. We found that those who had been in the hypocrisy condition were continuing to use condoms at three times the rate of those in the control condition.

My next hypocrisy experiment, with my graduate student Ruth Thibodeau, was designed to get students to conserve water. California was going through one of its periodic droughts, and the campus administration was urging students to use less water, again with little effect. We invited students to sign a poster urging everyone to conserve water by taking shorter showers. (Students were happy to sign the poster; after all, everybody believes in conserving water.) We then made half of them mindful of their hypocrisy by asking them to estimate how long their own most recent showers had been. Afterward, our confederates, who were loitering in the field-house shower room, surreptitiously timed the participants' showers. Students in the hypocrisy condition showered, on average, for three and a half minutes—a fraction of the time spent in the shower by those in the control condition.

The hypocrisy paradigm extended the reach of dissonance theory and proved to be a fruitful way of exploring human behavior, generating a plethora of interesting hypotheses. Yet I was inclined to let others test them. As for me, I felt it was precisely the right moment to say farewell to the social psychological laboratory. I had just turned sixty and realized that I had gradually been losing my zeal for the nuts and bolts of doing experiments. With the hypocrisy studies completed, I would be leaving on a high, just as an aging baseball player dreams of ending his career by hitting a home run his last time at bat. Once Jeff, Carrie, and Ruth had earned their doctorates and moved on to teaching positions at fine universities, I lost interest in mentoring new students and found myself more or less marking time as my laboratory rooms gathered dust.

As I might have predicted from the Life Cycle course that Ellen Suckiel and I had been teaching, my priorities had shifted. I had grown impatient with doing experiments because I no longer wanted to contribute one brick at a time to the edifice of our knowledge in social psychology. What I did want to do in my old age was put those bricks together, building on what I already knew. I had a strong desire to synthesize my knowledge and experience, by continuing to teach large lecture courses in the hope of inspiring undergraduates and by writing books for general audiences. My departmental colleague Anthony Pratkanis and I had long shared an interest in the uses and abuses of persuasion, so we collaborated on *Age of Propaganda*, a general-audience book in which we combined social-psychological findings with our insights and interpretations.

By this time some of my close friends had retired, but the thought of retirement had never crossed my mind. For several years after my brother died, I was certain that I too would die young. Who needs to think about retirement when he will die in his thirties? As the years rolled by, morphing into decades, I was forced to abandon that tragic-romantic self-image. Even so, I could not imagine leaving the university. I loved teaching so much that I was sure I would remain on that lecture platform until they had to carry me out feet first. I secretly harbored the fantasy that

I would collapse and die of a heart attack at ninety-five, while delivering an impassioned lecture on dissonance theory, in a packed auditorium, standing room only, as admiring students leaned forward, hanging on my every word.

My fantasy notwithstanding, by 1994 my changing priorities had created something of an ethical dilemma. I could take the easy way out by continuing to teach, writing books, and collecting the relatively hefty salary that the university was paying me. But one of the primary reasons that I had been hired was my ability to do research and train graduate students to be good scientists so that they could take positions in academia, where they could continue to produce research and train their graduate students to do the same. Should I give up training graduate students? This would mean shortchanging the university. Should I go through the motions of training them even though I had lost my enthusiasm for doing experiments? This would be shortchanging the students who would be coming to UCSC to work with me.

While I was wrestling with these questions, California fell into one of its recurring major financial crises (as common as its droughts). The legislature required all state universities to cut their expenditures drastically, and the universities responded by encouraging senior professors to take early retirement. Because the retirement fund, unlike the state budget, was flush, we could retire at approximately 75 percent of our annual salary. As an inducement to those who enjoyed teaching, they guaranteed that we could continue to teach our favorite course for at least five years, and perhaps indefinitely, for a small honorarium.

The offer resolved my ethical dilemma; I could teach without doing research. Still, the word "retirement" sounded noxious to my ears; it seemed final—like death. I therefore did what most participants in social psychological experiments do: I checked to see what other people were doing. Both of my most senior colleagues in psychology, Bill Domhoff and Tom Pettigrew, were strongly leaning toward taking early retirement. And so, like the elderly people I used to watch wading into the cold surf at Revere Beach when I was a boy, the three of us held hands and took the plunge together.

Bill, Tom, and I retired. But we were still teaching our favorite courses; Bill and Tom taught their seminars, and I had my introductory social psychology course with three hundred undergraduates. This arrangement lasted until a new chair of the department took over and unilaterally decided not to renew the teaching agreement, claiming that there was not enough money in the budget for the three of us. This explanation made no sense to me; intro social psychology was a basic course for majors and, because of my small stipend, was costing the university less than thirty dollars per student. The students were up in arms and protested vigorously, without success. I was out of a job.

Fortunately, as soon as the Stanford Psychology Department heard this news, they invited me to teach one course per year, as a distinguished visiting professor, for as long as I wanted to. On what must have been a slow news day in May 2000, the headline on the front page of the *Santa Cruz Sentinel* read "Famed Social Psychologist Elliot Aronson Leaves UCSC for Stanford." The article began, "Stanford University is snapping up esteemed psychology professor and author Elliot Aronson now that UC Santa Cruz is cutting him loose. The UCSC psychology department cited financial reasons for ending its relationship with the semi-retired Aronson, arguably the most famous living American social psychologist." The story was gratifying, but it barely soothed my sorrow at leaving the university I had served for twenty-five years and the feisty, teachable students I was so very fond of.

The Stanford Psychology Department went out of its way to make me feel at home, inviting me to teach anything I wanted. I chose a course on social influence, the first subject I'd ever taught as a new and nervous assistant professor at Harvard. The course attracted a great many students, graduates and undergraduates, across several disciplines. There was something sweet and satisfying about ending my teaching career at the very place where, forty years earlier, I had first become a social psychologist. However, my thoughts were not about the end of an era in my life; they were of a new beginning. My fantasy of teaching until age ninety-five might come true after all! But as Woody Allen is said to have said, "If you want to make God laugh, tell him about your plans."

CHAPTER TEN

The Roller Coaster

Elliot and Vera hiking in Yosemite, 2005.

One morning in the autumn of 2000, I woke up, and the world looked fuzzy. I thought old age had finally caught up with me and I might need my first pair of glasses, so I went to an ophthalmologist. After dilating my pupils, he peered into my retina, sighed, and shook his head gravely. "I'm afraid that glasses won't help you," he said. He sent me to a specialist who informed me that I had a rare kind of macular degeneration and that it was untreatable. He added that I might lose all of my central vision, but if I were lucky the deterioration might stop short of that.

For the next four years, every few months I experienced a sharp decline in my vision. With each decline, I felt an onslaught of dizziness and a loss of control as I bumped into furniture, tripped over minor cracks in the sidewalk, and could barely read. But with a great deal of effort, I would adjust. I would walk more slowly, pay more attention, enlarge the font on my computer, and get used to a world that increasingly looked like a fuzzy version of an impressionist painting on a foggy day.

And I would say, "Hey, I can handle this. If only my eyesight doesn't get any worse than this, I will be okay." Then, a few months later, my vision would undergo another sharp decline. Again I would gradually adjust, enlarging the font on my computer to the size of the E on an optometrist's chart, practicing with a cane to help me with curbs and avoid obstacles in my path, and looking into new computer technologies to help the blind. Friends and colleagues offered support, advice, and news of any breakthroughs in treatment that they read about, although my kind of macular degeneration was, and still is, untreatable. Finally, in 2004, my eyesight hit rock bottom. I lost my central vision completely. The good news is that it won't get any worse than this; the bad news is that it can't get any worse than this.

At first I was devastated by the horror of living in a dark and distorted world. My first important decision was what to do about Stanford. As my vision was declining, I had been rewriting my lecture notes, printing them by hand in block letters of ever-increasing size. But when my vision bottomed out, I could no longer read any of them, let alone see my students' faces and gauge their reactions. During that time of despair, believing there was no way that I could ever teach according to my own standards, I resigned. I realize now that this was an impetuous decision; in the years since then I have gradually trained myself to lecture without notes.

I can still see a little with my peripheral vision, but I can't recognize faces at a distance greater than ten inches. I need to move very close to someone to know who it is I'm talking to, and this occasionally causes a faux pas: Thinking it's a friend, I will suddenly find myself standing practically nose to nose with a stranger, and we both quickly pull back in amused embarrassment. This inability to differentiate people, though, is hardest on me when my four adorable little granddaughters are visiting; I often have difficulty telling them apart—a realization that never fails to break my heart. Because of experiences like these and the anxiety of being in bustling, unfamiliar environments, my blindness seems to have rekindled my childhood shyness, something that I thought I had succeeded in squelching in adulthood.

I used to think of blindness as simply a severe diminution of eyesight, but it is much more than that. I not only can't see things that are there but frequently see things that aren't there. For a few years I would see Hebrew words as if they were printed on a wall in front of me, not the usual kind as in a prayer book, but the ornate kind that appear in the Torah, beautifully hand-lettered works of art. (Of these, the most memorable to me was the Hebrew word *timshel*, which means "thou mayest.") Still today, every two or three minutes, a powerful burst of light goes off somewhere behind my eyes. These disconcerting visual auras have required imaginative coping skills. At first I tried poking fun at myself by pretending that I was being surrounded by paparazzi—hence all the flashbulbs. Now I just live with them.

If I learned anything from my older brother, Jason, it is the absolute refusal to complain about the hand I've been dealt, but to play the cards as well as I can. I have been trying to do this without resorting to denial at one extreme or wallowing in self-pity at the other. It certainly is no laughing matter for a "shy person" like me to be lost in airports or in unfamiliar cities, being forced to approach strangers and ask for directions. It is no joke for a scholar to be unable to skim a journal article to see if it contains anything of interest. But humor, combined with a little dissonance reduction, has carried me through the most difficult moments. There's an old Jewish joke that captures my feeling:

Two old friends meet on the street. "*Nu*, Jake," says Sol. "How are you feeling now that you have arthritis and cancer?"

"Terrible. But not so bad."

With every decrement in my eyesight, part of my adjustment has involved minimizing the importance of the things I can no longer do (who likes cocktail parties and journal articles, anyway?) and focusing on the things that I can do, like conversing with my friends and immersing myself in audiobooks. It is becoming easier for this shy person to ask strangers on the street for help, because I have learned that most people will respond with patience and kindness. If I can no longer catch a baseball, or even see one, I still can run—as long as I do it on the beach at the water's edge, early in the morning, when there are fewer toddlers to trip over.

One of the primary reasons I retired was to do more writing for the general public, and indeed I did—until my inability to read and edit my work made writing by myself extremely tedious. (Where do I put the fucking cursor?) In the past, I had enjoyed writing with colleagues, but now my inability to read forced the collaboration to take new and richer forms. Collaboration is about listening. My coauthors and I begin by talking out our ideas, arguments, and rebuttals. Once we have a first draft, my coauthor reads it aloud. The back-and-forth of the spoken word not only intensifies the exchange of ideas but also enhances the use of language: It is easier to spot clunkers by hearing them than by seeing them on a page. (In fact, I now recommend that all writers listen to their words as well as read them; you don't have to be blind to do that.) Using this process I have collaborated with two of my sons, Hal and Josh, in three revisions of *The Social Animal.*

After I went blind the first book I attempted from scratch, *Mistakes Were Made (but Not by Me)*, was written with my friend and colleague Carol Tavris. Even Carol, who is one of psychology's most gifted writers, was surprised and delighted at how much the oral back-and-forth improved the final product. This book has a special poignancy for me, because it reflects another kind of full-circle experience: It is an homage to my close friend and mentor Leon Festinger. In 1957, under duress, I had read *A Theory of Cognitive Dissonance* in manuscript form, and it changed my life. Leon was a great scientist but utterly uninterested in applying his science to better the human condition. In *Mistakes Were Made*, we showed how dissonance theory can explain why so many people can do harmful, foolish, self-defeating, or cruel things and still sleep soundly at night. Leon would not have cared about explaining why so many prosecutors won't accept DNA evidence showing that they put the wrong guy in prison, why some therapists justify the use of outdated methods that are harming their clients, why most scientists who accept money from industry convince themselves that they can't possibly be influenced by it, and why so many quarreling couples (and nations) cannot see the other's perspective. But I had always felt that dissonance theory was too powerful to leave in a laboratory, and so, in a sense, Carol and I dragged Leon, kicking and screaming, into the real world. Our book was published in 2007, exactly fifty years after the publication of *A Theory of Cognitive Dissonance*.

Today I realize that it is only my eyesight I have lost, not my vision. The first person to teach me this valuable lesson was my granddaughter Ruth, who was six years old in 2003, when my eyesight was almost completely gone. Although she is uncommonly bright, she was having difficulty learning how to read. She could not get the hang of it, and as the end of the school year approached, her teacher indicated that if she couldn't read, she would have to repeat the first grade. How could I help her grasp the essentials of reading, when I myself was nearly blind? The obvious hook was storytelling. Ruth was always begging me to tell her stories, stories I made up as I went along, so that I almost never told the same story more than once. The next time she asked for one, I suggested that we compose it together. She was excited by the idea. Then I said, "I have a terrible memory. As we go along, I had better write it down, so that if we are interrupted, we won't forget where we left off." I pulled out a stack of five-by-seven-inch cards, and as we composed, I carefully printed our words on the cards. It was hard for me to see, of course, so I needed to print in large, bold letters, only four or five words to a card. There we were, one of us not knowing how to read, the other barely able to decipher even oversized words.

Ruth asked if the story could be about me when I was a little boy, and she also insisted that she be one of the central characters. "How can you be a character in a story that happened before you were born?" I asked.

"C'mon, Grandpa, you can make something up." She was right, of course; I was thinking linearly. And so began *The Adventures of Ruthie and a Little Boy Named Grandpa*. Our story was an inside-out combination of *Hansel and Gretel* and *Jack and the Beanstalk*, where the old woman and the giant from the traditional fairy tales turn out to be nice people. Little Grandpa, because he is vaguely aware of the original stories, is suspicious and hesitant, while Ruth is trusting and adventurous.

After we had filled several cards, I told Ruth that I wanted to check how we had described the old woman. "Please shuffle through the cards to look for when the old woman makes her first appearance," I said. "Here is how you find the card with the old woman on it. The *O* sound in 'old' is a circle, so look for a word that starts with a circle." She found it. Then, a few minutes later, I would ask her to find the card with the word "oven" on it. I said, "It starts with the same circle, but then it has a *V* sound after the *O*; the *V* looks like an arrowhead pointed downward." Because we were engaged in a project that was of great interest to her, and because there was no pressure, Ruth was motivated to look for letters that previously had been meaningless and confusing. Within a few days, she was reading whole sentences. Within a month, there was no stopping her. She was reading everything in sight. Of course, she would have learned to read eventually without my help. Nonetheless, because it was such an exhilarating week for Ruthie and me, although for different reasons, I arranged for the story to be published by a vanity press, with the two of us as coauthors. That little book is a sweet reminder of one of my favorite teaching experiences.

It is not by accident that I lived near enough to my grandchildren to have developed such close relationships with them. When I reflect on my life, I see with the clarity of hindsight the intersecting strands of chance and intention that made our family as tight as it is. Our decision to move to Santa Cruz was based on the conscious reasoning that if the locale was attractive enough, our children would want to establish their own lives near us. But it was by chance that at the particular moment that Vera and I had decided to leave Texas, UCSC was looking for a professor with my combination of skills and experience. Today, so many years later, Hal, Neal, and Julie still live in or near this city with their spouses and children; Josh and his family visit at every opportunity.

Was it due to chance that we lost none of our children to the siren song of drugs and rebellion that claimed so many of their generation, or was it due to our child-rearing style, which can best be termed "vigilant laissez-faire"? Vera and I can't be sure. We tried hard to avoid meddling in their private lives while encouraging them to talk to us about anything and everything that concerned them. Even so, they kept many of their adventures, misadventures, explorations, and heartbreaks to themselves, telling us about them only years later. For example, we informed all our kids that when the bedroom door was locked, we were not to be disturbed— unless, of course, they needed us to drive them to the emergency room. In her thirties, Julie told us, with amusement, "When I was three years old, I sat outside your bedroom door for an hour, hoping you would hear me whimpering!" More seriously, Josh recently let us know that he had been picked on for a whole year by his fourth-grade teacher. "I wish you had known about it," he complained. Perhaps we should have been a little more vigilant and a little less laissez-faire. But all of our children somehow found their own way, forgiving us our mistakes and oversights, remaining close to us and to one another.

In adulthood, each of our children chose to do the kind of work that reflects his or her individual interest and proclivity. But their choices share an underlying belief that serving the common good is what it means to live the good life. Hal became an environmental sociologist and expert on solar energy; he is training minority teenagers, unemployed contractors, and autoworkers to become proficient in a technology that has a bright present and an even brighter future. Neal became a firefighter, a first responder in rescuing people from burning buildings, automobile accidents, and the devastation of earthquakes. Julie became an educational consultant, nurturing and evaluating innovative strategies adopted by primary and secondary schools. Joshua became a professor of social psychology. When I think of how many things come around again in our lives, I smile as I recall the Jensen episode at UCSC, years before Josh arrived as a student. Today, Josh's innovative research on developing interventions that raise the motivation and test scores of the most disadvantaged minorities is a far more effective riposte to Jensen's misguided ideas than I (or anyone else) could have come up with at the time.

A few years ago Vera and I managed to make contact with our old friend Dick Alpert. Dick had suffered a serious stroke that left him slow of speech and partially paralyzed. We met in a restaurant, he in a wheelchair and I walking hesitantly with a white cane. The waiters—perhaps out of curiosity about what an old blind guy and an old cripple had to say to each other, perhaps because they recognized Baba Ram Dass—hovered near our table, surreptitiously eavesdropping. We spoke of the many ways in which our lives had intersected, of religious belief (his) and skepticism (mine), and of his transformation from developmental psychologist to spiritual leader. Near the end of our meeting, he asked me kindly, "And you, Ellie? Are you going to end up as a social psychologist?" Without a moment's hesitation I said, "I don't intend to end up at all!" His face lit up, and with great effort he reached for my hand. I thought he wanted to shake it, but instead he brought my hand to his lips and kissed it.

Vera and I walked outside the restaurant and watched Dick's driver wheel him up a ramp and into the van. He looked frail and helpless, yet he was still the same bright, charming, charismatic guy I had known for most of my life. I admired the courage with which he was dealing with the debilitating effects of his stroke. Life is a roller coaster, I thought.

When I was twelve years old, Jason took me for my first ride on the roller coaster at Revere Beach. Although I had been nagging him to take me for more than a year, as the ride started, I was plenty scared. Jason, who was a veteran of thirty-odd roller-coaster rides, assured me that I had nothing to be afraid of. As usual, he was right; it was an exhilarating experience. When it was over I asked him, "What's your favorite part of the ride?"

"What's your favorite part?" he asked.

"I hate when you do that!" I said.

He smiled and said, "Do what?"

"I hate when you do that, too!" I shouted.

I was so annoyed at him I decided to give him the old silent treatment. But I was so eager to discuss the experience that the silent treatment lasted about thirty-four seconds. I said, "My favorite part was right after we went flying down that steep drop and we suddenly curved up again. It was so exciting I could feel my heart go right up into my throat."

"Yeah. I know what you mean," he said. "That used to be my favorite part, too. But you know what? After a few rides, it dawned on me that I wasn't enjoying the rest of the experience because I kept waiting for that part of the ride to show up. So then I played a trick on myself. I pretended that my favorite part was when we were just starting down that steep hill. But then I found myself waiting for *that* to occur and missing out on the enjoyment of the rest of the ride. So then I pushed it back another notch and pretended to myself that my favorite part was when we were climbing the hill . . . and then it dawned on me that it's stupid to have a favorite part. Because it's all the roller coaster—the ups, the downs, the climbing, the falling, the gradual turns, the sharp twists. It's all the roller coaster."

My brother was only fourteen when he said that. Although he may not have been fully aware of it, I can see, looking at it now, he might have been using the roller coaster as a metaphor for living.

What's my favorite part of this roller coaster I've been riding for seventy-eight years? As my fourteen-year-old mentor taught me, there is no favorite part. Another way of putting it is that it is all my favorite part. All of it—the plummets of blindness and loss, as well as the exhilaration that comes from giving a compelling lecture or making an important scientific discovery, and the warmth that comes from loving and being loved by my wife, kids, grandchildren, and friends. Indeed, if I were forced to choose one favorite part, I would say right now, but I guess I could have said that anywhere along the way.

Courtesy John Georgian. Used with permission.

ACKNOWLEDGMENTS

For writers, acknowledgments are never easy. The fear (bordering on paralysis) is that we might leave someone out and thereby earn an enemy for life. To avoid this dreadful outcome, the temptation is not just to thank the usual suspects but to heap praise on everyone who could possibly have contributed to the successful completion of our project: lawyers, barbers, certified public accountants, and the bartender at our local watering hole, who kept the booze coming during our frequent bouts of writer's block.

The problem is compounded when the work in question is an autobiography. How can I avoid thanking my first grade teacher, who taught me how to read, or my first employer, who fired me, thus closing the door on a career as produce manager at a supermarket, or my first girlfriend, who taught me that she didn't always want me to take no for an answer? But I will avoid that temptation. Indeed, I will acknowledge the efforts of only three people.

Bob Lescher is a literary agent of the old school: wise, experienced, patient, and courtly. A few years ago he took a look at a brief professional autobiography I had written for inclusion in *The History of Psychology in Autobiography*, and he was enthusiastic about turning it into a book. I knew it wouldn't be easy; my memory was sluggish and getting worse by the day. Moreover, I was certain that no publisher would be interested in the autobiography of an amnesiac whose name is not exactly a household word. "The damn thing will sell eleven copies," I said, "and all eleven buyers will be Aronsons." But Bob was at least half right: Publishers *were* interested. My friend and occasional coauthor, Carol Tavris, played a decisive role in the completion of this project. Indeed, if an autobiography could have a coauthor, she would be it.

By continually asking provocative questions, she succeeded in transforming my sluggish memory into a treasure chest of previously forgotten events and stories. Under Carol's prodding, entire dialogues came back to me verbatim. Carol also played a major role in shaping the work, helping me to eliminate irrelevant details and focus on specific themes that have run throughout my life. Her love for the project was sustaining and her assistance invaluable.

Finally, I was blessed with a brilliant young editor, Whitney Casser, who was adept at trimming away the fat of redundancy and overstatement and continually forced me to "show rather than tell" wherever possible. Her talent and good humor were a great asset to me and to the final product.

SELECTED PUBLICATIONS
BY ELLIOT ARONSON

References in boldface are described in some detail in the text.

MAJOR WRITINGS ON COGNITIVE DISSONANCE:
THEORY AND RESEARCH

"The Evolution of Cognitive Dissonance Theory: A Personal
Appraisal." In *The Science of Social Influence*, edited by
A. Pratkanis. New York: Psychology Press, 2007.

Mistakes Were Made (but Not by Me*): Why We Justify Foolish Beliefs,
Bad Decisions, and Hurtful Acts* (with C. Tavris). Orlando:
Houghton Mifflin Harcourt, 2007.

"Dissonance, Hypocrisy, and the Self-Concept." In *Cognitive
Dissonance: Progress on a Pivotal Theory in Social Psychology*,
edited by E. Harmon-Jones and J. Mills, 101–126. Washington,
DC: American Psychological Association, 1999.

"The Power of Self-Persuasion." *American Psychologist* 54 (1999):
873–884.

"The Theory of Cognitive Dissonance: The Evolution and Vicissitudes
of an Idea." In *The Message of Social Psychology*, edited by
C. McGarty and S. A. Haslam. London: Blackwell, 1997.

**"Inducing Hypocrisy as a Means of Encouraging Young Adults to
Use Condoms" (with J. Stone, A. L. Crain, M. P. Winslow,
and C. B. Fried).** *Personality and Social Psychology Bulletin* **20
(1994): 116–128.**

"The Return of the Repressed: Dissonance Theory Makes a
Comeback." *Psychological Inquiry* 3 (1992): 303–311.

"Taking a Closer Look: Reasserting the Role of the Self-Concept in
Dissonance Theory" (with R. Thibodeau). *Personality and Social
Psychology Bulletin* 18 (1992): 591–602.

"Using Cognitive Dissonance to Encourage Water Conservation" (with C. A. Dickerson, R. Thibodeau, and D. Miller). *Journal of Applied Social Psychology* 22 (1992): 841–854.

"How to Change Behavior." In *How People Change: Inside and Outside Therapy*, edited by R. Curtis and G. Stricker. New York: Plenum, 1991.

"Overcoming Denial and Increasing the Intention to Use Condoms Through the Induction of Hypocrisy" (with C. Fried and J. Stone). *American Journal of Public Health* 81 (1991): 1636–1638.

"Persuasion Via Self-Justification: Large Commitments for Small Rewards." In *Four Decades of Social Psychology*, edited by L. Festinger. New York: Oxford University Press, 1980.

"The Theory of Cognitive Dissonance: A Current Perspective." In *Cognitive Theories in Social Psychology*, edited by L. Berkowitz, 215–220. New York: Academic Press, 1978.

"A Two-Factor Theory of Dissonance Reduction: The Effect of Feeling Stupid or Feeling 'Awful' on Opinion Change" (with T. Chase, R. Helmreich, and R. Ruhnke). *International Journal of Communication Research* 3 (1974): 340–352.

"Opinion Change in the Advocate as a Function of the Persuasability of His Audience: A Clarification of the Meaning of Dissonance" (with E. Nel and R. Helmreich). *Journal of Personality and Social Psychology* 12 (1969): 117–124.

"The Theory of Cognitive Dissonance: A Current Perspective." In *Advances in Experimental Social Psychology*, edited by L. Berkowitz, 4:1–34. New York: Academic Press, 1969.

"Dishonest Behavior as a Function of Differential Levels of Induced Self-Esteem" (with D. R. Mettee). *Journal of Personality and Social Psychology* 9 (1968): 121–127.

"Dissonance Theory: Progress and Problems." In *Theories of Cognitive Consistency: A Sourcebook*, edited by R. P. Abelson, E. Aronson, W. J. McGuire, T. M. Newcomb, M. J. Rosenberg, and P. H. Tannenbaum, 5–27. Chicago: Rand McNally, 1968.

"Dissonance Theory and the Formation of Values." In *Contributions to General Psychology*, edited by C. D. Speilberger, R. Fox, and B. Masterson, 366–369. New York: Ronald Press, 1968.

"The Psychology of Insufficient Justification: An Analysis of Some Conflicting Data." In *Cognitive Consistency*, edited by S. Feldman, 109–133. New York: Academic Press, 1966.

"Communicator Credibility and Communication Discrepancy as Determinants of Opinion Change" (with J. Turner and J. M. Carlsmith). *Journal of Abnormal Social Psychology* 67 (1963): 31–36.

"Effect of the Severity of Threat on the Devaluation of Forbidden Behavior" (with J. M. Carlsmith). *Journal of Abnormal and Social Psychology* 66 (1963): 584–588.

"The Effects of Expectancy on Volunteering for an Unpleasant Experience" (with J. M. Carlsmith and J. M. Darley). *Journal of Abnormal and Social Psychology* 66 (1963): 220–224.

"Some Hedonic Consequences of the Confirmation and Disconfirmation of Expectancies" (with J. M. Carlsmith). *Journal of Abnormal and Social Psychology* 66 (1963): 151–156.

"Performance Expectancy as a Determinant of Actual Performance" (with J. M. Carlsmith). *Journal of Abnormal and Social Psychology* 65 (1962): 178–182.

"The Effect of Effort on the Attractiveness of Rewarded and Unrewarded Stimuli." *Journal of Abnormal and Social Psychology* 63 (1961): 375–380.

"Arousal and Reduction of Dissonance in Social Contexts" (with L. Festinger). In *Group Dynamics*, edited by D. Cartwright and Z. Zander, 125–136. 3rd ed. New York: Harper & Row, 1960/1968.

"The Effect of Severity of Initiation on Liking for a Group" (with J. Mills). *Journal of Abnormal and Social Psychology* 59 (1959): 177–181.

"Selectivity in Exposure to Information" (with J. Mills and H. Robinson). *Journal of Abnormal and Social Psychology* 59 (1959): 250–253.

See Also

Festinger, L., and J. M. Carlsmith. "Cognitive Consequences of Forced Compliance." *Journal of Abnormal and Social Psychology* 58 (1959): 203–210.

Festinger, L. *A Theory of Cognitive Dissonance.* Evanston, IL: Row, Peterson, 1957.

RESEARCH ON ATTRACTION

"Antecedents, Correlates, and Consequences of Sexual Jealousy" (with A. Pines). *Journal of Personality* 51 (1983): 108–136.

"The Reciprocation of Attraction from Similar and Dissimilar Others: A Study in Person Perception and Evaluation" (with E. E. Jones and L. Bell). In *Experimental Social Psychology*, edited by C. G. McClintock, 142–179. New York: Holt, Rinehart, & Winston, 1972.

"To Err Is Humanizing—Sometimes: Effects of Self-Esteem, Competence, and a Pratfall on Interpersonal Attraction" (with R. Helmreich and J. LeFan). *Journal of Personality and Social Psychology* 16 (1970): 259–264.

"Liking for an Evaluator as a Function of Her Physical Attractiveness and Nature of the Evaluations" (with H. Sigall). *Journal of Experimental Social Psychology* 5 (1969): 93–100.

"Some Antecedents of Interpersonal Attraction." In *Nebraska Symposium on Motivation 1969*, edited by W. J. Arnold and D. Levine, 143–173. Lincoln: University of Nebraska Press, 1969. (Won AAAS Socio-Psychological Prize for 1970.)

"Liking for an Evaluator as a Function of His Discernment" (with D. Landy). *Journal of Personality and Social Psychology* 9 (1968): 133–141.

"My Enemy's Enemy Is My Friend" (with V. Cope). *Journal of Personality and Social Psychology* 8 (1968): 8–12.

"Opinion Change and the Gain-Loss Model of Interpersonal Attraction" (with H. Sigall). *Journal of Experimental Social Psychology* 3 (1967): 178–188.

"The Effect of a Pratfall on Increasing Interpersonal Attractiveness" (with B. Willerman and J. Floyd). *Psychonomic Science* **4 (1966): 227–228.**

"On Increasing the Persuasiveness of a Low Prestige Communicator" (with E. Walster and D. Abrahams). *Journal of Experimental Social Psychology* 2 (1966): 325–342.

"Gain and Loss of Esteem as Determinants of Interpersonal
   Attractiveness" (with D. Linder). *Journal of Experimental
   Social Psychology* 1 (1965): 156–171.
"Opinion Change as a Function of the Communicator's
   Attractiveness and Desire to Influence" (with J. Mills). *Journal of
   Personality and Social Psychology* 1 (1965): 173–177.

RESEARCH ON ENERGY CONSERVATION

"Making Research Apply: High Stakes Public Policy in a Regulatory
   Environment" (with D. Archer and T. F. Pettigrew). *American
   Psychologist* 47 (1992): 1233–1236.
"The Social Psychology of Energy Conservation" (with M. H.
   Gonzales). In *Social Influence Processes and Prevention*, edited by
   J. Edwards. New York: Plenum Press, 1990.
"Using Social Cognition and Persuasion to Promote Energy
   Conservation: A Quasi-Experiment" (with M. H. Gonzales and
   M. Costanzo). *Journal of Applied Social Psychology* 18 (1988):
   1049–1066.
"Energy Conservation Behavior: The Difficult Path from
   Information to Action" (with M. Costanzo et al.). *American
   Psychologist* 41 (1986): 521–528.
"The Social-Psychological Foundations of Successful Energy
   Conservation Programmes" (with S. Coltrane and D. Archer).
   Energy Policy 14 (1986): 133–148.
"Improving Utility Conservation Programs: Outcomes,
   Interventions, and Evaluations" (with L. Condelli et al.). *Energy*
   9 (1984): 485–494.
"Residential Energy Conservation: A Social-Psychological Perspective."
   In *Families and Energy*, edited by B. Morrison and W. Kempton,
   11–24. East Lansing: Michigan State University Press, 1984.
"A Social-Psychological Perspective on Energy Conservation in
   Residential Buildings" (with S. Yates). *American Psychologist* 38
   (1983): 435–444.
"The Relative Effectiveness of Models and Prompts on Energy
   Conservation: A Field Experiment in a Shower Room" (with
   M. O'Leary). *Journal of Environmental Systems* (1982): 219–224.

RESEARCH ON THE JIGSAW CLASSROOM

"The Jigsaw Strategy in Action: Integrating Peer Providers into Traditional Service Settings" (with C. Macius, P. J. Barreira, C. F. Rodican, and P. B. Gold). *Journal of Mental Health Policy Research* 34 (2008): 494–496.

"Reducing Hostility and Building Compassion: Lessons from the Jigsaw Classroom." In *The Social Psychology of Good and Evil*, edited by A. Miller, 469–488. New York: Guilford, 2004.

"Building Empathy, Compassion, and Achievement in the Jigsaw Classroom." In *Improving Academic Achievement*, edited by J. Aronson. San Diego: Academic Press, 2002.

"The Jigsaw Classroom: A Cooperative Strategy for Reducing Prejudice" (with R. Thibodeau). In *Cultural Diversity in the Schools*, edited by J. Lynch, C. Modgil, and S. Modgil. London: Falmer Press, 1992.

"Desegregation, Jigsaw, and the Mexican-American Experience" (with A. Gonzalez). In *Eliminating Racism*, edited by P. Katz and D. Taylor. New York: Plenum, 1988.

"Teaching Students What They Think They Already Know About Prejudice and Desegregation." In *The G. Stanley Hall Lecture Series*, edited by V. P. Makosky. Vol. 7. Washington, DC: American Psychological Association Press, 1986.

"Modifying the Environment of the Desegregated Classroom." In *Motivation and Society*, edited by A. J. Stewart, 319–336. San Francisco: Jossey-Bass, 1984.

"Cooperation in the Classroom: The Impact of the Jigsaw Method on Inter-Ethnic Relations, Classroom Performance, and Self-Esteem" (with S. Yates). In *Small Groups*, edited by H. Blumberg and P. Hare. London: John Wiley & Sons, 1983.

"Cooperation, Prosocial Behavior, and Academic Performance: Experiments in the Desegregated Classroom" (with N. Osherow). *Applied Social Psychology Annual* 1 (1980): 163–196.

"Training Teachers to Implement Jigsaw Learning: A Manual for Teachers" (with E. Goode). In *Cooperation in Education*, edited by S. Sharan, P. Hare, C. Webb, and R. Hertz-Lazarowitz, 47–81. Provo: Brigham Young University Press, 1980.

"Jigsaw Groups and the Desegregated Classroom: In Pursuit of Common Goals" (with D. Bridgeman). *Personality and Social Psychology Bulletin* 5 (1979): 438–446.

"The Effects of Cooperative Classroom Structure on Student Behavior and Attitudes" (with D. Bridgeman and R. Geffner). In *Social Psychology of Education*, edited by D. Bar Tal and L. Saxe. Washington, DC: Hemisphere, 1978.

"Interdependent Interactions and Prosocial Behavior" (with D. Bridgeman and R. Geffner). *Journal of Research and Development in Education* 12 (1978): 16–27.

"Interdependence in the Classroom: A Field Study" (with N. T. Blaney, C. Stephan, R. Rosenfield, and J. Sikes). *Journal of Educational Psychology* 69 (1977): 121–128.

"Performance in the Interdependent Classroom: A Field Study" (with W. Lucker, D. Rosenfield, and J. Sikes). *American Educational Research Journal* 13 (1976): 115–123.

"Busing and Racial Tension: The Jigsaw Route to Learning and Liking" (with N. Blaney, J. Sikes, C. Stephan, and M. Snapp). *Psychology Today* 8 (February 1975): 43–50.

OTHER RESEARCH AND WRITING

Gonzales, Marti Hope, Carol Tavris, and Joshua Aronson. *The Scientist and the Humanist: A Festschrift in Honor of Elliot Aronson.* New York: Psychology Press, 2010. This collection of essays in honor of Elliot Aronson will bring readers up-to-date on the state of current research in the many areas of Elliot's pioneering discoveries, including cognitive dissonance theory, experimental methods, the Jigsaw classroom, social psychology and the law, attraction and relationships, energy policy, and prejudice and intergroup conflict.

"Fear, Denial, and Sensible Action in the Face of Disasters." *Social Research* 75 (2008): 1–18.

"Drifting My Own Way: Following My Nose and My Heart." In *Psychologists Defying the Crowd: Stories of Those Who Battled the Establishment and Won*, edited by R. Sternberg. Washington, DC: APA Books, 2002.

"Mindless Propaganda, Thoughtful Persuasion" (with A. Pratkanis). In *Social Psychology Annual*, edited by M. H. Davis. New York: McGraw-Hill, 2001.

"Adventures in Experimental Social Psychology: Roots, Branches, and Sticky New Leaves." In *Reflections on 100 Years of Experimental Social Psychology*, edited by A. Rodrigues and R. Levine, 82–113. New York: Basic Books, 1999.

"The Experimental Method in Social Psychology" (with T. Wilson and M. Brewer). In *The Handbook of Social Psychology*, edited by G. Lindzey, D. Gilbert, and S. Fiske. New York: Random House, 1998.

"On Baseball and Failure." *Dialogue* (Spring 1995): 4–5.

"Analysis, Synthesis, and the Treasuring of the Old." *Personality and Social Psychology Bulletin* 15 (1989): 508–512.

"Experimentation in Social Psychology" (with M. Brewer and J. M. Carlsmith). In *The Handbook of Social Psychology*, edited by G. Lindzey and E. Aronson. 3rd ed. New York: Random House, 1985.

"Attribution of Fault to a Rape Victim as a Function of Respectability of the Victim" (with C. Jones). *Journal of Personality and Social Psychology* 26 (1973): 415–419.

"Beyond Parkinson's Law: III. The Effect of Protractive and Contractive Distractions on the Wasting of Time on Subsequent Tasks" (with D. Landy and K. McCue). *Journal of Applied Psychology* 53 (1969): 236–239.

"The Influence of the Character of the Criminal and His Victim on the Decisions of Simulated Jurors" (with D. Landy). *Journal of Experimental Social Psychology* 5 (1969): 141–152.

"The Effect of Expectancy of Task Duration on the Experience of Fatigue" (with B. Walster). *Journal of Experimental Social Psychology* 3 (1967): 41–46.

"Further Steps Beyond Parkinson's Law: A Replication and Extension of the Excess Time Effect" (with D. Landy). *Journal of Experimental Social Psychology* 3 (1967): 274–285.

"Beyond Parkinson's Law: The Effect of Excess Time on Subsequent Performance" (with E. Gerard). *Journal of Personality and Social Psychology* 3 (1966): 336–339.

"Choosing to Suffer as a Consequence of Expecting to Suffer: An Unexpected Finding" (with E. Walster and Z. Brown). *Journal of Experimental Social Psychology* 2 (1966): 400–406.

"Self-Evaluation Versus Direct Anxiety Reduction as Determinants of the Fear Affiliation Relationship" (with J. M. Darley). *Journal of Experimental Social Psychology*, Supplement 1 (1966): 66–79.

"The Effect of Relevant and Irrelevant Aspects of Communicator Credibility on Opinion Change" (with B. W. Golden). *Journal of Personality* 30 (1962): 135–146.

"The Need for Achievement as Measured by Graphic Expression." In *Motives in Fantasy, Action, and Society*, edited by J. W. Atkinson, 249–265. New York: Van Nostrand, 1958.

INDEX